International Political Economy Series

General Editor: **Timothy M. Shaw**, Professor of Commonwealth Governance and Development, and Director of the Institute of Commonwealth Studies, School of Advanced Study, University of London

Titles include:

Leonard Seabrooke
US POWER IN INTERNATIONAL FINANCE
The Victory of Dividends

Timothy J. Sinclair and Kenneth P. Thomas (*editors*)
STRUCTURE AND AGENCY IN INTERNATIONAL CAPITAL MOBILITY

Kendall Stiles (*editor*)
GLOBAL INSTITUTIONS AND LOCAL EMPOWERMENT
Competing Theoretical Perspectives

Caroline Thomas and Peter Wilkin (*editors*)
GLOBALIZATION AND THE SOUTH

Kenneth P. Thomas
CAPITAL BEYOND BORDERS
States and Firms in the Auto Industry, 1960–94

Geoffrey R. D. Underhill (*editor*)
THE NEW WORLD ORDER IN INTERNATIONAL FINANCE

Amy Verdun
EUROPEAN RESPONSES TO GLOBALIZATION AND FINANCIAL MARKET
INTEGRATION
Perceptions of Economic and Monetary Union in Britain, France and Germany

Robert Wolfe
FARM WARS
The Political Economy of Agriculture and the International Trade Regime

International Political Economy Series
Series Standing Order ISBN 0–333–71708–2
(*outside North America only*)

You can receive future titles in this series as they are published by placing a standing order.
Please contact your bookseller or, in case of difficulty, write to us at the address below with
your name and address, the title of the series and one of the ISBNs quoted above.

Customer Services Department, Macmillan Distribution Ltd, Houndmills, Basingstoke,
Hampshire RG21 6XS, England

Egalitarian Politics in the Age of Globalization

Edited by

Craig N. Murphy
Professor and Chair of Political Science
Wellesley College

palgrave

First published 2002 by
PALGRAVE
Houndmills, Basingstoke, Hampshire RG21 6XS and
175 Fifth Avenue, New York, N. Y. 10010
Companies and representatives throughout the world

PALGRAVE is the new global academic imprint of
St. Martin's Press LLC Scholarly and Reference Division and
Palgrave Publishers Ltd (formerly Macmillan Press Ltd).

ISBN 0–333–79240–8

This book is printed on paper suitable for recycling and
made from fully managed and sustained forest sources.

A catalogue record for this book is available
from the British Library.

Library of Congress Cataloging-in-Publication Data
Egalitarian politics in the age of globalization / Craig N. Murphy,
editor.
        p. cm. — (Series in international political economy)
    Includes bibliographical references and index.
    ISBN 0–333–79240–8 (cloth)
    1. Social movements. 2. Equality. 3. Globalization. I. Murphy,
Craig. II. Series.
    HM881 .E34 2001
    303.48′4—dc21
                                                        2001035821

10   9   8   7   6   5   4   3   2   1
11   10   09   08   07   06   05   04   03   02

Printed and bound in Great Britain by
Antony Rowe Ltd, Chippenham, Wiltshire

Contents

Notes on the Contributors

Marc Blecher is Professor of Politics at Oberlin College and author of *China Against the Tides: Restructuring through Revolution, Radicalism and Reform* (1997).

Christine B. N. Chin is Assistant Professor of International Relations at American University in Washington, DC, and author of *In Service and Servitude: Women and the Malaysian Modernization Project* (1997).

Jane Dawson is Associate Professor of Political Science at Connecticut College and author of *Eco-Nationalism: Anti-Nuclear Activism and National Identity in Russia, Lithuania, and Ukraine* (1996).

Joel Krieger is Norma Wilentz Hess Professor of Political Science at Wellesley College and author of *British Politics in a Global Age: Can Social Democracy Survive?* (1999).

Katharine H. S. Moon is Associate Professor of Political Science at Wellesley College and author of *Sex Among Allies: Military Prostitution in US–Korean Relations* (1997).

Craig N. Murphy is Professor and Chair of Political Science at Wellesley College and past President of the International Studies Association.

William I. Robinson is Assistant Professor of Sociology at the University of California and author of *Promoting Polyarchy: Globalization, US Intervention, and Hegemony* (1996).

Mark Rupert is Associate Professor of Political Science at Syracuse University and author of *Producing Hegemony: The Politics of Mass Production and American Global Power* (1995).

Filomina C. Steady is Professor and Chair of Africana Studies at Wellesley College and president of the Womens' World Summit Foundation, a Geneva-based international organization helping to promote the Convention on the Elimination of All Forms of Discrimination Against Women and the Convention on the Rights of the Child.

Sylvia C. Tiwon is Associate Professor of Southeast Asian Studies at the University of California, Berkeley, and author of *Breaking the Spell: Colonialism and Literary Renaissance in Indonesia* (1999).

List of Abbreviations

AAWORD   Association of African Women Organized for Research and Development
AFL-CIO   American Federation of Labor and Congress of Industrial Organizations
AFP   *Agence France-Press*
Alt-WID   Alternative Women-in-Development
ANC   African National Congress
APFS   Asian People's Friendship Society
CEDAW   Convention on the Elimination of all Forms of Discrimination against Women
CEO   Chief Executive Officer
CIO   Congress of Industrial Organizations
CND   *China News Digest*
COWAN   Country-Women Association of Nigeria
CTIC   Catholic Tokyo International Center
CUEPACS   Congress of Unions of Employees in the Public and Civil Services
ECLAC   Economic Commission for Latin America and the Caribbean
EMU   Economic and Monetary Union
EPI   Economic Policy Institute
EU   European Union
FBIS   *Foreign Broadcast Information Service's China Daily Report*
FDI   foreign direct investment
FKTU   Federation of Korean Trade Unions
FNPR   Federation of Independent Trade Unions of Russia
FOMCA   Federation of Malaysian Consumers Association
FTUI   Free Trade Union Institute
GATT   General Agreement on Tariffs and Trade
IGO   intergovernmental organization
IMF   International Monetary Fund
ISA   Internal Security Act
JCMK   Joint Committee for Migrant Workers
KCTU   Korean Confederation of Trade Unions
LO   Landsorganisationen (Sweden)
MCA   Malayan Chinese Association

MIC	Malayan Indian Congress
MSP	Malay Special Privileges
MTUC	Malaysian Trades Union Congress
MWM	Migrant Workers' Movement
NAFTA	North American Free Trade Agreement
NCWS	National Council of Womens' Societies
NEP	New Economic Policy
NGO	nongovernmental organization
NNSMW	National Network in Solidarity with Migrant Workers
NOW	National Organization for Women
NSM	new social movements
NSP	New Social Policy
OECD	Organization for Economic Cooperation and Development
PAC	Pan African Congress
PDI	Partai Demokrasi Indonesia
PKI	Indonesian Communist Party
PPP	Partai Persatuan Pembangunan
SAP	Structural Adjustment Program
UMNO	United Malays National Organization
UNDP	United Nations Development Program
UN ECA	United Nations Economic Commission for Africa
UPI	*United Press International*
UPS	United Parcel Service
WIN	Women in Nigeria

Introduction: Globalization and the Double-Movement Hypothesis

Craig N. Murphy

This book is a collaborative, multiregional study of the strategies and impact of different types of egalitarian social movements over the last 20 years. It contrasts the recent experience of movements promoting democratization, women, labor and development in the USA, Western Europe, Latin America, the former Soviet Union, Africa, China, and parts of Southeast and Northeast Asia.

The project was triggered by patterns reported in *International Organization and Industrial Change* (Murphy 1994). That book argues that a series of stepwise changes has occurred in the scale of industrial economies, from the local and national economies of the early Industrial Revolution to the intercontinental markets linking the Organization for Economic Cooperation and Development (OECD) countries and the Third World in the Automobile and Jet Age of the mid-twentieth century. Each transition to a more encompassing industrial order has initially been marked by a period of relatively slow economic growth in which rapid marketization takes place, the state seems to retreat, and uncompromising versions of *laissez-faire* liberalism triumph. Until now, a second phase has always followed, one marked by the increasing role of a more socially oriented liberalism, the rise of which has been linked to the growing success of egalitarian social movements. This second phase, or, in Karl Polanyi's (1957) terms, the second part of this 'double movement', has also been associated with the consolidation of the whole range of 'governance' institutions, from the interstate level down to the shop floor. Those institutions, for a time, help maintain a period of relative peace and relative prosperity over a larger industrial market area in which a new generation of lead industries become dominant. Eventually, however, various social conflicts, including those that arise from the restraints on liberal innovation imposed by each era's governance institutions, lead to crises, to which a new generation of *laissez-faire* 'first movers' provide the initial, successful social response.

The two-stage pattern is consistent with core arguments of the liberal internationalist tradition that goes back to Adam Smith and Immanuel Kant. Both theorists expected that a social form of liberal republican state would contribute to prosperity and peace but that any putatively 'republican' state captured by the interests of profit-takers would be unable to sustain a liberal, highly productive economy. Instead, an economy based on cartels, monopolization and so on would take hold, as it had in company-run colonies of Smith's day. This is similar to the characterization of the current world economy put forward by the late Susan Strange in her *Retreat of the State* (1996). Within the logic of Smith and Kant's argument, powerful egalitarian social movements help restore the 'divided government' (the liberal, republican polities) that allows a liberal economy to be a source of prosperity, human dignity and peace.

With this perspective in mind, we could look at the last decades of the twentieth century – an era of relatively slow growth in most parts of the world, rapid marketization and the relative retreat of the state – as a stage in the development of a wider liberal 'world order'. Moreover, if the earlier pattern holds, the prospects for the movement to the next phase will be linked to the relative success of the whole range of egalitarian social movements: hence this project.

Even if the pattern no longer holds, there is sufficient reason to warrant interest in regional differences in the relative success of various egalitarian social movements. Looked at globally, women's movements and movements for democratization and the protection of human rights appear to have been markedly more successful in recent years than labor movements or movements concerned with development. Wage gaps between men and women have narrowed, and women's access to education and privileged labor markets has increased in almost all parts of the world (UN Development Program, or UNDP 1995; Tzannatos 1998). Similarly, the number of liberal democracies has greatly increased, as has the formal protection of human rights on almost every continent (M. Ward *et al.* 1999). On the other hand, compelling evidence indicates that income gaps within societies have grown in many parts of the world over the same period. The gaps between more and less privileged regions of the world, the 'developed' and the 'less developed', have grown in an equally startling way (Pritchett 1995; UNDP 1995; World Bank 1995; Milanovic 1999).

Over the past 20 years, the seemingly more successful women's movements and democratization movements have tended to pursue national or local goals through struggles linked by a transnational cadre who shared a worldview and used transnational conferences and the powers of intergovernmental and nongovernmental institutions to support local efforts. The proximate causes of the various narrowed gender gaps were changes in national legislation and in the practices of multinational firms and international aid agencies. In addition, however, women have been able to use the UN conference circuit since 1975 to develop links among separate regional struggles, create a flexible and well-connected transnational cadre of activists, agree on a surprisingly wide set of priorities, and insert those priorities into the work of significant intergovernmental organizations. Moreover, women have been unusually successful at building solidarity across lines of identity difference, be they race, religion or culture.

A somewhat similar story can be told about movements for democratization and human rights, although the linking institutions, cadres and ideas central to the story differ. In this case, central roles have been played by Western, liberal institutions – including private foundations supporting the goals of a free society – as well as by the Catholic Church. Neoclassical economists, human rights activists, some media figures, and officials of a number of Western governments have played roles at the center of a transnational cadre, allowing local struggles – in Eastern Europe, Latin America, and parts of Asia and Africa – to become linked.

The same cannot be said about the international labor movements or international movements for development. Labor movements and development movements have nothing like the unified transnational strategies or global cadre of the women's movement. In addition, lines of identity difference within many societies (as well as across them) create deep rifts among workers and between First World and Third World peoples.

Do these differences in organization and strategy account for a significant part of the differences in outcomes? To find out, I asked a group of regional specialists to identify the range of egalitarian social movements that has developed over the last 20 years within the regions of their expertise. Within the parts of the world they knew best, they investigated the goals and strategies of various movements, their relative success, and the reasons for it. They asked to what extent are changes in levels of inequality across different dimensions the consequence of differences in organization and strategy rather than of larger political and economic forces? They paid special attention to the impact of strategies and worldviews that make bridges across identity boundaries and those that foster international and transnational links.

What the regional specialists discovered confounded many of my hypotheses and ultimately painted a much more complex picture of contemporary egalitarian politics. Historical evidence had suggested that egalitarian social movements play a key role in Polanyi's double movement – first away from society and toward the market, then back toward society – that has marked the geographic expansion of capitalist industrialism. Although recent history does not refute this hypothesis, the case studies demonstrate something more interesting. Indeed, the marketization that has become characteristic of all societies over the last 20 years has, in many cases, resulted in organized responses by and on behalf of the disadvantaged. Reaching comparative conclusions about the efficacy of different manifestations of this egalitarian political response turns out to be quite difficult, however, if only because they are not truly independent cases.

Contemporary marketization is largely the manifestation of one or, at most, two or three transnational political and economic processes. It is the political program of neoliberal forces responding to political opportunities throughout the OECD and the Cold War-era dependent Third World that emerged with the breakdown of the Bretton Woods Western economic order in the 1970s. It is also the political program of the same social forces and their local allies responding to the differing crises of the Leninist political and economic model throughout Eastern Europe, the former Soviet Union and China.

The concurrent phenomena that provided our research puzzle – for example, that at an aggregate level, the number of formal democracies has increased and gender inequality has decreased whereas class-based and North–South inequalities have increased – can be explained in part by the different strategies typically employed by women's and democratic movements on the one hand, and by labor movements and development movements on the other. Yet this is not necessarily why, at a global level, women's movements and democracy movements may play a greater role in any move back toward society that came with the beginning of today's new industrial era, the so-called Information Age.

In many places, both democratization and women's empowerment are chimeras. The gap between women's and men's wages has narrowed, and women have access to more kinds of jobs in part because economic deprivation has forced more women to work for wages and competition-stretched firms have welcomed them. In other ways, perhaps less easily studied, the relative position of women has declined in many places as relatively gender-neutral state programs have been privatized and as the scope and significance of patriarchal family relations has increased. Similarly, liberal democracy and the protections for human rights that have been achieved in the last two decades must be recognized as only partial victories for popular forces. Everywhere, these political openings have come as part of a larger package that brings not only marketization and increasing class inequality but also the widespread conviction that 'there is no alternative' to the inegalitarian economic paradigm. In some parts of the world, multiparty elections and the organizations of a seemingly thriving civil society are manifestations of creative human responses to the funding requirements of increasingly powerful OECD donors. However, they should not be confused with effective local government by the people.

Globalization and marketization have undoubtedly energized real egalitarian social movements in many parts of the world. In the former Soviet sphere, however, the lack of traditions of political organization and the overwhelming burden of the struggle simply to survive in posttransition societies have combined to ensure minimal response. In China, the continuation of a repressive political order has also closed the political space for organized social movements, although a complex form of popular response does exist. Where globalization and marketization have energized social responses, the movements have often been relatively ineffective because organizing at a level beyond that of the national society has become difficult.

In the USA, Western Europe, Latin America and Northeast Asia, emergent examples exist of this form of organization, but it is too soon to say what their impact will be. Nevertheless, particular characteristics of this stage of globalization are likely to make women's movements (for example) more effective agents than traditional class-based movements. The complex identity politics of the USA, Western Europe, Africa and Latin America reveal these strengths, and they are linked to the specific histories of the transnational women's movements and democratization movements that have already had an impact in the last decades of the twentieth century.

The next nine chapters make this more complex argument. First, Chapters 1 and 2 consider the local patterns in the USA and Western Europe, the regions that have had the greatest impact on the contemporary era of globalization. Chapters 3 and 4 show the patterns of globalization and response in Latin America and Africa, the areas of the world that are, arguably, most closely linked to this North Atlantic core. In Chapters 5 and 6, the former Leninist states – the former

Soviet Union and China – provide the third set of cases, those where the contrasts to the North Atlantic core and its dependencies are the greatest. Chapters 7 and 8 concentrate on the newly industrializing countries of Asia (until the financial crisis in the late 1990s, considered the great success stories of the current era of globalization) and on their model, Japan. In Chapter 9, I conclude by returning to the transnational patterns that link these cases and the complex lessons for egalitarian politics that they suggest.

The collaboration that resulted in this book took place over a two-year period with the support of a number of institutions and individuals to which we are immensely grateful. The authors were able to meet in two conferences under the generous auspices of Wellesley College's M. Margaret Ball Chair in International Relations and the Thomas J. Watson Jr Institute of International Studies at Brown University and its director, Thomas J. Biersteker.

Professors Partha Chatterjee of the University of Calcutta, A. Richard Norton of Boston University and Wellington Nyangoni of Brandeis University were members of the group, but were unable to complete papers for this volume. We are deeply indebted to them for their outlines, drafts and conversations. Their ideas remain a central part of almost every chapter of this book.

An earlier version of chapter 1 was published in Mark Rupert, *Ideologies of Globalization*, Routledge 2000, and is published by permission.

Debra David, former managing editor of *Global Governance*, prepared the final manuscript. We are grateful for her experience and her invaluable help in unifying so many different voices from so many corners of the world.

Finally, we thank Tim Shaw of Dalhousie University for supporting the project from the beginning, for taking part in the second conference, and for finding a place for this book in this series. Many of us owe career-long debts to Tim, one of the most active, generous and consistent promoters of critical and truly global scholarship, especially by junior scholars. We hope these studies merit the faith he put in many of us when we were new to this field, and we dedicate this book to him.

1
Class, Gender and the Politics of Neoliberal Globalization in the USA

Mark Rupert

The sharp recession of 1979, which Paul Volcker and the Federal Reserve Board inflicted upon working Americans in order to 'squeeze inflation out of the economy' and protect the interests of the investor class, may, in retrospect, be seen as the first indication that volcanic processes were about to rearrange the landscape of the US political economy and its relations with the world economy (Greider 1987, 75–123; Wachtel 1990, 132–6). The subterranean transformations that, since the mid-1960s, had been restructuring the postwar national and international historic bloc – the alliances of classes, ideas and institutions governing the US-led world economy – erupted in 1979. Since 1979, they have destabilized the conditions of life for many Americans. Both blue-collar and white-collar workers have been rocked by waves of corporate restructuring, mass layoffs and plant closures, aggressive concessionary bargaining and union-busting, and increasing use of temporary and contingent forms of work, all set against a backdrop of a mythical (or at least 'mythic') process of 'globalization' that was just real enough to enable employers to make widespread use of the threat to relocate jobs if workers failed to be sufficiently responsive to the putative imperatives of global competition. At the same time, working people have been forced to struggle with the sacrifices required for 'global competitiveness', corporate profits have been extraordinarily handsome, chief executive officers (CEOs) and investors have made money hand over fist, and Wall Street has indulged in a long-term, record-setting bull market. It is in this context that inequalities of both income and wealth in the United States have attained extreme levels not seen since the 1920s. In such conditions of tension and flux, the hegemonic ideology of postwar liberal capitalism may seem increasingly hollow to some Americans, and its established routines of political

7

practice may no longer contain them effectively. The present situation contains the potential for an organic crisis of the postwar hegemonic order, a crisis that opens a range of political possibilities that would have seemed utopian or dystopian 20 years ago.

From the perverse populisms of Ross Perot and Pat Buchanan and the revolutionary rhetoric and violent potential of the patriot and militia movements (see Rupert 1997), to an apparent resurgence of the labor movement in the Teamsters' 1997 United Parcel Service (UPS) strike, and transnational labor–consumer alliances in the current antisweat-shop campaigns and the Seattle and Washington protests against the World Trade Organization and the International Monetary Fund (IMF)/World Bank, the crisis of the old hegemony is giving birth to a range of counterhegemonic or antihegemonic political projects. The rhetoric of these movements is sharply critical of the project of liberal globalization and often includes representations of arrogant and abusive corporate power. Yet the terms in which these critiques are constructed differ dramatically and so, therefore, do the political futures they are able to imagine. In this chapter, I contrast the implications of these various antihegemonic ideologies for global political economy, with particular attention paid to their ability to support dialogues and coalitions across national boundaries and potentially also across boundaries of gender and race. Although I would not wish to minimize the importance of race to progressive politics in the United States (see, for example, Goldfield 1997), my primary concern in this chapter will be the potential for a progressive political convergence of the politics of class and gender.

Fordism and class politics in twentieth-century America

Following Antonio Gramsci, I understand Fordism to be a sociopolitical regime, a set of institutionalized relationships between the social organization of production, on the one hand, and social self-understandings and political organizations, on the other. Gramsci (1971, 280–1) was among the first theorists to recognize the potential political and cultural significance of 'an ultra-modern form of production and of working methods – such as is offered by the most advanced American variety, the industry of Henry Ford'.

Displacing predominantly craft-based production in which skilled laborers exercised substantial control over their conditions of work, Fordist production entailed an intensified industrial division of labor, increased mechanization, and coordination of large-scale manufacturing processes (for example, sequential machining operations and converging assembly lines) to achieve a steady flow of production. It also entailed a shift toward the use of less skilled labor performing, *ad infinitum*, tasks minutely specified by management and the potential for heightened capitalist control over the pace and intensity of work.

In the mid-1920s, one production worker described as follows the relentless pace and intense effort that his job required and the consequences of failing to meet that standard on a daily basis:

> You've got to work like hell in Ford's. From the time you become a number in the morning until the bell rings for quitting time you have to keep at it. You can't let up. You've got to get out the production ... and if you can't get it out, you get out. (Quoted in Rupert 1995, 111)

At the core of the Fordist reorganization of production, then, was the construction of new relations of power in the workplace. To the extent that these relations of power could become established parameters of the work process, capital would reap the gains of manifold increases in output per hour of wage labor.

The promise of massive increases in productivity led to the widespread imitation and adaptation of Ford's basic model of production through the industrial core of the US economy. The institutionalization of such a system of production required a combination of force and persuasion: a political regime in which trade unions would be subdued, workers might be offered a higher real standard of living, and the ideological legitimation of this new kind of capitalism would be embodied in cultural practices and social relations extending far beyond the workplace (Rupert 1995).

In the 40 years following the first experiments in line assembly at Ford's Highland Park plant, industrial struggles focusing on issues of unionization and the politics of production waxed and waned throughout the industrial sectors of the US economy. The relationship of industrial workers to the corporate giants that dominated the manufacturing heart of the economy was not effectively stabilized until the militant industrial unions that arose in the 1930s were deradicalized, incorporated into the social infrastructure of the economy, and became junior partners in the coalition that established US global hegemony in the postwar world. The relationship of industrial labor and US global power was consummated during the early years of the Cold War when the Congress of Industrial Organizations (CIO) purged its leadership of radicals and expelled entire unions that were perceived to be under communist leadership or influence (for example, because they criticized the country's emerging global role). In the context of rising Cold War fears and access to an unprecedented affluence (rising real wages secured for unionized industrial workers through pattern bargaining, the linking of wages to productivity growth, cost-of-living adjustments, and so on), the challenge of industrial labor was contained within the bounds of a vision of liberal capitalism as the social system best able to secure – on a global basis, and with the active collaboration of 'free trade unions' – individual rights and liberties and a more generalized prosperity. Cold War anticommunism was the ideological cement that bound industrial labor together with internationally oriented segments of corporate capital in the project of reconstructing the world economy along liberal capitalist lines (Rupert 1995).

Political ambiguities of Fordism in America

The political institutions of Fordism were profoundly ambiguous. On the one hand, they enabled working people to have some collective voice in the conditions under which they sold their labor-power, and they provided organized labor with some recognition and influence within one of America's major political parties. These are real historical victories, hard won and not to be taken lightly (as labor learned painfully during the Reagan–Bush years of Republican rollback). But the democratizing potential of Fordist political institutions was severely constrained. The collective bargaining fostered and channeled by these institutions was of an economistic nature – limited for the most part to wages, benefits and working conditions – and was premised upon an acceptance of capitalist control of the labor process (in the form of a 'workplace rule of law') and the prioritization of private profits as the primary social value (Rupert 1995). Whereas the industrial union movement of the 1930s and 1940s was a vibrant and polyvocal grassroots movement, central to which were political tendencies that envisioned a broad-based democratization of the capitalist economy under the banner of 'industrial democracy', the unionism institutionalized under the Fordist regime was a bureaucratic and economically oriented 'business unionism'. 'This metamorphosis,' Kim Moody explains, 'involved the suppression of internal political life, the ritualization of the bargaining process, the expansion of the administrative apparatus to unprecedented levels, and the abandonment of the concept of social unionism that had been the public face of the CIO' (1988, 41).

Under the Fordist regime, then, organized labor was both empowered and disempowered. It was empowered to bargain over wages and working conditions, and thus to attempt to secure for its members a larger share of the social surplus that the Fordist organization of production made possible. But the condition of this empowerment of industrial unions was the disempowerment of their rank and file on the shop floor and within the increasingly hierarchic unions themselves, and the exclusion and repression of more broadly based, explicitly political, transformative visions of what the union movement could be. Industrial unionism was empowered to cast its organized support behind the Democratic Party and its modest agenda of social reform. But it was disempowered in other ways. Insofar as labor lacked any real political alternative to the Democratic Party, the Democrats were well aware that they could afford to take organized labor's support for granted without major or sustained exertions on labor's behalf. And organized labor became politically dependent upon a Democratic Party that was unprepared to challenge business hegemony in America or promote an agenda of transformative democratization.

The politics of Fordism were also ambiguous insofar as even its limited forms of empowerment were unevenly distributed across the working class, made available to some workers while excluding many others. These processes of inclusion and exclusion have not been race- or gender-neutral, and this segmentation of the working class has been politically consequential. David Gordon, Richard Edwards and Michael Reich (1982, 192–210) document the emergence within the postwar US industrial economy of a sectoral division between an industrial 'core' and an industrial 'periphery'. In the core, large and concentrated manufacturing firms enjoyed a growing productivity advantage over smaller manufacturing firms in the more fiercely competitive peripheral sector. Core firms tended to be more densely unionized than the periphery, paid significantly higher wages (further, the core/periphery wage gap grew wider between 1958 and 1973–75) and offered somewhat greater job security. These latter tendencies are likely to have been mutually reinforcing for core firms, because unionization and higher wage rates create incentives for firms to invest in productivity-enhancing technology even as higher productivity enables these firms to purchase labor peace through collective bargaining with industrial unions.

As women and African–Americans entered the industrial labor force in greater numbers, segregation by race and gender interacted with labor market segmentation. Women and African–Americans were disproportionately represented in peripheral sector employment; and although they were also present in the core industries, they tended to be concentrated in the least rewarding and least secure activities. According to Gordon, Edwards and Reich (1982, 210), 60 per cent of black workers were employed in secondary jobs (peripheral manufacturing or low-paid service sector) in 1970. Still more extreme was gendered division: 'Four categories of female workers – those in the peripheral manufacturing industries, in retail trade, in clerical occupations, and in the health and educational sectors – accounted for 95 per cent of all female employment in 1970' (1982, 206). Their concentration in less unionized industries (non-goods producing) has much to do with the fact that female workers are substantially less likely to belong to unions than males (R. Freeman and Medoff 1984, 26–8).

Nevertheless, it is too simple to claim that Fordist unions have been a white man's preserve or that their overall effect has been to increase inequality by creating a privileged industrial aristocracy. 'Nonwhite' workers, for example, have been more likely than 'whites' to belong to industrial unions (Freeman and Medoff 1984, 27–30). And belonging to a union has tended to shield those workers, as well as unionized female workers, from the full effects of labor market discrimination: using Labor Department data for 1997, the American Federation of Labor and Congress of Industrial Organizations (AFL–CIO) reports that the union wage benefit (the difference between union and nonunion wages) is 34 per cent for all workers, 40 per cent for women, 44 per cent for African–Americans, and 53 per cent for Latino workers (AFL–CIO, 1998). These data also reveal that even within the unionized workforce, however, the median weekly earnings of male workers are substantially higher than the overall median ($683 versus $640), and that men ($683) tend to be paid more than women ($577), African–Americans ($533) or Latinos ($506).

Despite these ambiguities, the authoritative study by Richard Freeman and James Medoff argues against the labor aristocracy thesis. Rather, they argue that three effects attributable to unions contribute to overall income equalization: 'union wage policies lower inequality of wages *within* establishments; 'union wage policies favor equal pay for equal work *across* establishments; and union wage gains for blue-collar labor reduce inequality between white-collar and blue-collar workers' (1984, 78). My own conclusion is more ambiguous. It seems to me that the unions of the Fordist regime have lessened inequalities based on race and gender but have also at the same time failed to eliminate such inequalities and, to that extent, may be said to have institutionalized them.

Finally, the politics of Fordism were ambiguous insofar as securing a livable wage for working-class families came at the expense of women. Fordism reinforced the ideology of female domesticity by emphasizing a 'family wage' sufficient to support the dependents of the breadwinner. In this way, an understanding was normalized of 'the family' as comprising dependent women and children as well as a male breadwinner. In the words of Martha May:

> The family 'living wage' for male workers assumed that all women would, sooner or later, become wives, and thus it was legitimate to argue for the exclusion of women from the labor force. Working women were believed to devalue wages, making a 'living wage' difficult to achieve and upsetting a natural sexual order. (1990, 277)

Thus, the family wage ideology implied the norm of a privatized life of domestic dependency for women, and it justified paying female workers lower wages, because the implicit norm suggested that women either were or should be provided for by the family wage earned by a husband or father.

In all of these ways, then, the politics of Fordism were deeply ambiguous: progressive perhaps in some ways but divisive and disempowering in others. No matter, the historical structures underpinning such politics were not to last.

Decline of Fordism and possibilities of class politics

As the new millennium begins, the Fordist world order is under great strain. Following on the disintegration of the 'Evil Empire', the Cold War has been officially pronounced to be over: anticommunism no longer serves as a crucial ingredient in the ideological cement binding together the postwar historic bloc. Further, the postwar prosperity that US industrial labor had enjoyed as a result of its participation in the hegemonic bloc is evaporating. Unions, the central institutions of 'industrial democracy' in Fordist America, have been attacked by the state and capital, memberships are in long-term decline, and real wages have been effectively reduced even as productivity growth rebounded during the 1980s (Mishel, Bernstein and Schmitt 1997, 131–5, 166–8). With the mutation of the postwar historic bloc such that transnational financial and industrial capital are increasingly predominant and industrial labor within the United States is no longer a relatively privileged junior partner, sociopolitical relations and popular ideologies that once seemed firmly grounded are now increasingly up for grabs.

In sharp contrast to the central presuppositions of Fordist hegemony, working Americans increasingly realize that they live in an environment where corporate profits need not correspond to rising standards of living or improved quality of life for themselves and their coworkers, and that their ability to exercise any control at all over their economic futures is, under current institutional arrangements, quite limited. Mounting evidence of long-term tendencies toward transnational production, corporate 'restructuring', subcontracting and outsourcing, plant closures and layoffs, concessionary bargaining and union-busting, increasing exploitation of part-timers and contingent workers, declining real wages, widening and deepening poverty and intense economic uncertainty among average Americans has in recent years been juxtaposed to news of resurgent corporate profits, happy days on Wall Street, and breathtaking inequalities of income and wealth. The liberal vision of a transnational order institutionalizing the values of freedom and prosperity – most firmly embedded in popular common sense during the postwar decades – may begin to seem bitterly ironic to growing numbers of Americans.

Once solidly hegemonic, the liberal narrative of globalization is now increasingly vulnerable to challenge. The liberal narrative associates capitalism and globally competitive markets with prosperity and liberty (understood in terms of individual choice). In the sociopolitical circumstances of the new century, however, average Americans might be more likely to find some plausibility in narratives that claim global capitalism can be relied upon to deliver neither prosperity nor liberty or, rather, to deliver these to socially privileged groups at the expense of the majority.

A constellation of factors – including deindustrialization and the shift toward service employment, deunionization and increasing vulnerability to trade and the transnational mobility of capital – has contributed to a palpable shift in social power in favor of capital and capitalists and to the disadvantage of workers, communities and unions. Indicators of this shift are not hard to find. After rising steadily through the postwar decades, the real wages of production and nonsupervisory workers have been declining more or less steadily since 1973.[1] Further, after dramatic reduction between 1964 and 1974, the proportion of workers earning wages insufficient to support a family of four above the official poverty level increased by 50 per cent between 1974 and 1990. By the latter year, according to more conservative estimates, almost one in five year-round full-time workers was earning below-poverty wages (US Census Bureau 1992, 3; compare Mishel, Bernstein and Schmitt 1997, 149–56).

The proportion of the workforce engaged in provision of services has increased from around 50 per cent in 1950 to about 75 per cent in 1990; manufacturing employment has also declined from about 35 per cent to about 22 per cent of the labor force. This is significant because the service sector is typically less productive and pays substantially lower wages than manufacturing. In 1993, average hourly compensation (wages plus benefits) in services was $15.51, compared with $20.22 in goods production (Folbre 1995, 2.2–2.3). So a shift in the composition of the economy away from manufacturing and toward services would tend to lower overall productivity and overall wages.

However, declining overall rates of productivity growth resulting from an increasingly service-based economy cannot explain why compensation has lagged behind productivity since the mid-1960s. During the 'golden years' of postwar Fordism, real wages rose steadily along with productivity (Rupert 1995, 179). That relationship has since been severed: productivity continues to rise (albeit more slowly than during the 'golden age'), while real wages have been declining and total compensation (wages plus benefits) have stagnated (Mishel, Bernstein and Schmitt 1997, 131–8). Doug Henwood, editor of *Left Business Observer*, explains:

> We're constantly told by economists and pundits that the key to getting wages up again is raising productivity. But over the last several decades, productivity – the inflation-adjusted value of output per hour of work – has risen much faster than real compensation (wages plus fringe benefits adjusted for inflation) … Here's another way to think about the growing gap between productivity and wages. According to the World Bank, in 1966, US manufacturing wages were equal to 46 per cent of the value added in production (value-added is the difference between selling price and the costs of raw material and other inputs). In 1990, that figure had fallen to 36 per cent. (Henwood 1997b)

Workers in post-Fordist America, it seems, are less able to lay claim to the fruits of their growing productivity. This intensified exploitation of workers is a large part of the explanation for higher corporate profits, a roaring stock market, and growth in executive compensation so extravagant that even the business press seemed embarrassed.

The labor-oriented Economic Policy Institute (EPI) concurs that a significant power shift in favor of capital has occurred. According to EPI economist Lawrence Mishel (1997), whereas 'labor's share of corporate sector income rose from 79.2 per cent in 1959 to 83.9 per cent in 1979', it had declined to about 81 per cent by 1996. In the manufacturing sector, the reversal has been sharper still. Correspondingly, EPI reported that corporate profit rates have hit record peaks over the last eight-year business cycle, up more than 50 per cent from the profit peak of the previous business cycle (substantially higher, that is, than the profit peak of the rabidly probusiness Reagan–Bush years):

> Corporate profit rates reached a new peak in 1996 and are now at their highest level since these data were first collected in 1959 ... In no previous period in US history have profit rates experienced such a rapid sustained rise ... The rise in profit rates results from two factors: a shift in income from wages to profits, and a decline in the relative size of the capital stock due to low levels on investment ... In 1988, 14.07 per cent of corporate income went to profits. In 1996, this proportion had risen by more than a full percentage point to 15.16 per cent. This shift from wages to profits created a gap between wage growth and productivity growth, and took away approximately one quarter of the wage gain that workers would have realized over the last eight years if their wages had kept pace with productivity. (EPI 1997; see also Baker and Mishel 1995)

Conditions favoring extraordinary levels of corporate profitability have translated into rich rewards for investors. According to Henwood (1997a), recent record highs on Wall Street (the Dow surging past 10 000) represent the crest of a wave that has been building for years:

> Over the last 15 years, the real (inflation-adjusted) Standard & Poor's 500 index, a proxy for blue-chip corporate America, is up 574 per cent, by far the biggest 15-year real rise since good statistics start in 1886; in 1964, it was 434 per cent; in 1929, 205 per cent. By most conventional measures of whether stocks are reasonably priced, the market is at or near historic extremes.

Not only have investors made substantial profits through the appreciation of their assets but they have also been receiving generous dividends: 'Firms are paying out near-record shares of their profits to their stockholders, 70 per cent of after-tax profits since 1982, [almost] twice historical averages.' Henwood suggests that, Federal Reserve Board chairman Alan Greenspan notwithstanding, this 'exuberance' in the markets is not altogether 'irrational', but rather 'stock markets are celebrating the political triumph of capital worldwide'.

It is sometimes claimed that growing participation in mutual funds and pension plans have 'democratized' the ownership of capital, implying that the benefits of a booming stock market might trickle down at least as far as the 'middle class'. It is important to remember, however, that ownership of financial and business assets remains highly concentrated among the very rich, and the great bulk of the gains from the stock market boom have accrued to the top 10 per cent of US households (see Mishel, Bernstein and Schmitt 1997, 287–92).

If the 1990s have been good to members of the investor class who derive the bulk of their income from the ownership of financial and business assets, they have also been happy times for corporate executives (who, as recipients of large stock options, are also members of the investor class). In 1978, the average American corporate CEO earned about 60 times as much as the average worker; by 1995 the average CEO was making 172 times as much as his workers. The compensation of the average CEO grew by 152 per cent between 1978 and 1995, rising to more than $4.3 million annually (Mishel, Bernstein and Schmitt 1997, 226).

The classical Marxian concept of class based upon relationship to the means of production surely has some purchase in the contemporary US political economy. Bowles and Edwards (1993, 105) report that in 1988, the richest 1 per cent of US families, enjoying annual incomes of more than one million dollars, received almost three-quarters of their income from property ownership in the form of profit, interest, capital gain, rents and royalties. This contrasts markedly with the great majority of families, who are primarily dependent upon wage labor to supply the necessities of life and who are, therefore, fully subject to the manifold relations of power and domination that are inherent in the capitalist wage relation. In 1988, the 46 million families whose incomes fell between $20 000 and $75 000 received almost 84 per cent of their income from labor.

In an environment where the rewards to corporate managers and investors have far outstripped the wages of working people, it should not be surprising to discover that inequalities of income and wealth are at historically high levels. According to the US Census Bureau, income inequality increased markedly between 1968 and 1994, such that the income gap between rich and poor was wider in 1994 than at any time since 1947, when it began collecting such data (US Census Bureau 1996; see also Wolff 1995, 28; Mishel, Bernstein and Schmitt 1997, 52–64).

Inequality of wealth is even starker than the income gap. According to Federal Reserve data for 1995, the wealthiest 10 per cent of the population owned 84 per cent of the stock and 90 per cent of the bonds owned by individuals (including indirect ownership through mutual funds), as well as 92 per cent of business assets. The top 1 per cent now control more wealth than the bottom 90 per cent of the population (Henwood 1997c; see also Wolff 1995, 7; Mishel, Bernstein and Schmitt 1997, 278–81).

Working people have not shared in this bounty; in fact, it has been predicated upon their resubjugation to more direct forms of class-based power. Formerly privileged as junior partners in the postwar hegemonic bloc, unions have been the object of a sustained assault in recent decades (Moody 1988) and have seen union membership in decline since the 1950s. Recent figures show the continuing decline of the union movement from over 20 per cent of wage and salary workers in 1983 to 14.5 per cent in 1996. This is directly related to declining real wages, because unionized workers enjoy a substantial pay advantage over the nonunionized (and create significant 'spillover' effects into nonunionized workplaces); in 1996, median weekly earnings for unionized workers were $615, compared to $462 for workers without union representation (US Bureau of Labor Statistics 1997). But even unionized workers have been on the defensive since the early 1980s, negotiating dramatically smaller pay increases and demonstrating ever more reluctance to invoke the strike weapon (Rupert 1995, 183–7). This decline of union power translates into a lessened ability for working people to bargain collectively and thereby to have a voice in determining the conditions of their labor (Mishel, Bernstein and Schmitt 1997, 198–203).

The EPI claims that increased trade, especially imports of manufactured goods from developing countries, has contributed to deindustrialization and job losses in the United States and has put downward pressure on the wages of industrial workers (Mishel, Bernstein and Schmitt 1997, 190–7). But the effects of globalization go far beyond the 11 per cent of the US economy accounted for by imported manufactures. Employers throughout the economy are fully aware of the fearful dependence of working people upon their jobs; and in an era of transnationalized production, managers are prepared to exploit this economic insecurity as a source of workplace power. This is clearly demonstrated through the now common threats by employers to close plants and eliminate jobs when they are faced with unionization drives or new collective bargaining situations. According to one of the most comprehensive and systematic studies of unionization campaigns undertaken in the period since the founding of the North American Free Trade Agreement (NAFTA), this type of workplace extortion has taken a variety of forms:

> Specific unambiguous threats ranged from attaching shipping labels to equipment throughout the plant with a Mexican address, to posting maps of North America with an arrow pointing from the current plant site to Mexico, to a letter directly stating that the company will have to shut down if the union wins the election.

One firm shut down a production line without warning and 'parked thirteen flat-bed tractor-trailers loaded with shrink-wrapped production equipment in front of the plant for the duration' of the unionization campaign, marked with large hot-pink signs reading 'Mexico Transfer Job'. Between 1993 and 1995, such threats accompanied at least half of all union certification elections (Bronfenbrenner 1997, 8–9). In the words of one auto worker contemplating his future in a transnationalized economy, the threat of runaway jobs 'puts the fear in you' (quoted in Rupert 1995, 195); and, indeed, it is intended to do so. It is the threat of transnational capital mobility and job loss, combined with the ideologies of 'global competitiveness' and 'workplace cooperation', that represents the articulation of coercion and consent in the post-Fordist workplace (Moody 1997).

That something profound was happening to Fordism's version of 'the American Dream' was brought home to many people by waves of corporate 'restructuring', often involving massive layoffs of blue-collar workers and middle managers. The Institute for Policy Studies released a report showing that CEOs who engineered major layoffs received higher than average pay raises (including stock options), that Wall Street tended to reward layoffs by bidding up the stock prices of these firms when layoffs were announced, and that CEOs and investors together enjoyed windfalls from these bouts of job destruction (S. Anderson and Cavanagh 1996). For a time, this theme received intense media attention. Many of the news items were narratives of the profit motive run amok, of corporate power and arrogance overriding the simple decency of average working people. Media attention to these issues seemed to reach a crescendo in early 1996, when the *New York Times* published its 'Downsizing of America' series, and Pat Buchanan made the plight of

American working people one of the primary themes of his right-populist presidential campaign. During this period, stories about corporate downsizing were commonplace in the mainstream media, sometimes coming close to questioning the presumptive priority of profit maximization as a social norm. *Newsweek* ran a controversial cover story on the architects of major corporate restructuring plans whom it identified as 'the Hit Men': the story highlighted the tens of thousands of jobs recently liquidated by top corporate CEOs and juxtaposed these figures with their million-dollar salaries (26 February 1996).

There is some evidence that these experiences and their interpretation in terms of arrogant and unresponsive corporate power have begun to effect changes in popular common sense, changes that may not bode well for the hegemonic ideology of liberal capitalism. The 1997 strike of package handlers and drivers at UPS evoked much greater sympathy from the public at large than other major industrial actions of recent decades. In its representations of strike issues, the Teamsters highlighted the usage of lower-paid part-time workers by UPS to create a two-tiered wage system. This issue appears to have resonated with people attempting to make a living in a post-Fordist America where many fear being relegated to the growing sector of part-time, temporary or contingent workers, earning substantially lower hourly wages and more meager benefits than full-time 'core' employees (Mishel, Bernstein and Schmitt 1997, 257–61, 265–71; Uchitelle 1997; Carre and Tilly 1998). Survey data suggest that a majority of the public claimed to support the striking Teamsters' union, whereas just over one-quarter voiced support for UPS management.

This reflects what may be a longer-term reorientation away from a core element of Fordist hegemony: the presumptive identification of American working people with the interests and profits of employers. In 1984, 34 per cent of the public claimed to generally support labor in industrial disputes, whereas 45 per cent said they favored management; in 1996, responses to a similar survey question suggested that 44 per cent favored workers, whereas only 24 per cent were predisposed toward management. John J. Sweeney, president of the AFL–CIO, explained how the expansion of corporate profits at the expense of the American Dream has made working people more responsive to the union's message: 'People understand when you talk to them about the transition from full-time, middle-income jobs to part-time, low-income jobs' (Greenhouse 1997a). When you speak to people now about the death of the American Dream as they had come to know it during the postwar decades, they are increasingly ready to listen.

This, then, is the historical-structural context in which battles over the meaning of *globalization* are being waged. The hegemonic bloc of the Fordist period is being restructured, and organized labor in the United States finds itself shut out of its once privileged position, denied access to the affluence it took for granted during the postwar 'golden years' and deprived of a voice in the conventional political process. The agenda of capital accumulation dominates both major parties just as capital itself dominates the economy. Ordinary Americans find themselves struggling with social power relations obscured from, and by, the hegemonic ideology of liberal capitalism. Under these circumstances, it seems to me unwise to presume that the formerly dominant ideology will continue to define the ways in which globalization will be interpreted and acted upon. Rather, the meanings assigned to globalization, and the kinds of political projects enabled by these worldviews, will be determined by struggles waged on the terrain of popular common sense. To what extent might these struggles begin to bridge the chasms separating the politics of class and gender in the United States?

Intersections of gender and class

In contrast to those who would reify gender relations by deploying a transhistorical notion of patriarchy as near-universal male domination, as well as those who would subsume gender relations as but one of the areas where capitalism secures its functional reproduction, Michele Barrett proposes a Marxian feminism in which gender and capitalism are understood to be mutually irreducible but historically intertwined. 'No one would want to deny that there are physiological differences between the sexes, but what is at issue is how these differences are constructed as divisions by human social agency' (Barrett 1988, 250). The social construction of gender difference did not begin with capitalism, but capitalist relations of production emerged from (conflictual and open-ended) historical processes that included the reworking of socially constructed gender relations, such that they became interwoven with the social fabric of capitalism:

> It is clear that on the one hand the wage relation characteristic of capitalism, and the accompanying separation of home and workplace, have historically made a substantial contribution to the formation of the present sexual division of labor in which women's position is located principally in relation to responsibility for domestic labor and

dependence upon a male wage-earner. On the other hand, some elements of this sexual division undoubtedly existed before the development of capitalism; they have not been totally constructed by capitalism. In addition to this historically prior sexual division of labor, upon which capitalism has built a more rigidly segregated division, we can isolate many points of struggle in which the eventual outcome is not pre-given in terms of the requirements of capital. (Barrett 1988, 137)

A model of women's dependence has become entrenched in the relations of production of capitalism, in the divisions of labor in wage work, and between wage labor and domestic labor. As such, an oppression of women that is not in any essentialist sense 'pre-given' by the logic of capitalist development has become necessary for the ongoing reproduction of the mode of production in its present form. Hence the oppression of women, although not a functional prerequisite of capitalism, has acquired a material basis in the relations of production and reproduction of capitalism today (Barrett 1988, 249).

Under capitalist relations of production, women are seen to have a 'dual relationship' to class structure: they may be wage laborers themselves, directly exploited through the sale of their own labor-power, or they may be involved in a mediated relationship of exploitation through their dependence upon a male wage-earner and their responsibility for domestic labor and child care, or both (Barrett 1988, 139, 151). The dependent position of women in the context of modern capitalism is thus produced both in the workplace and in the family.

In the workplace, women are subject to a 'vertical' division of labor in which they are subordinated to men in terms of power and remuneration and a 'horizontal' division of labor in which women are overrepresented in some types of work and underrepresented in others. Evidence from the US political economy strongly supports the existence of these divisions: at every level of education, women are paid substantially less than men; and women tend to be concentrated in clerical and service jobs and in the relatively lower-status and lower-paid professions such as nursing and teaching (Albelda and Tilly 1997, 4–6, 46–7).

Both the vertical and horizontal divisions of labor are related to women's positioning within the family. Insofar as women are assigned primary responsibility for child rearing and domestic labor, they may be more likely to work part-time or to leave the workforce altogether for extended periods, and correspondingly they may be less powerful and more insecure at work, less able to develop and defend job skills, to form ties of solidarity and bargain from a position of (relative) strength, to accumulate seniority, and to be promoted along a career track parallel to that traveled by many men. 'Furthermore, the construction of a family form in which the male head of household is supposedly responsible for the financial support of a dependent wife and children has militated against demands for equal pay and an equal "right to work" by women' (Barrett 1988, 157). According to Randy Albelda and Chris Tilly (1997, 4–5), women in the United States make about two-thirds of men's hourly wage, but women tend to work fewer hours a year than men, primarily because of their domestic burdens, which means that women's average annual earnings are about one-half those of men. The ideology of domesticity also affects the 'horizontally' gendered division of labor, insofar as women may be disproportionately assigned to areas of work that involve service or caring and hence are understood in terms of this ideology as quintessentially 'female'.

Barrett (1988, 219) points toward the 'family-household system' (uniting kinship with cohabitation and, under capitalism, separating residence and consumption from waged work) as the primary historical locus of women's oppression, for it is here that the material relations of dependence upon male wage-earners, and the ideological construction of women as domestics and care-givers, have been situated. Women have been enveloped in a privatized domestic sphere that is culturally defined as the home of all that is feminine at the same time as they have been effectively blocked from equal participation in the labor force and thus rendered economically dependent. 'The family–household system has resulted in the "double shift" of wage labor and domestic labor for many working-class women, and the assumption of their household dependence has left many "unsupported" women in a very vulnerable position.'

This division of the labor force by gender has been politically consequential not just for the disempowerment of women but for the working class as a whole. Gendering the division of labor in these ways has meant the relative privileging of male workers and the concomitant assignment of women disproportionately to the ranks of the poorly paid and the insecure. The real, if also partial, gains that organized (predominantly male) workers have won are made vulnerable under conditions in which a feminized 'reserve army of labor' can be employed by capital to undercut the power of the labor movement (Barrett 1988, 171, 218, 258; compare Sayer and Walker 1992).

Overturning this situation requires de-reification and restructuring of the family–household system such that domestic and child-care responsibilities are no longer gendered in the same way that they have been. This, in turn, implies massive changes in the gendered divisions of labor in the workplace and in the state policies that support them; in short, a gendered emancipatory project entails transforming much of the contemporary political economy of capitalism as well as 'domestic' life. This creates considerable potential, Michele Barrett argues, for the confluence of feminist and socialist political projects.

Linda McDowell (1991) has argued that the restructuring of Fordist political economy in Britain has entailed a dismantling of a corresponding set of historical structures, to which she refers as the Fordist gender order: 'That old order, based on a stable working class, on the nuclear family supported by a male breadwinner and by women's domestic labor underpinned by Keynesian economic and welfare policies that ensured the reproduction of the working class, is passing from view' (403). The classic conceptualization of patriarchy, wherein men appropriate the unpaid domestic labor of women – the product of which is the labor-power sold by male workers as if it were entirely their own – may have been most appropriate to the Fordist form of capitalism with its institutionalized norm of the family wage. In recent decades, restructuring of capitalist enterprise has undermined the family wage and women have entered the labor market in growing numbers, especially among the ranks of part-time and contingent workers. At the same time, the neoliberalism of Thatcher and Reagan resulted in abandonment of the Keynesian policies that supported the regime of the family wage, and reductions in the social services and benefits that contributed to the reproduction of working-class families. The gendered effects of these transformations thus include a heightening of the double burden upon women, a condition that might be described as a sort of 'social speed-up' (416).

During the 1980s, for the many working-class women propelled into the labor market by economic necessity and by a desire for greater independence, two incomes were essential to maintain their previous standard of living. This means that these families are now doing three jobs for the price of one previously: two in the paid labor force and one unpaid at home – the labor of household work and child rearing – if it is accepted that previously the male 'family wage' reflected some contribution toward the unpaid domestic labor of female partners (McDowell 1991, 415).

These burdens have not been equally distributed among all women. Rather, it is working-class women who bear the brunt of the social speed-up, whereas those middle-class women who are able to gain access to core labor markets and professional occupations may be able to purchase on the market commodities and services formerly produced within the household (perhaps, ironically, by employing working-class women relegated to the lowest-paying segments of the service sector). These processes of restructuring, then, have included the degradation of the labor market position of many working-class men, social speed-up for working-class women, and labor market progress for middle-class women, all of which adds up to 'a widening of class divisions and a narrowing of gender divisions in the labor market' (McDowell 1991, 411). McDowell suggests that this points toward a possible convergence of class and gender politics: 'In this latest round in the continuous struggle over the control of women's labor, the majority of women *and* men are losing. Capital is the beneficiary' (416).

Evidence suggests that tendencies similar to those described by McDowell are at work in the United States. It remains true that women are more likely than men to earn low wages:

> In 1995, 36.8 per cent of women earned poverty-level wages or less, significantly more than the share of men (23.3 per cent). Women are also much less likely to earn very high wages. In 1995, only 6.1 per cent of women, but 13.5 per cent of men, earned at least three times the poverty level wage. (Mishel, Bernstein and Schmitt 1997, 151)

Nevertheless, the wages of formerly privileged male workers have been under relentless pressure for 20 years, driving the wages of most male workers closer to those of women:

> From 1979 to 1989, the median hourly wage fell $1.25 for men and rose $0.49 for women. These moves led to a growth in the hourly wage ratio between men and women by 10.3 percentage points, from 62.8 per cent in 1979 to 73.1 per cent in 1989, representing a sizable reduction in gender wage inequality. (Mishel, Bernstein and Schmitt 1997, 147)

Since 1989, the median wage for both male and female workers has been falling but female wages have fallen more slowly, leading the gender wage ratio to rise still further to 76.7 per cent. Although the gender gap has been compressed by the deprivileging of all but the most highly paid male workers, inequality has increased among women working outside the home. In the period 1979–89, the bottom 20 per cent of female wage earners lost ground, the middle deciles gained modestly, and the wages of the top 20 per cent grew rapidly. In the period 1989–95, on the other hand, only the top 20 per cent of female wage workers experienced any growth at all (with the exception of the very bottom 10 per cent, which may have benefited from minimum-wage legislation). So there has been a marked dispersion among female wage earners since 1979, with the top 20 per cent pulling away from the rest (Mishel, Bernstein and Schmitt 1997, 145–7). Economic restructuring has had the effect of reducing, if hardly eliminating, gender divisions within the waged workforce, while heightening the class-based oppression of both men and women workers.

Johanna Brenner (1993) has provided an analysis of contemporary US feminism that is in many ways complementary to Barrett's under-standing of a socialist-feminist project and McDowell's analysis of the demise of the Fordist gender order. Brenner argues that gendered aspects of the current wave of transnational capitalist restructuring and the retrenchment of the welfare state in the United States have combined to place great political-economic pressures upon women, especially working-class women and women of color.

In this 'new gender order', two major tributaries of 'second wave' feminism may appear to have run dry. Liberal feminism, with its demands for abstract equality of women and men, has been largely 'institutionalized and culturally incorporated as women's right to com-pete and contract free from limitations imposed on account of our sex' (Brenner 1993, 102). Enabling women to participate in the market more fully, however, may seem something of a Pyrrhic victory in an era when the conditions surrounding the sale of labor-power are dramati-cally worsening for all but the most privileged workers. Moreover, 'a politics which focuses *exclusively* on discriminatory treatment is inevitably class and race biased because it ignores women's differential resources for competing in the market' (Brenner 1993, 117). However, 'social welfare feminism', which seeks to go beyond abstract equality and more directly address material issues which affect working women (for instance, advocating government assistance in securing paid parental leave, universal healthcare and quality child care) is hobbled by its strategic dependence upon a Democratic Party whose concern for working people (much less working women) is ambiguous at best, and duplicitous at worst.

Brenner (1993) concludes that these two wings of 'second wave' feminism should be supplanted by a new, more broadly-based strategy, 'a serious and disruptive challenge to capital, a broad and militant "rainbow movement", including new, more social and political forms of trade union struggle and national political organization independent of the Democratic Party' (103). She envisions the development of a 'third wave' politics that 'combines the liberatory moments (the demand for individual self-expression, self-determination, and democratic participation) of the movements for democratic inclusion (feminism, civil rights, gay/lesbian rights) with new struggles over material needs (for healthcare, for childcare and paid prenatal leave, for living-wage jobs, for a clean environment)' (Brenner 1993, 157). Crucial to this renewed socialist-feminist agenda is the fostering of 'grassroots networks and solidarities', which will be enabling and which will support a kind of snowball effect whereby those engaged in organized struggle grow and develop as members of more self-determining communities. Organization, then, is not to be understood instrumentally but as part of a self-transformative process: 'The main point of organizing people around their immediate needs is to develop the capacities of women activists, their critical understanding and confidence in collective action, their commitments to ways of organizing social life that are democratic and participatory' (149). And among the conditions of a healthy and vibrant democracy are social commitments for shared domestic and child-care responsibilities to enable equalized access to economic and political life for both men and women.

To what degree have these sorts of materialist feminist critiques and positions been reflected in the debates surrounding globalization?

Feminist activists challenge neoliberal globalization

Mainstream US women's groups such as the National Organization for Women (NOW) were late in coming to the public deliberations on issues of globalization, and in particular were conspicuously absent from the NAFTA debates. Marianne Marchand (1996) has argued that this may have been a consequence of the manner in which the NAFTA debates were discursively framed. According to Marchand, these debates were cast largely in the peculiar language of economics, econometric models of job losses or gains were accorded a privileged position in the deliberations, and less 'scientific' or quantifiable considerations (such as gender) were effectively marginalized.

However, this marginalization was contested. The gendered effects of North American free trade – and the neoliberal policy regime that it reflected – were analyzed and publicized by smaller activist groups such as the Alternative Women-in-Development (Alt-WID) working group, working in cooperation with *Mujer-a-Mujer* in Mexico and Canada (on which see Gabriel and Macdonald 1994, 559; Runyan 1996, 248). Alt-WID argued that exploitation of Mexican women workers (some 60 per cent of the extremely low-wage labor force of the *maquiladora* [export-oriented industries near the Mexican border], was linked to increasing economic vulnerability of women and the feminization of poverty in Canada and the United States, and that NAFTA would accelerate and intensify these tendencies. North American women, among the most vulnerable of the continent's workers as a result of the pervasive effects of gendered divisions of labor, would be set in competition against one another, ultimately lowering the floor under all workers:

> Society's devaluation of women's work in and outside of the home has been a crucial factor at the heart of this trend to lower wages. In all three countries, the pursuit of a low wage strategy is made easier because women's income is seen as secondary. Also, traditional women's jobs are considered 'un- or low-skilled,' thereby supposedly justifying lower wages. Because of the multiple home, work, and community demands placed on them, women have been less able to organize effectively to protect their rights ... Women are forced to juggle household responsibilities with the need to earn an income, so they often seek temporary and part-time work, which companies use as a means to lower their overall wage and benefit costs ... For women, part-time, temporary, contract or contingent work means lower wages, no benefits, and little protection. (Alt-WID 1993, 3–4)

Further, Alt-WID argued that the free-market political agenda underlying NAFTA, and its dynamic of downward harmonization, would result in reduced levels of public services available to poor families and single mothers in all three countries.

> Public provision or subsidy of child care, housing or training all might be contested as barriers to trade for any country which tries to provide a safer and higher standard of living for its people. This particularly hurts women and the children they care for. First, because women (at least in Canada and the United States) tend to be disproportionately poor. Secondly, because publicly provided services often substitute for domestic work and relieve women's burden at home.

So, when public services are reduced or eliminated, often women have to compensate in the home and/or as community volunteers. (Alt-WID 1993, 11)

Finally, Alt-WID argued that NAFTA and neoliberalism more generally were potentially disempowering for women, and profoundly anti-democratic in their political implications. 'The policies that NAFTA proposes would subordinate democratically developed standards to those created by supranational and democratically unaccountable entities. The "impact on trade" would be the only yardstick for judging a large body of public laws with those who benefit from free trade as the judges' (Alt-WID 1993, 12). Alt-WID called for transnational organizing initiatives to address these and related issues directly, providing practical suggestions for organizing and contacts for networking in all three countries.

In recent years, gendered critiques of neoliberalism have become more common. A wide-ranging critique of neoliberalism by Pamela Sparr, an activist-researcher associated with Alt-WID and the Women's Alternative Economic Network (WAEN), was published in *Ms.* magazine, for example, in 1992. Sparr explicitly linked the gendered effects of Reagan–Bush era policies to ongoing tendencies of worldwide capitalist restructuring and 'structural adjustment' in the global South. She argued that neoliberalism in both North and South tended to increase economic and domestic burdens upon women, and most cruelly upon the poorest women: 'What US women are now experiencing bears a striking similarity to what women of highly indebted nations in the "South" have been experiencing for quite some time' (Sparr 1992, 32).

Similarly, Shea Cunningham and Betsy Reed (1995) – of Focus on the Global South and *Dollars and Sense*, respectively – have argued that a preoccupation with debt reduction, fiscal conservatism and austerity characterizes the policies of the US government as well as the World Bank and IMF, with especially disastrous consequences for women on a global scale. The Structural Adjustment Programs (SAPs) set up for poor countries by the World Bank and IMF generally require cutbacks in government spending, wage containment, deregulation of the economy and privatization of state-owned enterprise, and increased openness to the world economy in order to attract foreign investment and earn export revenues with which to repay debt. 'Since the budget slashing, pro-business SAPs hurt the poor, and, according to the 1995 UN Development Report, 70 per cent of the world's 1.3 billion people living in poverty are female, women have suffered disproportionately from their [the IMF and World Bank's] austere measures' (Cunningham and Reed

1995, 22). Under SAPs women are increasingly drawn into the export sector, working for wages much lower than those typically earned by male workers: 'As a worldwide average, women are paid nearly 40 per cent less than men for the very same work' (24). Further, SAPs typically reduce the level of public services available, increasing the weight of the double burden on women who must then provide more of the 'caring' services needed by family members as well as engage in intensified productive activity. And this has implications for the reproduction of gendered divisions of labor and ideologies of domesticity in future generations: 'Among children, it is females again who bear a disproportionate share of the burden. As women must extend their work day ... school attendance among girls in particular tends to drop as mothers depend on their daughters to ease their own time constraints' (1995, 24). Cunningham and Reed liken the effects of SAPs to those of the US government's social welfare policies, forcing poor women into the lowest paid strata of the workforce and intensifying the double burden they must bear.

Along very similar lines, the transnational women's solidarity organization MADRE has associated globalization with 'the raw violence of economic exploitation' and suggested that the same neoliberalism that draws women to work in Third World export enclaves also dismantles social welfare systems in the rich countries, driving women into low-wage labor and undermining wage levels more generally. According to MADRE, intensified inequality both within countries and on a global scale has been a direct result of this heightened exploitation. MADRE represents globalization as a political challenge that can be met by a broad-based democratizing response:

> Multi-national corporations are able to trample the social and economic rights of the world's majority because the global arena lacks any countervailing democratic structures through which to oppose them. In fact, the creation of effective mechanisms to win transparency, accountability and representation for ordinary people in the workings of the global economy is a central challenge of today's progressive movements. (Susskind 1998, 8)

Mainstream feminist organizations begin to catch on

Ms. magazine, the first mass-circulation feminist periodical in the United States, began publication in 1972. 'Using the funding and circulation that a mass-media magazine offered, the *Ms.* founders intended to harness capitalism for the feminist movement. The risk, however, was that capitalism – more specifically, advertisers, would harness *Ms.* first' (Farrell 1995, 54). And, according to Amy Farrell's intensive study of the history and politics of *Ms.*, that is just what happened. For its first 17 years, *Ms.* was torn by its contradictory location, attempting to mediate between a diverse and vibrant women's movement on the one hand and, on the other, advertisers who were primarily interested in representing women to themselves as consumers. In the uneasy symbiosis that emerged, the women's movement was portrayed as struggling for inclusion of women in the corporate capitalist world of work, and advertisers 'drew on some of the most compelling themes evoked by feminism – equality, freedom, personal transformation, and sisterhood – to justify a consumer ethic' (Farrell 1995, 56). In the representations predominating in *Ms.*, women were liberated to the extent they achieved career goals and were able to purchase commodities that marked them as successful. In short, *Ms.* had become a cheerleader for the liberal feminism of middle-class, predominantly white women, despite its editorial pretensions to include the voices of 'all women, everywhere' (quoted in Farrell 1995, 60). Farrell documents that many *Ms.* readers were painfully aware of the contradictions of 'their' magazine and voiced strong criticisms in letters published in the magazine.

By the late 1980s, the chronic financial difficulties at *Ms.* were becoming an acute crisis, and the magazine was purchased by a mass-media firm that intended to resolve its problems by moving it away from its roots in the feminist movement and making it more attractive to advertisers and to more upscale readers. The strategy failed as advertisers continued to desert the magazine, and the commercial version of *Ms.* folded in 1989. *Ms.* re-emerged, phoenix-like, in 1990 as a non-commercial publication with no advertising content.

Since then, the new *Ms.* has published a number of articles that depart from the liberal feminist model of equal opportunity and individual advancement, and present instead a direct critique of interwoven relations of class and gender in the era of capitalist restructuring and neoliberalism. In addition to Pamela Sparr's broad-ranging critique of transnational neoliberalism (1992), *Ms.* published a gendered critique of trade liberalization which pointedly observed that 'women – who fill most of the world's low-pay, low-skill jobs – are most often exploited as a result of unchecked global economic integration'; yet 'the National Organization for Women never offered any comment on [1993's] crucial NAFTA vote' (Kadetsky 1994, 15). Another feature in the new *Ms.* focused upon one of the gendered aspects of post-Fordist restructuring, highlighting the overrepresentation of women among the growing ranks of underpaid, insecure and vulnerable part-time and contingent workers (Judd and Pope 1994). The following year, *Ms.* published Cynthia Enloe's devastating critique (1995) of Nike and the pervasive exploitation of mostly female workers by the transnational sports shoe industry. Enloe saw such practices as indicative of larger tendencies within globalizing neoliberal capitalism: 'Big business will step up efforts to pit working women in industrialized countries against much lower-paid working women in "developing" countries, perpetuating the misleading notion that they are inevitable rivals in the global job market' (1995, 11–12). In contrast to the neoliberal ideology of relentless competition, Enloe praised the efforts of working women to adopt positions of transnational solidarity and mutual support. Enloe's feature article was accompanied by a shorter attack on the General Agreement on Tariffs and Trade (GATT) authored by Mary McGinn (1995), a radical labor activist associated with the journal *Labor Notes*. 'Unfortunately', McGinn argued, 'most US women's advocacy groups took no position on GATT [during the 1994 ratification debate]. But clearly, all women have a lot to lose: expanded freedom for multinational corporations jeopardizes social justice everywhere' (1995, 15). Since the appearance of the articles by Enloe and McGinn, *Ms.* has published at least six articles of varying lengths that focus attention on the return of sweatshops in the neoliberal world economy and the particular threat this poses to the health and welfare of women workers and their families.

Although *Ms.* was becoming more hospitable to critiques of neoliberal globalization, the mainstream feminist organizations appeared largely inert in the major public debates surrounding NAFTA (1993) and GATT (1994). Finally, in 1997, Global Exchange (see A. Ross 1997) succeeded in organizing a coalition of 15 women's organizations, including NOW, the *Ms.* Foundation, the Feminist Majority, the Black Women's Agenda and the Coalition of Labor Union Women, all of which joined in taking a public stand against sweatshops, directly addressing Phil Knight, CEO of Nike. In a striking gesture of transnational solidarity, they pointed to the stark contradiction between Nike's advertising strategies, which portray Western women as strong, capable and independent, and its exploitation of a predominantly female labor force in the Asian factories where its shoes are produced. 'While the women who wear Nike shoes in the United States are encouraged to perform their best, the Indonesian, Vietnamese and Chinese women making the shoes often suffer from inadequate wages, corporal punishment, forced overtime and/or sexual harassment' (quoted in Greenhouse 1997b; see also Feminist Majority 1997). They called upon Nike to accept independent monitors to ensure that its subcontractors pay a livable wage and observe basic standards of worker rights and workplace health and safety. The Feminist Majority has continued to encourage transnational solidarity against sweatshops and maintains a Feminists Against Sweatshops web page designed to educate American women on the dangers of global sweatshop labor and present resources for anti-sweatshop activism (http://www.feminist.org/other/sweatshops.html). Although it is not at all clear that mainstream feminist organizations in the United States are adopting as a central part of their agenda a radical critique of neoliberal globalization, it is nevertheless difficult to deny that such critiques have found their way into the feminist press and have fostered some very real, if also as yet somewhat limited, gestures of transnational solidarity.

Christina Gabriel and Laura Macdonald (1994, 536) argue that women across North America share common aspects of gendered social subordination: 'Systematic discrimination gives women unequal access to resources; women's participation in economic activities is largely governed by the sexual division of labor within the household; gender underpins definitions of skills; and women's work in reproduction and production is undervalued.' These commonalities of gendered oppression might provide the material basis on which to construct relations of solidarity and mutually supporting struggles. However, Gabriel and Macdonald caution that women in North America are differently situated in relation to the international political economy, that 'gender, class and race position groups of women differently and mediate the effects of trade liberalization'.

Viewed in relation to Mexican women, women in Canada and the United States have been relatively privileged, benefiting from higher general living standards, more extensive social safety nets (especially in Canada), and more actively mobilized women's movements. As a consequence, many women in northern North America were somewhat less violently affected by global economic crisis and restructuring than most Mexican women have been. Restructuring has exacerbated differences among northern women, as some middle-class professional, technical and managerial women have done well, while working-class women and women of color have been disproportionately assigned to the ranks of more intensively exploited secondary or contingent workers. In Mexico, rural and indigenous women bear the brunt of liberalization.

Because of such differences – as William Robinson also discusses in Chapter 3 – 'there can be no axiomatic unity between groups of women' (Gabriel and Macdonald 1994, 539). Rather, political unity becomes the product of ongoing negotiation, a problematic process of recognizing and mediating these differences in order to realize the potential for solidarity.

Conclusion

Although I have written from an analytic perspective informed by my readings of Marx and Gramsci (similarly, see Rupert 1998; Solomon and Rupert 1999), I do not presume that capitalist globalization will generate simple and unproblematic class identities to be the ready-made bases for political struggle. Rather, I would argue that people in different social and historical settings have been incorporated into global capitalism in a variety of ways, articulating their own historical relations and cultures with those of core capitalism. I believe that the various forms of subordination to transnational capital nevertheless entail structural commonalities that create the possibility for common political horizons, common interests and transnational democratizing projects to be negotiated (Moody 1997). If such strategies are to be successful, they must encompass not just the workplace but also the intersections of public and private spheres, of production and reproduction, linking work, home and community.

In pursuing this kind of transformative project, anticapitalist progressives have much to learn from feminist and women's movements and, in particular, the transnational organizing efforts of the Canadian National Action Committee on the Status of Women, as chronicled by Gabriel and Macdonald (1994). In an era of globalizing capitalism and neoliberal restructuring, the intersections of gender and class have become the most significant array of sites for fruitful scholarly and political labor.

Notes

1. The wage gains generated by tightening labor markets at the peak of the current business cycle have been much ballyhooed. However, the EPI puts this wage growth in perspective:

   Even with these recent gains, the pay of the typical worker in mid-1998 is still not as high as it was in 1989, the year of the last business cycle peak. Moreover, these recent wage gains, dependent upon current tight labor markets, low inflation, and one-time increases in the minimum wage, are unlikely to withstand the inevitable shift in the business cycle. (Mishel, Bernstein and Schmitt 1997)

These conjunctural wage gains, then, do not portend a significant shift in what we might call the 'underlying fundamentals' of the US political economy: the relative disempowerment of people who depend upon wages to live.

2
Egalitarian Social Movements in Western Europe: Can They Survive Globalization and the Economic and Monetary Union?

Joel Krieger

In the past two decades, increasing tensions worldwide over the distribution of economic and political goods and a proliferating set of demands by diverse social actors have fueled dissatisfactions and encouraged the revitalization of egalitarian social movements. The uncertain and destabilizing processes of globalization and the formation of strategically malleable, context-dependent hybrid collective identities (associated with a process I call 'political modularity') have created tremendous political volatility and inspired popular pressure in both domestic and transnational settings – through new social movements (NSMs) and nongovernmental organizations (NGOs) – for specific policy remedies.

At the same time, intergovernmental organizations (IGOs) and the European Union (EU) – the most powerful among them – have exerted monumental political influence. The EU sets agendas and implements policies that configure the goals and shape the strategies and prospects for success of egalitarian social movements in Western Europe. It also serves as an arena for debate and the object of sometimes-intense mobilization for the discontent of significant constituencies that cannot achieve success through traditional domestic political venues. The juxtaposition of the EU as a new polity, alongside existing national systems for the representation of interests, raises captivating questions about the emergent pattern of opportunity structures for collective action (Aspinwall and Greenwood 1998).

Nevertheless, because of distinct organizational genealogies reinforced by largely noncommunicating scholarly literatures, relatively little systematic attention has been paid to the interactive effects of domestic social movements on the one hand, and transnational processes on the other, including interstate regionalization, globalization, and the role of IGOs and NGOs. Equally problematic are efforts to explain how the processes of globalization and, in the European case, EU-led regional integration influence the formation, proliferation and success of social movements. Moreover, these efforts often remain trapped within specific policy domains – and attendant concepts of interest-based politics – that are narrowly or traditionally defined. Thus, the significance and potential mobilization force of context-dependent identities and interests are neglected.

This chapter represents a preliminary and selective effort to locate the analysis of Western European egalitarian social movements in the context of EU responses to globalization and to address some of the analytical oversights that limit the utility of existing comparative approaches to the study of social movements. First, I consider the analytic framework that West Europeanists have frequently applied to the study of social movements and suggest some areas for potentially fruitful refinement. Second, I discuss the setting for egalitarian social movements shaped by context-dependent processes of identity formation and the modularization of politics on the one hand, and by the interactive effects of globalization and EU regional integration initiatives on the other. Third, I introduce two case studies: wage-earner feminism in Sweden and a 'Eurostrike' that erupted over Renault's announced closure of a Belgian plant in 1997. Finally, I briefly use these examples to extract some tentative observations about conditions of success – both the prospects and limits of cross-border mobilization – that confront contemporary egalitarian social movements in Western Europe.

Analytical and conceptual framework: the comparative study of social movements

A vibrant and theoretically rich literature has emerged from comparative political studies of social movements. It provides an important starting point, as well as some highly developed understandings of the fluid interplay between social movements and more institutionalized domestic politics. As becomes clear, its explanatory power for understanding social movements in an era of EU regional integration and globalization suffers from its lack of attention to transnational developments.

Comparative social movements

Through much of the 1980s, new social movement literature (for example, Offe 1985; Dalton and Kuechler 1990) claimed a categorical distinction between emergent social movements (for example environmental, women's and antinuclear movements) and traditional social movements (principally labor movements and, in the USA, the civil rights movement). NSM activists, as compared with traditional movement activists, it was argued, emerged from different social strata (professional occupations rather than a working-class or underclass milieu) and embraced different value orientations (postmaterialist values as distinct from traditional distributive bargains and interest intermediation). Distinctions were claimed also with reference to the scope of critical perspectives: that NSM activists raised far-reaching critiques of society which could not be resolved by alternation of government or distributional bargaining between left and right. Initially, in organizational terms, NSMs were said to be more participatory, nonhierarchical, democratic and less goal-oriented: value change was as important as policy change.

Some literature on international social movements, such as that by Paul Wapner (1996) on the environmentalists and Amy Higer (1997) on feminists, confirms the significance of these putative categorical distinctions between the traditional and the new social movements. These scholars argue that environmentalist movements and women's movements are held together by a 'Northern' cadre of activists, with the occupations and values that typify new social movements. Nevertheless, in recent years, significant scholarship has challenged these premises of NSM literature, arguing that inherent distinctions between women's or environmental movements and labor movements must be revisited at the very least, because the traits associated with 'new' and 'old' are inconsistently and fluidly distributed (Klandermans 1986; Rochon 1990; Kriesi *et al.* 1995).

Political opportunity structures

Although the concept has emerged almost exclusively from the domestic social movement literature (Kitschelt 1986; Klandermans 1986; Rochon 1990; Tarrow 1994, 1995; Kriesi *et al.* 1995; Rucht 1995), political opportunity structure (POS) can be applied productively to both domestic and transnational social movements. POS generally refers to the whole range of 'signals to social and political actors which either encourage or discourage them to use their internal resources to form social movements' (Tarrow 1995). It introduces analytical tools to study the degree of openness of a domestic or global governance system to interventions by social movement actors. It also attempts to operationalize and analyze the way in which political systems structure the mobilization capacity, shape the behavior and goals, and condition the success of movements.

The domestic social movement literature emphasizes distinctive national cleavage structures (existing patterns of political conflict), institutional arrangements and alliance patterns emanating from the political system (Kriesi *et al.* 1995), implying distinctive national patterns of social movement mobilization. Where similarities in the patterned behavior are observed among women's movements or environmental movements, for example, these are attributed to common policy agendas and goals or the emulation of strategy and leadership across national boundaries.

By neglecting the international dimension, the POS approach reifies the increasingly problematic distinction between domestic and international politics, and neglects the interactive influences of domestic and international opportunity structures on egalitarian social movements.[1] In contrast, the perspective here applies a simple POS approach to the emergent 'composite polity' of EU Europe, where uncertainty over group rights and territorial boundaries and multiple, overlapping authorities and structures of political opportunity open up new possibilities for contentious political action by ordinary people (Tarrow 1998).

The context-dependency of egalitarian social movements

To come to terms with the experiences and alternative futures of contemporary social movements, we need to refine and open up the analytical framework. We also need to broaden the frame of reference. Above all, the political opportunities and strategic options available to social movements are radically structured – at once constrained and enabled – by a set of multiple distinct (but related) processes. These include European integration shaped by the European Economic and Monetary Union (EMU), the competitive pressures of globalization and modular politics. Thus, egalitarian social movements are triply context-dependent in ways that may open up new strategic opportunities but create daunting challenges as well.

EU and globalization

European integration is the movement toward economic and monetary union symbolized by the introduction of a single currency, and globalization is the global reorganization of production and redistribution of the workforce and the increased extent and intensity of international trade, finance and foreign direct investment. Taken together, both are likely to have chilling effects on egalitarian movements. Thus there is a tendency toward a discouraging convergence, explicitly advanced by the EU and reinforced by the logic of globalization.

The macroeconomic and social policies mandated by the EMU convergence criteria and the subsequent Stability and Growth Pact play havoc with the post-World War II settlement and distributional bargains and social democratic politics that have thus far encouraged egalitarian movements. In fact, if left uncontested, this neoliberal, market-driven agenda for deepening European integration nullifies the full-employment, Keynesian, welfare regime (Streeck 1997). Insofar as this context compels national polities to pursue price stability and avoid public debts and deficits, one observer said, 'it may well be possible to speak of a new transnational anti-inflationary monetary "regime" which has replaced its Keynesian predecessor' (G. Ross 1998, 176).

Assuming that greater equality involves the upper adjustment of wages (the narrowing of relativities and differentials) and implementing costly adjustments in social programs (for example, paying women 'equal value' or comparable worth, providing extensive parental leave, administering pensions with high replacement ratios, and so forth), then the EMU convergence criteria and the anti-inflationary regime set up significant anti-egalitarian barriers.

Globalization tends to produce similar downward pressures by favoring national systems such as those of Britain and the USA, which rely more on private contractual and market-driven arrangements and less on state capacity and political bargaining to determine distributional outcomes. At the same time, global investment strategies ostracize markets such as Germany or the Scandinavian countries, which rely more on citizenship status, institutionalized bargaining and coordination, and state-sponsored arrangements. Globalization increases the mobility of capital and labor across borders, and expresses its deregulatory and anti-institutional bias in dramatic patterns of foreign direct investment (FDI), which very substantially favor Britain over Germany, for example (Krieger 1999). In this way, the processes of globalization tend to dissolve negotiated coordination between nationally based capital and labor, challenge progressive distributive bargains, and punish countries with more egalitarian policy legacies and institutional capacities.

Can propitious national institutional contexts overcome these pressures for anti-egalitarian convergence? Do cross-national differences in institutional contexts result in significant variation?

Far more research is needed to provide compelling answers to these questions. Yet it seems likely that institutional and policy legacies at the country level will not be as significant as they were before the current period of intensified globalization and European integration, at least among the 15 member countries of the EU. The case of Swedish social democracy offers a chastening illustration. Sweden's reluctant entry in 1995 into the EU symbolized the end of its commitment to egalitarian exceptionalism based on solidaristic wage bargaining, grand schemes for collective share ownership through the build-up of wage-earner funds, and a comprehensive redistributive welfare regime. For Sweden, EU membership came in the post-Maastricht era of intensive EMU pressures and was coterminous with economic liberalization measures, including financial deregulation and a disastrous anti-inflationary monetary policy pegged to the German mark. If Sweden is brought on-line in this manner – despite its unparalleled solidaristic legacy, capacities for highly egalitarian returns to labor, and concerted efforts to reduce gender-based inequalities – then the pressures elsewhere may prove nearly overwhelming.

Moreover, on the reasonable assumption that egalitarian distribution of economic resources correlates with political regulation of the market and institutionalized capacities for negotiated and cooperative outcomes, processes of globalization such as patterns of FDI may tend to produce a dreary paradox. Countries such as Sweden (and, to some extent, Germany) that have the institutional capacities and the political will to support egalitarian movements are increasingly stretched for resources. In contrast, deregulatory and weakly institutionalized countries, such as the UK and the USA, which are favored by globalization, experience less resource pressure but lack the effective organization of interests and political-cultural values to sustain egalitarian movements.

A recent comparative study of the crisis and future prospects of social democracy in four of the most advanced cases (Austria, Norway, Finland and Sweden) confirms that changes in the international economies since the 1970s – with run-on effects on domestic economies – have eroded the institutional moorings of the social democratic model. The authors convincingly argue that the multinationalization of capital and the internationalization of financial markets have robbed governments of key policy instruments to implement countercyclical macroeconomic policy and, most important, on the supply side, to increase reinvestment in production (Huber and Stephens 1998).

Political modularity

The prospects of egalitarian social movements in Western Europe are also shaped by critical changes in political identity formation. These transformations are not uniformly negative for the prospects of egalitarian movements. Nevertheless, they do complicate politics and shift the political opportunity structures, even as they challenge traditional fixed or unitary conceptions of politics, policy and mobilization strategies.

In his book *Conditions of Liberty: Civil Society and its Rivals*, Ernest Gellner (1994) presents a wonderfully playful conceit that helps deepen our understanding of the volatility of contemporary politics, the transitory character of allegiances, and the malleability of identity formation. He begins simply enough by contrasting modular furniture to ordinary furniture. Gellner explains that modular furniture 'comes in bits that are agglutinative'. Initially, you purchase one piece that can function on its own, but when preferences or circumstances change, you can tack on another piece to what is already there, and 'the whole thing will still have a coherence, aesthetically and technically'. Further, you can combine and recombine the bits at will. The contrast with ordinary furniture is clear. 'With the old kind, if you want coherence you have to buy it all at once, in one go, which means that you have to make a kind of irrevocable commitment, or at any rate a commitment which it will be rather costly to revoke,' observes Gellner. 'If you add a new bit of non-modular furniture to an old bit, you may end up with an eclectic, incoherent mess.' It is difficult to adapt or modify traditional furniture and achieve coherence: success requires the 'careful and possibly arduous search for new stylistically compatible items' (Gellner 1994, 97).

The concept *modular politics*[2] helps provide a framework for understanding the increasingly fluid and situational interplay of collective identities. By referring to identities as modular, I mean, as Eric Hobsbawm (1996, 41) states, that 'in real life identities, like garments, are interchangeable or wearable in combination rather than unique and, as it were, stuck to the body'. Although the term *identity politics* usually suggests that one identity determines or dominates politics, modular politics implies multiple identities that are combined and ordered without fixed priority, perpetually recombined and modified, and alert to political assessments and alliance prospects.[3]

In recent decades, discussion of nonclass collective identities has mushroomed, as have preoccupations with identity politics. One camp advances identity politics and features those influenced by postmodern theory. This camp has claimed that the diversity of real-life experience and the terrifying failure rate of progressive political projects render enlightenment expectations meaningless or obsolete. This camp rejects class politics and the transformative project it represents, along with other providential 'grand narratives' that sustain political beliefs (Wolin 1988; Norris 1990). In place of class politics, it privileges the more immediate attachments of gender, sexuality, race and other 'subject-positions' built on the 'ruins of the old universal values of modernity' (Aronowitz 1992, 12).

Others, relying on more grounded historical and sociological analysis, suggest that racial, ethnic or cultural identities have gained a compensatory salience as traditional sources of identity such as nation, class, family or community rupture or dissolve. Daniel Bell was among the first to make this argument, over 25 years ago, when he observed, 'The breakup of the traditional authority structures and the previous affective social units – historically nation and class ... make the ethnic attachment more salient' (1975, 171). In a similar vein, Stuart Hall (1992, 75) has argued that people seek attachments – a sense of 'belonging to' a group – to offset the dislocating effects of the processes of globalization. These contribute to the fragmentation of the 'cultural landscapes of class, gender, sexuality, ethnicity, race and nationality which gave us firm locations as social individuals'.

Class analysis suggests that the irreducible facts of exploitation and a putatively common relationship to the means of production unifies class interests, despite differences in actual work experiences, as well as in ethnic or gender identities. Class organizes politics. In common usage, the term identity politics usually suggests that identities located in gender, race, nation and ethnicity are separate and distinct from class. Moreover, identities 'trump' class and dominate politics. They comprise the postmaterialist values widely ascribed to new social movements that are distinct from the materialist values and historical materialist analysis of a class-based model of collective action. They are also distinct from a traditional scheme of postwar settlement and distributive politics that involve negotiations between state actors and the organized representatives of class interests over how to distribute the 'economic pie'.

Modular politics emphasizes the interactive effects of gender, ethnicity and workplace experiences. It assumes that beliefs, cultural orientations, collective memories and, especially, real-life experiences of a group's members shape values, interests, political agendas and mobilization. Identities are hybrid, fluid and context-dependent; they are also strategic. Modular politics implies multiple identities that are perpetually combined and ordered without fixed priority, as well as recombined and modified in response to political contexts. Modular politics also implies the importance of particular issues and the strategies required for political mobilization. Shifting, hybrid, context-dependent identities organize politics, in general, and egalitarian social movements in particular.

Case studies

Although I cannot establish the claim convincingly here, I want to suggest the critical significance of these three dimensions of context-dependency – globalization, EMU and modularity – on the fate of egalitarian social movements in Western Europe. How they play out depends on the specifics of the cases and the relevant political opportunity structures, as the following cases demonstrate.

Swedish wage-earner feminism

The case of wage-earner feminism must be set within the context of the growth, consolidation and deepening crisis of the Swedish model of social democracy. As one observer put it, 'For much of the postwar period, the Swedish labour movement stood as the exemplar of labour strength and innovative capacity' (Mahon 1996, 547). Through its close links with the Social Democratic Party, which governed Sweden from 1932 to 1976 and again from 1982 to 1991, the Swedish labor movement, organized through powerful trade union confederations (especially the '*Landsorganisationen*', or LO, representing blue-collar workers), advanced a strategy of egalitarian wage agreements ('solidaristic wages') backed by macrolevel economic and social policy initiatives.

In this context, the Social Democrats' electoral strength, combined with labor corporatism and solidaristic wage bargaining strategies, led to a vast array of comprehensive, egalitarian and universal welfare provisions (Esping-Andersen 1990). The Swedish case also famously included an attempt at democratic control of investment through the Meidner Plan, a far-reaching proposal endorsed by the LO congress of 1976 that called for the gradual collectivization of private ownership of industry through the build-up of wage-earner funds. It is therefore not surprising that when European comparativists speak of the 'limits of Social Democracy' they point to Sweden, with the Social Democratic Party so dominant for six decades until 1991, its high union density, and its impressive package of reform initiatives, as the *locus classicus* (Pontusson 1992).

'Wage-earner feminism' emerged powerfully in Sweden only after cracks began to appear in the Swedish model. The 1980s brought intensified competitive pressures, the loss of LO hegemony, the erosion of solidaristic wage bargaining, and the search for a progressive post-Fordist compromise that might serve as an alternative to the neoliberal model that was taking hold elsewhere. The demands of wage-earner feminism for political parity, pay equity and a renewal of the welfare state to extend the frontier of gender equality in all areas of social policy gained prominence because external pressures for competitiveness, deep-seated normative values that rejected the TINA ('there is no alternative') approach to neoliberalism, and the erosion of the Swedish model created the possibility for effective mobilization.

Women experienced the brute edge of globalization and deindustrialization by their overrepresentation in low-paying service sector employment and part-time or casual wage sectors, thus providing an underlying rationale for their claims. But the conditions faced by women, and their status as quintessential 'postindustrial' workers, do not explain why the predominantly 'male manufacturing' union leadership was so responsive. Rather, the political opportunity was there because industrial and organizational structures had weakened and powerful, new political incentives and resources created a new political space. The radical demands of women wage earners became politically influential, and critical to LO's strategy, because women could convincingly be 'represented as the ones who have the most to gain from, and [are] most likely to be protagonists for, the unions' alternative vision of a post-Fordist workplace, a vision inspired by the largely male, and certainly industrial, Metalworkers' Union, Metall' (Mahon 1996, 546). This strategic opening made the particular needs of women workers the basis for robust across-the-board mobilization (Mahon 1991, 1996).

One might add that the needs around which wage-earner feminists mobilized are widely supported by women throughout Western Europe. For example, as research in the UK shows clearly, the political agendas of women are driven by modular politics as an imperative to reconcile the demands of work and family responsibilities in a way that meets actual needs that are driven by the interactive effects of gender and class identities. Recent studies that have attempted to identify the political agendas of women in Britain provide findings that may be relevant for understanding the emergent prospects of egalitarian social movements. First, the studies suggest that women's foremost social concerns (for example child care, the rights and pay of part-time workers, equal pay, support for family care givers, domestic violence) are not high priorities on the mainstream policy agendas that are defined by political parties, although they are discussed in documents aimed specifically at women. Second, to the extent that women and men care about the same broadly defined issues, women often understand the issues differently from men and express different priorities. For example, whereas men consider unemployment the central employment issue, women emphasize equal pay and pensions, access to child care, and the rights of part-time workers. Third, the research indicates the emergence of distinct sets of issues with special importance for the political agendas of particular groups of women voters. For example, older women are most concerned about pensions and transportation. Due to the overrepresentation of women in lower-paid, part-time jobs, working women express particular concern about the minimum wage and the treatment of part-time workers. Mothers find the level of child benefits more important than tax cuts. Finally, younger women express much support for policy innovations that would help them balance the responsibilities of work, family and child care (Lovenduski 1997).

Whether in Britain, Sweden or elsewhere, women may have the most to gain from a more democratic and participatory post-Fordist alternative, from a struggle against the endemic casualization of work, and from a recognition of the organic connection between work and domestic life. They also might benefit the most from the changes wage-earner feminism could inspire in welfare, labor market and industrial relations policy, but they would hardly be alone in achieving desirable results.

Will Swedish unions in a time of trouble have the capacity to advance renewed egalitarian aims framed in terms of a comprehensive and quite radical alternative to the market-driven, deregulatory, managerial flexibility of the dominant neoliberal post-Fordist model? The result of their efforts will say a lot about the fate of egalitarian social movements in Western Europe.

The 'Eurostrike' against Renault

When the French automobile manufacturing company, Renault, announced on 27 February 1997 that it planned to close a plant in Vilvoorde, Belgium, the reaction was instantaneous, dramatic and more far-reaching that anyone could have expected. Within days, the Belgian prime minister accused the French of chauvinism. The Belgians exploded in anger when they learned that the French government had known about the closure plans for six weeks or more, and that Renault was planning to use EU structural funds simultaneously to build a new facility in Spain.[4]

Almost immediately, both the European Parliament and the president of the European Commission contributed strongly worded rebukes, which were soon joined by those of the director-general for competition (as luck would have it, a Belgian). The Spanish government quickly withdrew plans to subsidize Renault's plant in Valladolid and even the French government began to backpedal.

All this was only a prelude to the main drama: workers in Vilvoorde occupied the plant, 'kidnapped' cars ready to be shipped, sent 'commandos' to France, and demonstrated with French Renault workers who traveled to Belgium to express solidarity. Mass demonstrations with international delegations followed, and newspapers throughout Europe heralded the 'Eurostrike', emphasizing the importance of the dispute as a European issue. Workers took the firm to court in France and in Belgium for violating EU plant closure regulations, and won in both countries. In the end, under pressure from the courts, the Belgian government, the demonstrators, the EU, and the French (center-right) prime minister cracked in less than a month. On 20 March, he announced a compensation package of 800 000 francs per worker, and in July – after a socialist government had taken office – the workers accepted the offer.

What is the significance of this case of qualified success in resistance to a plant closure? For a start, it suggests the need to cast the net widely in describing the political opportunity structures that frame social movement mobilization and success. Resistance achieved some success because it pushed all the buttons to raise the visibility of a commonplace, antilabor corporate decision and, most important, to *Europeanize* it. As a consequence, the workers' dispute signaled to a host of external actors – national governments, national courts, EU institutions, and French workers whose narrow interests were actually served by the closure – that there would be a political cost to sitting out this struggle. Once the media helped frame the issue as an affront to continental norms of social protection with far-reaching European implications, the door swung open to decisive interventions by an unlikely ensemble of institutional *qua* political actors. As Sidney Tarrow (1998, 20) observes, 'In the Vilvoorde story, the EU entered a contentious encounter not only as a formal authority but as a set of political players, providing opportunities for and constraints upon different actors.'

Finally, in an almost uncanny way, the Vilvoorde Eurostrike exploited the opportunities for the context-dependent mobilization that taps fluid modular identities: the drama has class, nationality, and emergent European identities written all over it. Globalization pressed Renault to act. European integration unleashed powerful institutional and political pressures. Ultimately, a volatile mix of collective identities inflamed by class and national outrage – and facilitated by the social rights of an emergent European citizenship – inspired massive political mobilization.

Conclusion

At first glance, the two case studies seem to provide salutary evidence for those seeking in egalitarian social movements the political agency to advance a more progressive, less marketized, world order. Surely an assault on neoliberal post-Fordism in the name of wage-earner feminism, and a workers' victory against a powerful, if ailing, multinational company in the name of transnational solidarity and 'social Europe' (not to mention a somewhat edgy nationalism) are powerful examples which indicate that, at least occasionally, there is an alternative.

Unfortunately, one has to consider the more pessimistic reading that these cases are exceptions that prove the rule. Swedish social democracy may simply be *sui generis* in the resonance of solidaristic egalitarian strategies and in the innovative capacity of union leadership to offer positive alternatives that place capital on the defensive. To put the Swedish mobilization in context, there is plenty of evidence that British female wage earners want what their Swedish counterparts have convinced the LO to pursue. But there is not a jot of evidence that the Trades Union Congress (tepid British cousin to the LO) will take up the struggle for a comparable post-Fordist alternative or see in women workers much more than a reserve army of increasing casualized employees suitable for recruitment (C. Howell 1996, 2000).

Similarly, it is not clear that the Vilvoorde Eurostrike is easily replicable, in part because European multinationals are likely to take heed of the lessons, observe the letter of EU consultative regulations, and think twice before inflaming modular identities replete with class, national and supranational overtones. Old-fashioned class or industrial resistance is a quite different and far more manageable process. It is a woeful sign of the times that the Renault strike is cast as a success, although the plant remained closed.

Ironically, Volvo may help tip the scales toward neoliberal, hard-edged corporate practices. Seeking to increase productivity and profits and move aggressively into developing markets, the once proudly egalitarian and innovative Swedish automaker announced in December 1998 that it would lay off 5300 workers (more than 7 per cent of its workforce) by mid-1999. Even more startling, in January 1999, Volvo and Ford announced the purchase of Volvo's car business by the world's second largest automobile manufacturer. Although the deal with Ford is designed to provide an infusion of capital into the Swedish motor company to expand its more profitable truck and bus operations, Volvo immediately declared its intention to close its Irvine, Ayrshire, truck production plant in Scotland by July 2000 and transfer assembly operations to the continent. Will a second massive Eurostrike defeat the streamlining efforts of another ailing European automobilecum-truck manufacturer? The initial expressions of outrage by Scottish unions, combining pleas for reconsideration with threats of consumer boycotts, seemed unlikely to scare Volvo into altering its competitive strategies. It does not appear that the ingredients are in place – sharp and fast EU interventions and the politics of national resentment – to push contention beyond the framework of a conventional and confinable labor dispute.

The lessons from Western Europe in the era of EMU about the transformative role of egalitarian social movements are chastening. There is growing resistance on the continent to the EU's 'market-monetarist austerity policies', notably in France, whatever the government, and more episodically in Gerhard Schröder's Germany after the departure of Oskar Lafontaine. Many leading European economists reckon that the EMU, like economic orthodoxies of the 1930s, will drive high levels of unemployment even higher. Political observers add that increased unemployment and resulting social dislocation threaten to intensify social polarization, which already finds expression in tough immigration and asylum policies, xenophobic movements and a Fortress Europe mentality (Gill 1998, 6).

That said, although restive European citizens increasingly use EU policies and directives to pressure national governments, there is little evidence of the 'transnationalization of social movement activity' (Tarrow 1998, 15) which would be needed to radically amend the Growth and Stability Pact from below. Meanwhile, elite bargaining among the finance and economic ministers who comprise Ecofin, and the leaders of the national governments they serve, will determine the fate of the EMU and decide whether the European Central Bank is forced to put aside its monetarist bible and concern itself with growth and jobs.

On present evidence, there is little reason to see the current period as an interregnum before the emergence of a new more humane order, or at least not as far as European initiatives are concerned.

Notes

1. For exceptions see Aspinwall and Greenwood (1998) and Tarrow (1998).
2. It should be noted that Gellner uses the term 'modular man'. I substitute the term 'modular politics' both to efface any gendered connotation and to focus attention on broader systemic processes rather than voluntary acts.
3. Of course, the claim that modularity affirms the social construction of categories of identity should not be read as an endorsement of the unrestricted plasticity sometimes implied by postmodernism: see Gilroy (1993).
4. Both the account of this strike and much of the analysis are drawn from the discussion by Tarrow (1998).

3
Latin America in an Age of Inequality: Confronting the New 'Utopia'

William I. Robinson

'If the immediate effect of a change is deleterious, then, until proof to the contrary, the final effect is deleterious.'

Polanyi (1957)

The gales of global capitalism have hit Latin America hard. The region has been ravaged by a new market apartheid characterized by a striking contradiction. Social movements of every type have proliferated in an increasingly dense civil society and are vibrant protagonists. But the accomplishments of social movements in organizing the popular classes have not been matched by an ability to offset the dramatic sharpening of social inequalities, increased polarization, and the growth of poverty brought about by globalization. How do we account for this paradox?

I argue that by liberating transnational capital from the compromises and commitments placed on it by diverse social forces in the nation-state phase of world capitalism, globalization has dramatically altered the balance among class and social forces in each nation. This has occurred at the global system level, away from popular majorities and toward transnational capital and its representatives. The exercise of real (structural and direct) power has increasingly shifted away from civil and political societies in nation-states and specific regions to the global system. This is the structural context of the paradox: the real ability of social movements to intercede and force change in national and regional social structures has declined. Latin American social movements have begun to transnationalize, yet how much will they be able to intercede in emergent transnational civil and political society as the real locus of change in the age of globalization, and how might this change increase their ability to force structural change?

Globalization and the liberation of capital from nation-state constraints

In his master study, *The Great Transformation*, Karl Polanyi summed up the previous historic change in the relationship between the state and capital, and society and market forces, that took place with the maturation of national capitalism in the nineteenth and the first half of the twentieth century. We now witness another great transformation, the maturation of transnational capitalism.[1] The world economy, in which nations were linked via commodity exchange and capital flows in an integrated international market, is giving way to a new global economy, in which the production process has become increasingly globalized. The global mobility of capital has allowed for the decentralization and functional integration around the world of vast chains of production and distribution, the instantaneous movement of values, and the unprecedented concentration and centralization of worldwide economic management, control and decision-making power in transnational capital. From a world structure characterized by capitalism as the dominant mode within a system of 'articulated modes of production', globalization is thus bringing about a world integrated into a single capitalist mode. Economic globalization brings with it the material basis for the transnationalization of political systems, civil society, social classes and cultural life. As a new global social structure of accumulation transforms existing national ones, integration into this emergent global economy and society is the causal macrostructural dynamic that underlies recent social change worldwide.

By making it structurally impossible for individual nations to sustain independent, or even autonomous, economies, political systems and social structures, globalization reconfigures world social forces in a very dramatic way. The globalization of capitalism seems to be replicating globally the sequence of historic development identified by Polanyi. As capitalism emerged, the unregulated market, with its naked quest for gain, unleashed its fury on the social bonds and institutions that allowed for individual survival and social reproduction.

The movement that extricated the economy from society in the last century in Europe and liberated the market from social constraint was followed by a 'second movement' that curtailed these deleterious effects by bringing a measure of social regulation to the forces of capitalism. But the 'double movement' was possible because capital, restricted by territorial, institutional and other limits bound up with the nation-state and the nation-state system, faced a series of constraints that forced it to reach a historic comprise with society. That compromise took the form of the Keynesian or 'New Deal' states and Fordist production in the cores of the world economy and of their Third World variant, multiclass 'developmental' states, and diverse populist projects in the periphery. The Keynesian states of the North and the developmental states of the South were able to capture and redirect surpluses through interventionist mechanisms that were viable in the nation-state phase of capitalism. Popular classes operating through mass social movements could apply pressure on national states to respond to their interests, to place controls on capital, and to attenuate some of the worst effects of the free market.

The global decentralization and fragmentation of the production process and the concomitant processes unfolding under the global economy redefine the phase of distribution in the accumulation of capital in relation to nation-states. They also fragment national cohesion around processes of social reproduction and shift the site of reproduction from the nation-state to transnational space. The 'utopia' of a self-regulated market that was brought under control by the double movement in the centers of world capitalism at the end of the nineteenth century has re-emerged with the lifting through the process of globalization of nation-state constraints on (transnationalized) capital. This liberation has freed emergent transnational capital from the compromises and commitments placed on it by the social forces in the nation-state phase of capitalism. Moreover, it has dramatically altered the balance of forces among classes and social groups in nations throughout the world toward an emergent transnational capitalist class.

In assessing the experience of social movements and the prospects of a new second movement, we should recall that this globalization is not unfolding as some predetermined structural process insofar as structural change is shaped by agents attempting to influence the process from below and from above. Indeed, the restraints on accumulation imposed by popular classes worldwide in the nation-state phase of capitalism were what drove capital to transnationalization in the first instance. The transnational capitalist class – as the primary agent of the global economy – controls the levers of global decision-making. Its class program is to create the conditions most propitious to the unfettered functioning of global capitalism and, since the mid-1980s, this has taken the form of neoliberalism. The neoliberal model seeks to achieve the conditions in each country and region of the world for the mobility and free operation of capital. The neoliberal SAPs sweeping

Latin America and the South are the major mechanism of adjusting national and regional economies to the global economy.

In the neoliberal model 'stabilization', or the package of fiscal, monetary, exchange and related measures, is intended to achieve macroeconomic stability, an essential requisite for fully mobile transnational capital to function simultaneously across numerous national borders. It is followed by 'structural adjustment': (1) liberalization of trade and finances, which opens the economy to the world market and to transnational capital; (2) deregulation, which removes the state from economic decision-making; (3) privatization of formerly public spheres that could hamper capital accumulation if criteria of public interest over private profit are left operative. This model thus generates the overall conditions for the profitable ('efficient') renewal of capital accumulation through new globalized circuits. Neoliberalism is the 'grease' by which global capitalism tears down all nonmarket structures that have in the past placed limits on, or acted as a protective layer against, the accumulation of capital. Nonmarket spheres of human activity – public spheres managed by states and private spheres linked to community and family – are being broken up, commodified and transferred to capital. By prizing open and making accessible to transnational capital every layer of the social fabric, neoliberalism extricates the global economy from global society, and the state defers to the market as the sole organizing power in the economic and social sphere.

However, outcomes are the result of social forces in struggle, even when the agency of dominant groups may appear as uncontested. There is no reason to assume that a change will come from the centers of power and privilege in the global system, which are commanded by a transnational capitalist class, together with a transnationalized bureaucratic and state elite that runs local governments and international institutions. To focus on the real and prospective agency of subordinate groups in global society is to ask what are those social forces that could force through a double movement against the gales of the global market? Such change will come only when it is forced on the global system by mass pressure from popular majorities violently uprooted from preglobalization local and national structures. These majorities are increasingly organized in diverse egalitarian social movements that often mediate directly between the state and the popular majority, and they are powerful agents of social change.

The universal penetration of capitalism through globalization draws all peoples not only into webs of market relations but also into webs of resistance. Kees van der Pijl (1997) has identified three moments in the process of the subordination of society and nature to the reproduction of capital: (1) original accumulation; (2) the capitalist production process; and (3) the process of social reproduction, each of which generates its own form of 'countermovement' resistance and struggle. We should turn to the social forces from below, which resist at all three of these moments, in anticipation of any counterhegemonic impulse that could develop into an effective double movement in Latin America and in global society at large. In the following sections, I explore social movements and inequality in Latin America, with respect to development, capital and labor, gender, and democratization and human rights. I then return briefly in the conclusion to the prospects of a counterhegemony.

Regional development in a world of polarized accumulation: Latin America's growing marginality in the global economy

Globalization has played a determinant role in the shift in Latin America from a regional model of accumulation, based on domestic market expansion, populism and import-substitution industrialization, to the neoliberal model based on liberalization and integration to the global economy, a *laissez-faire* state, and export-led development (Robinson 1998b). The transition from the predominant worldwide model of Keynesian or Fordist accumulation to post-Fordist 'flexible' accumulation models involves a process in each region of internal adjustment and rearticulation to the global system. It has accelerated diversity and uneven development among countries and regions in accordance with the matrix of factor cost considerations and the configuration of diverse social forces in the new globalized environment. The particular form of rearticulation to the global economy, including new socioeconomic structures and a modified regional profile in the global division of labor, has varied from region to region.

The dismantling of the preglobalization model of development and its replacement by the neoliberal model began in Latin America in the 1970s. But the imbroglio in Latin America's development was at its height in the 1980s, which is often referred to as Latin America's 'lost decade'. At the beginning of the decade, Latin America was hit by an economic crisis unprecedented since the 1930s crisis of world capitalism, and one that endured throughout the decade. Latin American development not only stagnated in absolute terms but, perhaps more significantly, the region has experienced backward movement in relation to the world economy. Some have referred to the region's marginalization as the 'Africanization' of Latin America, a reference to Africa's severe marginalization from the centers of world power and wealth and the increasing structural similarity of the two regions in the global system.

Latin America's share in world trade and production has declined steadily since 1980. Income and economic activity has contracted relative to the global system. As growth stagnated worldwide during the world recession that began in 1973, Latin America fell behind developing countries as a whole. The average annual growth of real GDP per capita in Latin America dropped to -0.4 per cent, compared to 2.3 per cent in developing countries (World Bank 1991, 1997).

Between 1980 and 1989, world economic activity expanded by an annual average of 3.1 per cent. Growth in Africa dropped from 4.2 per cent (1965–80) to 2.1 per cent (1980–89), and in Latin America it dropped even more precipitously, from 6.1 per cent (1965–80) to 1.6 per cent (1980–89: World Bank 1991, 1992). Between 1980 and 1990, Latin America's share of manufacturing value added fell from 6 per cent of the world total to 4.9 per cent (UN Industrial Development Organization 1993).

Latin America's share of world exports and imports has declined steadily from 1950 but dropped precipitously from 1980 into the 1990s (Wilkie 1995). In contrast, the volume of Latin American exports increased significantly throughout the 1980s and 1990s. In other words, Latin Americans have worked harder and produced more for the global economy, even as they have become more impoverished and marginalized. Between 1983 and 1985, the volume of the region's exports rose by 16.2 per cent, but the value of these same exports dropped by 9.9 per cent. Between 1992 and 1994, the volume rose by 22.3 per cent but the value increased by only 3.3 per cent (Economic Commission for Latin America and the Caribbean, or ECLAC 1988, 1989, 1990, 1991, 1994–95). The steady deterioration of the terms of trade for Latin America must be understood as a consequence of the region's increasingly asymmetric participation in the global division of labor at a time when adjustment has shifted resources toward the external sector (ECLAC 1990, 1994–95).

Latin America's increasing marginality in the global system should not be confused with its contribution to global capital accumulation. Latin America was a net exporter of capital to the world market throughout the 1980s, exporting $219 billion between 1982 and 1990 (ECLAC 1994–95). Ironically, therefore, Latin America continues to be a supplier of surplus for the world and an engine of growth of the global economy. In a liberalized global capitalist economy, surpluses may be transferred just as easily as they are generated, which reminds us that growth alone does not mean development. The permanent drainage of surplus from Latin America helps to explain the region's stagnating economy, declining income and plummeting living standards. The poor have to run faster just to remain in the same place. The social crisis in Latin America is not as much a crisis of production as it is of distribution. We should recall that inequality is a social relation of unequal power between the dominant and the subordinate and, more specifically, the power of the rich locally and globally to dispose of the social product.

Latin America experienced renewed growth and a net capital inflow of $80 billion between 1991 and 1994 (ECLAC 1994–95). But the vast bulk of the inflow of capital is not a consequence of direct foreign investment that could have helped expand the region's productive base as much as it is a consequence of new loans. It also did not result from the purchase of stock in privatized companies and speculative financial investment in equities and mutual funds, pensions, insurance, and so on (Veltmeyer 1997). The dominance of speculative financial flows over productive capital, reflecting the hegemony of transnational finance capital in the age of globalization and its frenzied 'casino capitalism' activity in recent years, gives an illusion of 'recovery' in Latin America. In addition, Latin America continued to export annually between 1992 and 1994 an average of $30 billion in profits and interests. Although there has been a resumption of growth, recovery has not generated new employment opportunities but has been accompanied by increased poverty and inequality (ECLAC 1994–95).

Given the outward drainage of surplus combined with liberalization and deeper external integration, it is not surprising that the external debt has continued to grow throughout the late 1980s and into the 1990s, and that its rate of growth is again increasing in the 1990s (ECLAC 1985, 1994–95).

Between 1980 and 1990, average per capital income in Latin America dropped by an unprecedented 11 per cent (World Bank 1997, 2), so that by 1990 most of the region's inhabitants found that their income had reverted to 1976 levels. Poverty levels also increased throughout the 1980s and early 1990s. Between 1980 and 1992, some 60 million new people joined the ranks of the poor, as the number of people living in poverty went from 136 million to 196 million, an increase from 41 per cent to 46 per cent of the total population.[2] Among those living in poverty, the level of indigence, defined as those who are unable to meet the daily minimum nutritional and related needs required for mere survival, also increased (Comision Economica para América Latina 1993).

Most telling in this data is the jump in poverty between 1989 and 1992. By the end of the 1980s, Latin America had resumed growth rates and attracted a net inflow of capital following the stagnation and decline during much of the decade. In the early 1990s, representatives from the international financial agencies began to speak of recovery, by which they meant that growth had resumed in most countries. The pattern in the 1980s and 1990s was not merely 'growth without redistribution'; it amounted to growth with further polarization and an expansion of poverty.

Latin America's development debacle is clearly linked to the crisis of global accumulation, which also hit Africa in the 1980s and finally caught up with the 'miracle economies' of East Asia, starting with the currency crises of 1997. Yet there are also region-specific considerations. The particular preglobalization structures and the form of articulation to the world economy help shape each region's fate under globalization. Africa's relegation to a world preserve for mineral and agricultural raw materials placed that region at a severe disadvantage as globalization unfolded. East Asia and Latin America shared a more advanced level of import-substitution industrialization (ISI). But East Asia's ISI model was based on the simultaneous expansion of the domestic market and increasingly higher value added exports for the world market, along with growing sectoral articulation and forward-backward linkages, a pattern that it sustained into the mid-1990s. Latin American ISI, in contrast, was characterized by an internal–external dualism: industrial expansion largely for the domestic market and continued articulation to the world economy through primary exports (Gereffi and Wyman 1990).

By eliminating the domestic market as a factor in development, globalization has placed Latin America in a structural situation parallel to that of Africa. But this is only part of the story. Regional adjustment in Latin America to the global economy has been effected through the neoliberal program, which is most advanced in this region, and is based on creating the optimal environment for private transnational capital to operate as the putative motor of development and social welfare. The fact that the domestic market is not of strategic importance in development and accumulation has important implications for class relations and social movements, and is, I suggest, at the heart of the development crisis in Latin America.

Labor: dimensions of inequality and new capital–labor relations in Latin America

Neoliberal reform has involved a restructuring of capital–labor relations in Latin America, in step with the intensified hegemony of capital and new patterns of post-Fordist accumulation in the globalized economy. The contraction of domestic markets, the dismantling of 'uncompetitive' national industry, the growth of the informal economy, revised labor codes directed at making labor flexible and austerity programs have resulted in the informalization of the workforce, mass underemployment and unemployment, a compression of real wages, and a transfer of income from labor to capital.

Inequality in Latin America, although high historically, further increased throughout the 1980s and 1990s. World Bank data for 18 Latin American countries indicates that the Gini coefficient rose from 0.45 in 1980 to 0.50 in 1989 (World Bank 1997). But income inequality is only one dimension, and often not the most important, of social inequality. Added to income polarization in the 1980s and 1990s there is also the dramatic deterioration in social conditions resulting from austerity measures that have drastically reduced and privatized health, education and other social programs. Popular classes whose social reproduction is dependent on a social wage (public sector) have faced a crisis, whereas privileged middle and upper classes become exclusive consumers of social services channelled through private networks.

The escalation of deprivation indicators in Brazil and Mexico, which together accounted for over half of Latin America's 465 million inhabitants (in 1995), is revealing. Between 1985 and 1990, the rate of child malnutrition in Brazil, where nearly 48 per cent of the country's 160 million people lived in poverty in 1990 (UNDP 1995), increased from 12.7 to 30.7 per cent of all children (World Bank 1997). In Mexico, where over 50 per cent of the country's 90 million people are in poverty, the purchasing power of the minimum wage dropped 66 per cent between 1982 and 1991. It was calculated that in the mid-1990s it took 4.8 minimum wages for a family of four to meet essential needs, yet 80 per cent of households earned 2.5 minimum wages or less. Consequently, malnutrition has spread among the urban and rural poor (Barkin, Ortiz and Rosen 1997).

The neoliberal development model ties internal accumulation to global circuits of accumulation and to external world market demand. By removing the domestic market and workers' consumption from the accumulation imperative, restructuring involves the demise of the populist class alliances between broad majorities and nationally based ruling classes that characterized the old development model. The new development model seeks to achieve a comparative advantage for Latin America through pliant cheap labor corresponding to the new capital–labor relationship.

Several factors contribute to the general secular decline in urban wages in the region. In integrating their countries into the global economy, local elites and, in particular, the transnationalized fractions of these elites that came to power in the 1980s and 1990s, base development on the exclusive criterion of achieving maximum internal profitability as the essential condition for attracting transnational capital. Profitability in this regard means achieving a comparative advantage in cheap labor and in state-subsidized access to the region's abundant natural resources. Globalized production such as the *maquila,* border-area export, sector involves a new situation whereby host countries offer only cheap labor to the global economy, compared with earlier periods in the world economy in which they offered limited markets along with fertile land and resources.

Successful development and the continuation of the privileged status of elites depend more than ever on expendable cheap labor. Established and aspiring economic and political elites thus see the erosion of labor's income, the withdrawal of public services and the curtailment of political demands as requirements for the region's successful integration into the global economy.[3] A comparison of the evolution of urban real minimum wages in select countries in Latin America from 1983 to 1992 showed a significant decline in real minimum wages in all cases, except for Chile (Wilkie 1995). In the logic of global capitalism, the cheapening of labor and its social disenfranchisement by the neoliberal state become conditions for development.

Capital has all but abandoned reciprocal obligations to labor in the employment contract with the emergence of a new post-Fordist political regime of accumulation. And states, transmutating from developmentalist to neoliberal, have all but abandoned public obligations to poor and working majorities under the new social structure of accumulation.[4] There has been an explosion of the informal sector, which has been the only avenue of survival for millions of people thrown out of work by the contraction of public sector employment, the dismantling of national enterprises, and the uprooting of remaining peasant communities by the incursion of capitalist agriculture. National and international data collections report those in the informal sector as 'employed', despite the highly irregular and unregulated character of the informal sector, characterized by low levels of productivity, low earnings, generally well below legal minimum wages, and precariousness, usually amounting to underemployment (World Bank 1988, 1990, 1993). The International Labor Organization estimates that four out of every five jobs generated from 1980 to 1993 in Latin America were in the informal sector (Veltmeyer 1997, 220).

The accelerated informal loosening of the labor market has been accompanied by the increase of labor flexibility in the remains of the formal sector. This has also been accompanied by more frequent use of contract work and contingent labor over permanent employment and collective contracts, with a consequent decline in the role of trade unions in the labor market and of working-class negotiating power. As Henry Veltmeyer notes (1997, 222), 'the increased international competitiveness of a number of Latin American economies is not, as in the East Asian NICs [newly industrialized countries], a function of rising wages ... The compression of wages has been the major mechanism of internal adjustment throughout the region.'

In comparison, it seems that Africa's marginality in the global economy is as a result of chronic political and social instability, which is itself a function of tensions generated by severe inequalities and an extremely disadvantageous relation to the global system. However, Latin America's growing marginality is as a result of the *success* of its 'race to the bottom' in wage compression, which has been combined with a modicum of social and political stability achieved by the destructuring and dispersal of labor.

Entering the global economy has resulted in a breaking down of the traditional Latin American working class. This breaking down entails a dramatic weakening of labor in relation to capital and a change in the correlation of class forces. Marginality is an unpropitious condition for mounting organized resistance, but the restructuring of the labor–capital relationship has also led to a change in the center of gravity of the working class. This center is no longer in the strategic sectors of national production or in the equally strategic sector of public services, but rather in the unproductive and low-productive informal sectors of the burgeoning urban economy. Labor resistance to neoliberalism shifts from the old places of work such as factories and offices, to new places such as the streets and communities, where labor becomes less distinguishable as a particular organized constituency within the new social movements. Ironically, globalization is generating the conditions for a new 'social unionism', and alliances with other social movements are increasingly the fulcrum of the labor movement.[5]

Women: advances and emerging dilemmas

The 1980s and early 1990s in Latin America witnessed a flourishing of participation by women in diverse social movements, along with a burgeoning of women's and feminist organizations (Stephen 1998). Women have mobilized to address collective problems that they, their children, and poor people face, and also to address the special forms of gender oppression and inequality that they suffer as women. In their diverse forms of mobilization, women have effectively articulated the central concerns of daily life: access to housing, health care and employment, freedom from violence against women and against the poor, and democracy and environmental preservation. Women have struggled as workers in trade unions, as mothers, as citizens in human rights movements, as housewives in shanty towns, as leading organizers and spokespeople for the indigenous movement, and as guerrillas in armed movements. The best known case of women in the vanguard of human rights movements is, perhaps, the Mothers of the Plaza de Mayo in Argentina, an organization that played a decisive role in the defeat of the military dictatorship in Argentina in 1983. But similar human rights organizations organized and led by women have arisen in Brazil, Chile, Guatemala, Honduras, Uruguay and other Latin American countries.

Reinforced by global communications, internal and international migrations, rising levels of formal education for women and increased personal autonomy and mobility, feminism has become a powerful social movement in its own right. The current feminist era in Latin America opened symbolically in 1975 in Mexico City at the *Conferencia Mundial del Año Internacional de la Mujer* (World Conference on the International Year of the Woman). The conference kicked off the UN Decade for Women (1975–85), and had led by the end of the 1980s to feminism's 'second wave' in Latin America (the first occurred in the late nineteenth and early twentieth centuries). By the 1990s, hundreds of feminist organizations were operating locally, nationally and transnationally in Latin America, linked into a powerful hemispheric network and to broader global networks (Jelin 1990; Jaquette 1994).

Women have made tremendous gains in *formal* equality, as measured, among other indicators, by the UN's gender development index. This composite index ranks nations according to the share of total income that women earn, women's life expectancy and literacy compared to men's, as well as women's enrollment in primary, secondary and tertiary schools (UNDP 1995).

In 1991, Argentina became the first country to institute affirmative action for political office, passing a quota law requiring that at least 30 per cent of political parties' candidates be women. Meanwhile, similar laws are being debated in other countries. In 1997, women held as few as 6.6 per cent and as many as 25.3 per cent of legislative seats. Women also held 6 per cent of cabinet posts (*Latinamerica Press* 1997). Although these figures indicate just how far women still have to go in securing full formal equality and equal representation, they also indicate significant progress, considering just how excluded women have been historically from positions of public authority. 'It is no longer strange to hear about a woman running a company, directing a university or campaigning for public office,' noted a recent issue of *Latinamerica Press* (1997, 2).

Yet dramatic improvements in education, in legal equality, in the percentage of women in leadership positions, in the availability of birth control and other tangible gains have not resulted in less inequality. The expectation is that the improvements necessarily would reflect certain modernization assumptions and that a sexual equalization of market conditions would be sufficient to eliminate inequality. Moreover, as Fernández-Kelly (1994) has noted:

> Those perspectives do not address problems stemming from ideologies that emphasize personal independence and fulfillment through paid employment. In countries where jobs are scarce and working conditions unsuitable for both men and women, the diffusion of ideologies that stress individualism can actually exacerbate women's vulnerability by charging them with new economic obligations that are difficult to meet with the wages they receive

The larger structural context to the upsurge in women's struggles is the dramatic change in the status of women in Latin America in recent decades. Globalization has major implications for the sexual division of labor, for gender relations and for the transformation of the family itself. The percentage of women in the labor force has grown in most regions of the world under globalization (UN Department for Economic and Social Information and Policy Analysis 1995). Increased formal sector female participation has resulted from several factors. Among them are the predictable pattern that accompanies capitalist development in general: that is, the need for families to send an increasing number of family members into the labor market with the decline in real wages and household income, the predilection of transnational capital to hire 'docile' female labor, particularly in *maquila* production, and so on.[6]

With the decline in male employment and real wages brought about by neoliberal restructuring, women have assumed a growing absolute and also relative importance as wage earners, and their contribution to household economies has increased. The reorganization of production on a global scale is feminizing the labor force and changing the previous gender demarcation of domestic and wage labor. Gender inequality is reproduced in the workforce and at the same time it continues in the household: the systematic subordination of women in the reproduction sphere is coupled with the systematic inequality of women in the production sphere. It is clear that under globalization there is a transformation of the sexual division of labor. New forms of labor market segmentation between men and women and wage differentials in the formal sector converge with unpaid domestic labor and hardship imposed in the sphere of gendered social reproduction, resulting in a deterioration of the status and social condition of most women. From the *maquilas* of Mexico, Central America and the Caribbean, to the new transnational agri-business plantations in Chile and Colombia, and the new industrial complexes in Brazil's northeast, women in Latin America disproportionately – and in some cases, exclusively – engage in unskilled, labor-intensive phases of globalized production.

The decline in wages and work conditions associated with new capital–labor relations at the production site takes place at a time when women increasingly make up the ranks of the workforce. At the same time, the costs of reproduction of the labor force are assumed by women without compensation, and these costs rise dramatically to the extent that neoliberal adjustment removes state and public support for that reproduction, which becomes 'privatized' and reverts more exclusively to the household. The state's withdrawal from providing basic services linked to social reproduction takes place at a time when the need for these services has grown with the rapid increase in urbanization and commodification.

These twin processes – stated in simplified terms, the deterioration of wages and social wages – have had a devastating impact on women and children (Cornai 1987; Benería and Feldman 1992). Women have disproportionately borne the burden of neoliberal restructuring, and the feminization of poverty has affected women in all Latin American countries. It is estimated that 70 per cent of the poor are women (Veltmeyer 1997, 224). Women in Latin America have a 34 per cent probability of belonging to the bottom 20 per cent of the income distribution, as compared with a 15 per cent probability for men (World Bank 1997, 48). As women have entered the formal labor force, the data indicates that they encounter a gender-segmented labor market in which women are disproportionately concentrated in low-wage employment and excluded from high-wage employment. This inequality in labor force participation aggravates other gender-based social inequalities (World Bank 1997, 197–202).

As women enter the labor force they are also disproportionately relegated to the informal economy, as part-time domestics, laundresses, street vendors, industrial homeworkers, and so on. Women account for fully 70 per cent of all new jobs in the informal sector (Veltmeyer 1997, 220), and by the 1990s an estimated 130 million women and children were eking out a living in the informal sector (Miller 1995). The transformation in the status of women, and particularly women's increasing centrality in production and reproduction along with the 'double burden', has galvanized poor and working women and fused women's movements with feminist movements in dynamic new social movements throughout the hemisphere. The women's movement in Latin America has experienced a remarkable dynamic. Through struc-tural circumstance, it has engaged in a synthesis of the particular strug-gle against women's oppression with the struggle against the deleterious effects of capitalist globalization at each of the three levels of resistance to capitalism identified by van der Pijl (1997). As women have entered the workforce *en masse* in recent decades, they have been at the van-guard of popular struggles around the process of production and exploitation, such as in the *maquiladoras*. But, in step with the essence of gender inequality and subordination, women remain locked into the sphere of reproduction even as their participation in production becomes formal. Hence women are at the forefront of battles over social reproduction that take place in the 'private' (household) and 'public' (community, workplace, and state) spheres.[7] Helen Safa (1995, 228) argues in this regard that the primary area of confrontation for women's social movements in Latin America 'has been not with capital but with the state, largely in terms of women's reproductive roles as wives, mothers, and consumers, both of state services and of private consumer goods'. And women have also played a major role in struggles against the incursion of capitalism and its disruption of community and autonomy, as epitomized in the mass participation and leadership roles of women in the Zapatista and other revolu-tionary movements or in the peasant-based Landless Movement (MST) of Brazil.

Feminist scholars in Latin America have debated as to whether capitalist globalization has acted to increase opportunities for women and break down some of the structures of gender subordination, or to increase the oppression and exploitation of women (K. Ward and Pyle 1995). Dialectically speaking, these assessments are both accurate and not mutually exclusive. On the one hand, the achievement of legal equality and the incorporation of women in the formal labor force and other changes have helped to break up traditional extended patriarchal family structures and the gender relations they embody. More egalitarian conjugal relations have developed where women's economic contribution to the household has increased. On the other hand, the actual status of women continues to deteriorate dramatically as the burden of survival steadily increases (Safa 1994). There is doubtless a gap between *de jure* equality and daily life that disguises an almost deleterious deterioration of women's status. 'Feminism confronted a tension between women's individual claims and the needs of their communities,' Fernández-Kelly notes (1994), in discussing the differences between the mobilization of middle-class and poor women:

The uneasy relation between individual and communal demands exposes class differences: for comparatively affluent women in Latin America, the agenda resembles that forged by feminists in advanced industrial countries; for impoverished women in rural and urban environments, an emphasis on equality with men skirts questions about the meaning and consequences of equality in deprived environments.

This 'emerging dilemma' underscores the dramatic growth under globalization of group and class inequalities and opportunities that cut across the gender divide, and place both poor and better off women in a contradictory situation. To the extent that gains in formal equality and opportunity improve the condition of women *as women*, gender inequality is increasingly fused with class and group inequality under globalization.[8] This only partly explains the mass participation and leadership role of women at every level in the struggle of popular classes and in all of Latin America's social movements. This also partly explains the paradox of tremendous gains in the Latin American women's movement, alongside the deterioration of the status of social conditions of women under globalization.

The original double movement that spawned Keynesian national social structures of accumulation embedded gender inequalities in the negotiated class relations between (male) employers and (male) employees. The family wage that became incorporated into Keynesian capitalism institutionalized the sexual division of labor based on the domestic/wage labor dichotomy. Globalization undermines the family wage as it drives down workers' wages and the social wage, and at the same time thrusts women into the labor market. Any new double movement cannot reinstitutionalize the dichotomy between production and reproduction that was structured into the original double movement earlier this century (Fernández-Kelly 1994). On the contrary, the emancipation of women requires a protective movement not only against global capital (perhaps its overthrow) but also (barring its overthrow) against any protective arrangements. Such protective measures force global capitalism into reciprocal and accountable relations with labor that are constructed on the basis of abolishing gendered dichotomy between production and reproduction, linking female subordination in the former and slavery in the latter.

Human rights and democratization: the antinomy of polyarchy

By the late 1970s, authoritarianism as the predominant mode of social control in Latin America faced an intractable crisis (Robinson 1996b). On the one hand, mass popular movements for democracy and human rights besieged the authoritarian regimes and threatened to bring down the whole elite-based social order along with the dictatorships, as happened in Nicaragua in 1979. This threat from below, combined with the inability of the authoritarian regimes to manage the dislocations and adjustments of globalization, generated intra-elite conflicts that unraveled the ruling power blocs. The crisis of elite rule was resolved through transitions to polyarchies that took place in almost every country in the region during the 1980s and early 1990s.

Reflected in these contested transitions was an effort by transnational dominant groups to reconstitute hegemony through a change in the mode of political domination, from the coercive systems of social control exercised by authoritarian and dictatorial regimes to more consensually based (or at least consensus-seeking) systems of the new polyarchies. At stake was the type of a social order – the emergent global capitalist order or some popular alternative – that would emerge in the wake of authoritarianism. Emergent transnationalized fractions of local elites in Latin America, with the structural power of the global economy behind them and the direct political and military intervention of the

USA and other transnational actors, were able to gain hegemony over democratization movements and steer the break-up of authoritarianism into polyarchic outcomes.

The transnational elite in the South is promoting polyarchy as the political counterpart to neoliberalism. Transitions to polyarchy should be seen in the light of the changing nature of transnational social control under globalization. Interaction and economic integration on a world scale are obstructed by authoritarian or dictatorial political arrangements, which are unable to manage the expansion of social intercourse associated with the global economy. Authoritarian systems have tended to unravel as globalizing pressures break up embedded forms of coercive political authority, dislocate traditional communities and social patterns, and stir masses of people to demand the democratization of social life. With its mechanisms for intra-elite compromise and accommodation and for hegemonic incorporation of popular majorities, polyarchy is better equipped in the new global environment to legitimize the political authority of dominant groups and to achieve a minimally stable environment for global capitalism to operate. The 'democratic consensus' in the new world order is a consensus among an increasingly cohesive global elite on the type of political system most propitious to the reproduction of social order in the new global environment.

The transitions from authoritarianism to polyarchy in Latin America afforded transnational elites the opportunity to reorganize state institutions and create a more favorable institutional framework for a deepening of neoliberal adjustment. Without a single exception in Latin America, the new polyarchic regimes – staffed by state managers tied to the transnational elite (the new 'modernizers' and 'technocrats') – have pursued a profound neoliberal transformation. The transnational elite has demonstrated a remarkable ability to wield the structural power of transnational capital over individual countries as a sledgehammer against popular grassroots movements for fundamental change in social structures.

In Haiti and Nicaragua, mass popular movements were impotent to change the social structure because the global economy and the transnational elite could dictate the internal conditions in these countries (Robinson 1996b) We should recall in this regard that transitions to polyarchy include transitions from left-wing nationalist and popular regimes that might provide a more favorable environment for egalitarian social movements as much as they do transitions from right-wing authoritarian regimes. The veto power of the global system overrides the ability of social movements to achieve egalitarian outcomes through the institutions of polyarchy. Indeed, it is the structural power of global capitalism to impose discipline through the market that (usually) makes unnecessary the all-pervasive coercive forms of political authority exercised by authoritarian regimes.

However, it is unclear whether polyarchy can be maintained under neoliberalism or whether global capitalism is compatible with a regime of human rights. The new model of development by insertion into new global circuits of accumulation does not require an inclusionary social base. Socioeconomic exclusion is inherent in the model since accumulation does not depend on a domestic market or internal social reproduction. This is a fundamental structural contradiction between the globalization model of development and the effort to maintain polyarchic political systems that require the hegemonic incorporation of a sufficiently broad social base. The neoliberal model generates social conditions and political tensions – inequality, polarization, impoverishment, marginality – which are conducive to a breakdown of polyarchy.

The human rights situation in Latin America is better than under the dictatorships, but this should not obscure our objective analysis. Social relations in daily life are violent and ordered on authoritarian hierarchies. Human rights violations are still systematic and widespread in Latin America, as the annual reports by the various human rights monitoring groups make clear (*Latinamerica Press* 1995). The new victims are now as much the social and economic outcasts as they are political dissidents, leading one observer to describe the new regimes as 'democracies without citizenship' (Pinheiro 1996).

Others have written about what 'social cleansing' of the poor and undesirable has involved. The mass murder of street children in Guatemala, Brazil and elsewhere by police and by death squads hired by affluent businessmen and local politicians is an infamous example (Scheper-Hughes and Hoffman 1994; Scheper-Hughes 1997). Thousands of poor people have died – the vast majority as they await trial – in countless prison uprisings in penitentiary systems that are unfit for human habitation (*Latinamerica Press* 1998). Another such grisly scandal concerns the round-up and the execution by security forces in Colombia in 1995 of homeless individuals and the delivery of their bodies to a private medical school as specimens for medical students to practice autopsies on (Dudley 1998). An indigenous leader in Brasilia was burned alive in early 1997 by upper-class teenagers for apparent amusement, and they were acquitted of homicide (*Latinamerica Press* 1997).

None of these cases is an anomaly: they are all manifestations of the social power of a minority wielded against the outcast in a socioeconomic system that by its very nature violates the human rights of a majority of society's members. When the very right to life is denied by the social order, discussion of human rights as a political abstraction becomes philistine.

When we speak of democracy and human rights, we should recall that the worldwide inequality in the distribution of wealth and power is a form of permanent structural violence against the world's majority. This structural violence generates collective protest that calls forth state repression. This repression transforms, on a regular basis, structural violence into direct violence. The structural violence of the socioeconomic system and violations of human rights are different moments of the same social relations of domination.

State repression claiming thousands of lives has been used throughout Latin America to repress protest against neoliberal structural adjustment. Almost every Latin American country has experienced waves of spontaneous uprisings, generally triggered by austerity measures such as the formation of urban poor political protest movements in the shanty towns and a resurgence of mass peasant movements and land invasions. These actions fall outside the formal institutions of the political system and almost always involve violent clashes between states and paramilitary forces and protesters. Moreover, these uprisings highlight the relationship between the violation of socioeconomic rights and the violation of 'traditional' human rights. Social polarization brought about by neoliberalism has generated mass conflict that the neoliberal states have not been able to control without resorting to human rights violations (Calderon 1995).

Latin America's polyarchic regimes face growing crises of legitimacy and governability. But the changed correlation of class and social forces brought about by the modification of Latin America's articulation to the global system helps to explain the continued survival of the new polyarchies. The fragmentation and weakening of the popular classes through restructuring and marginalization, along with the neoliberal culture of individualism and consumerism, contribute to the social control of the dispersed and atomized victims of global capitalism in Latin America.

Egalitarian social movements continue to push for democratization. Their struggles range from participation in electoral processes to mass movements against the exclusionary neoliberal states. The popular uprising that forced the corrupt Ecuadoran president, Abdala Bucaram, to resign in February 1997, and the mass movement that led to the impeachment of the corrupt Brazilian head of state, Fernando Collar de Mello, in 1993 exemplify just two results. Moreover, popular masses have struggled to preserve polyarchic structures in the face of attempts by civilian elites to usurp more dictatorial powers. Examples of this are the movement that forced the Guatemalan president, Jorge Serrano, to flee the country in 1993 after he dissolved congress, and the movements that prevented *coups d' état* in Argentina in the late 1980s and in Paraguay in 1997. In their electoral battles, mass movements face processes tightly controlled from above, such as elites that count on vastly superior resources and the immanent class advantage accrued from linkage to the transnational elite and the global economy, continued state repression, and the demobilizing effects of mass impoverishment and marginalization.

The mass pro-democracy movements of the 1970s and 1980s unraveled once dictatorships were replaced by polyarchies. Yet egalitarian social movements, in their struggle to win the power necessary for the effective transformation of the social order, have discovered that democratization and social emancipation are not separable. Diverse social movements, with the challenge to the established order that their demands for social and economic justice constitute, are themselves, by definitional fiat, democratization movements.

Conclusion: hegemony and counterhegemony

Popular classes have risen through egalitarian social movements and through other forms of organizations in civil society throughout Latin America, demanding a 'double movement'. In this study a limited number of social movements have been examined, but Latin America has also seen the burgeoning of indigenous, environmental, peasant, community associations of the urban poor, as well as other key social movements that will play a central role in forcing any prospective egalitarian outcome. It is also worth noting that less coordinated mass protest is also the order of the day throughout the region. Hunger strikes, sit-ins, land invasions, marches, blocked streets and mass meetings in both the cities and the countryside are regular occurrences. One question is how much these more inchoate opposition forces will be mobilized into the existing and new social movements and augment their capacity to force structural change.

Fernando Calderon (1995) argues that global economic and technological change have created a more fragmented and heterogeneous

social structure that engenders particularist, decentralized and disconnected forms of collective action. Latin American social movements are
too partial to mount a hegemonic challenge or to contest the systemic
logic of transnational power, which reveals the fundamental contradiction between the global concentration of power and wealth and
the diverse but decentralized forms of resistance under global capitalism. This explains only some of the irony of the inverse movement
between deepening inequalities and polarization and a proliferation of
social movements. The ability of social movements to contest the
neoliberal order, in my view, depends on breaking the hegemony of
this order through the development of a viable alternative program,
along with the transnationalization of popular movements in the
struggle to impose that alternative.

Neoliberalism had by the mid-1990s achieved a certain hegemony in
global society. The much-touted 'Washington consensus' in the Western
Hemisphere, for instance, reflects agreement over the project of the
transnational elite among an increasingly cohesive hemispheric elite.
This consensus is clustered in governments, the private sector and international financial and political agencies active in the hemisphere, such
as the UN, IMF, World Bank, Inter-American Development Bank and
the Organization of American States. It was forged through the course
of restructuring, debt renegotiation and 'transitions to democracy'
during the 1980s and early 1990s (Williamson 1990, 1993). It was
indeed a consensus, because it represented a congruence of interests
among the hemisphere's dominant groups, and these interests were
being advanced through institutions that command power (the hemisphere's states and the international financial institutions). The consensus also achieved ideological hegemony by setting the parameters
for, and the limits to, debate among subordinate groups on options
and alternative projects for the hemisphere.[9] In this sense, the
Washington consensus reflected the emergence of a new hegemonic
historic bloc in the hemisphere – and in global society – under the
leadership of the transnational elite.

Developing a viable, alternative socioeconomic program is not
enough. Social forces operating through nationally based social movements clearly need to transpose their mobilization and their capacity to
transnational space to place demands on the system, because it is at the
transnational level that the causes are to be found of the conditions
that these movements seek to address. Moreover, these two are linked.
The specifics of an alternative are not yet clear, but it would need to be
a new type of redistributionist project. It also would need to be one that

was transposed from the earlier national to the new transnational space, one that challenges the logic of capitalist hegemony, and one that develops an ideology along the lines that Christopher Chase-Dunn (1998) proposed for a new 'egalitarian universalism'.

What is the real negotiating power of popular majorities within a transnational setting? To ask this is to ask what are the prospects that key social movements, such as those of women, labor, democracy and human rights, and development and social justice, will develop the mechanisms that allow for transposition of local and national organizing strength to a transnational space. Latin American social movements had, in fact, begun to transnationalize in the 1990s, moving to create alliances, networks and organizations that transcended national and even regional borders. For instance, cross-border organizing has been extended and systematized in the wake of multinational US–Canadian–Mexican trade union coordination against NAFTA in 1993. In Central America, community-based social movements have formed the Central American Federation of Community Organizations (FCOC) to coordinate strategy and action throughout the Isthmus, and the peasant movements in South America have formed the Latin American Peasant Confederation (CLOC).

One strategy put forward for a more egalitarian outcome under globalization is the tempering of neoliberalism by the infusion of global Keynesian perspectives, presumably through social movements and other international actors, into the network of IGOs (see, for example, Murphy 1994). But we should be wary of the potential for the emerging set of global governance institutions to provide transnational political and organizational space for egalitarian social movements. Conversely, the network of reformed Bretton Woods bodies, the UN system agencies, trade organizations and so on constitute an incipient transnationalized state apparatus that functions to impose the implacable logic of global capitalism on the world's peoples, with an impunity made possible by its immunity from the types of constraint that could earlier be exercised at the nation-state level. Far from providing space and coordinating mechanisms for counterhegemonic development, the network of IGOs act to subvert a transnational counterhegemony. They are partisans in the battle for hegemony being waged in an increasingly transnationalized civil society. Dominant groups have operated through networks of IGOs and national and international NGOs that link together local, national and transnational space. We have seen in the 1990s a division of labor between the IGOs that strive to construct consensus and the general conditions for global capitalism at the international level and NGOs in each country and region. This is the new organizational form through which the transnational elite is attempting to construct its hegemony.

For instance, to undercut the type of opposition and alternative visions that could come from a counterhegemonic movement, the international financial institutions have recently called for SAPs to be 'redesigned' to give them a 'social dimension', not unlike the Basic Needs approach launched by World Bank under the direction of Robert McNamara in 1973 (Stahl 1996; Petras 1997, 1997–98; Veltmeyer 1997). Each SAP in Latin America now includes an adjunct 'social fund,' such as Pronasol (or Solidaridad) in Mexico, the social fund program (FOSOS) in Chile, and others. These funds are usually financed jointly by local governments and the multilateral agencies and putatively intend to 'target' the poor.

The New Social Policy (NSP) programs have not been able to ameliorate the spread of poverty and deprivation. They operate within the logic of the neoliberal model, largely as temporary relief to those marginalized by the new economic model, but without modifying the structural causes of that marginalization. The key institutional mechanism of the NSP programs is the privatization of social services that were earlier universalized and administered by states, and their decentralized administration as charities through new NGOs that act in partnership with local governments.

These programs are not the beginnings of a double movement but an ineffectual tinkering from above. Their aim is to contain the discontent generated by adjustment, to depoliticize popular grassroots constituencies, and to neutralize opposition from the 'bottom up' in synchronization with state and transnational activity that operates from the 'top down'. The spread of NGOs in Latin America and around the world has been hailed as an awakening and empowerment of civil society.

We should recall that civil society is the site of the battle for hegemony among antagonistic social forces. Without hegemony in civil society, the neoliberal project cannot be stabilized. NGOs do not invariably defend popular sectors and often represent dominant groups in civil society. The NSP programs utilize the rhetoric of 'empowering' local communities and 'participatory' development, but in practice they mediate relations between grassroots organizations and states in constructing the hegemony of the neoliberal order at the grassroots level. This is part of a shift in domination from above to below and from political to civil society.

In searching for a viable alternative to the neoliberal status quo, we should recall that the extent of social change may be fixed by historic structures, but the outer limits of these structures are always established and re-established by collective human agency. Our intellectual labor as a form of social action may constrict just as it may extend the proclaimed limits of the possible. Critical globalization studies should set as their objective elucidating the structural and historical context of the crisis of civilization we face, as well as the real inner workings and the contradictions of the emergent global social order. In this way, we may exercise a 'preferential option' for the subordinate majorities of emergent global society and for the future that is latent within them.

Notes

1. For more detailed discussion on the themes in this section, see Robinson (1996a, 1998a).
2. Population growth accounts for only 50 per cent of the increase in poverty. Whereas the number of poor people grew by 44 per cent during this period, the rate of total population growth was only 22 per cent. See Veltmeyer (1997, 225).
3. As calculated from data reported in Veltmeyer (1997), Wilkie (1997), UN Department for Economic and Social Information and Policy Analysis (1995).
4. On the hegemony of capital and political regimes of accumulation, see Buroway (1979). On social structures of accumulation, see Kotz, McDonough and Reich (1994).
5. For an extended analysis of this new 'social movement' unionism in the context of the restructuring of the global working class, see Moody (1997).
6. If female labor initially is (or is perceived to be) more easy to control, it is the result of gender socialization, combined with real relations of patriarchy and gender inequality and pre-existing sexual divisions of labor that render female workers less powerful than their male counterparts. The following is a typical statement made by a *maquiladora* manager:

   [Because of] their mothering instincts, women are ... more responsible than men; they are raised to be gentle and obedient, and so they are easier to deal with. They are also more nimble and meticulous and they don't get tired of doing the same thing nine hundred times a day ... We hire them because we know we'll have fewer problems. (Fernández-Kelly 1994, 1)

7. For example, women have been at the forefront of the social movements of urban poor, such as in the communal kitchens for food distribution and other popular self-help organizations that sprang up in Chile, Peru and elsewhere in the 1980s. Safa reports (1995, 229) that there were an estimated 1383 *Organizaciones Económicas Populares* (OEP, Popular Economic Organizations) in Santiago, Chile, alone in 1986, operating with almost exclusively

female leadership and participation. These organizations have become important in the survival strategies of women and families. In this way, these female-led community organizations become clearing houses for social movements and popular struggles of the urban poor. To the extent that they place demands on the state, they also become targets of government efforts at social control of women and the poor and thus sites for contesting hegemony. In this way, the women's movement has become a catalyst and a centripetal force for popular social change.

8. Safa (1994, 228) argues that prominence of women in the new social movements 'is based primarily on gender rather than on class', because in her assessment 'the bulk of poor women who participate in these movements are conscious of both class and gender exploitation but tend to legitimize their concerns over issues such as human rights or the cost of living primarily in terms of their roles as wives and mothers rather than as members of a subordinated class'. But this is a strictly subjective conception of the nature of social mobilization, which seems to deny the possibility that gender and class, far from being mutually exclusive, become fused in the mobilization of women. Indeed, as Safa notes, it is not 'women' who participate in these movements as women *per se*, but *poor* women. Moreover, the transformative potential of diverse women's movements goes well beyond women, affecting the entire social structure and polity.

9. Williamson (1993, 1330) ridicules heretics who do not agree with this consensus as 'flat earthers'. He says, 'The proof may not be quite as conclusive as the proof that the Earth is not flat, but it is sufficiently well established as to give sensible people better things to do with their time than challenge its veracity.'

4
Engendering Change through Egalitarian Movements: The African Experience

Filomina C. Steady

In much of modern Africa, authoritarian rule, capitalist economic systems and Western-style patriarchal structures bolstered by persistent economic dependence on former colonial powers and their allies have replaced the colonial system. Economic restructuring and globalization exacerbate the situation. A study of women's egalitarian movements therefore must recognize the domination of countries as well as of people. When women organize to challenge structures of domination in Africa, their agenda extends beyond concerns about gender equality.

In this chapter, I examine inequality based on gender while recognizing the linkages to inequalities based on class, political authoritarianism and position in the world economy. I begin with the general characteristics of African women's movements, and next I discuss four major forces that contribute to inequality and their impact on women. To further explore these forces, I discuss in detail three countries: Kenya, Nigeria and South Africa. I then look at movements that cut across national boundaries to challenge the inegalitarian tendencies of the world economy.

Characteristics of African women's movements

Observers often ask, 'Is there really a women's movement in Africa or is this a projection of the Western feminist discourse?' In Africa, women's movements are quite real, but they tend to take on more than gender issues. They promote humanistic and economic development objectives that concern the whole of society. African women's movements are primarily, though not exclusively, urban-based, multiethnic and multi-class. They can present themselves as large structured organizations as well as in informal groups and networks dedicated to advancing causes of importance to women. They usually seek to engage the state by trying to influence, become part of, challenge, change (or, if necessary, overthrow) the government.

African women have always mobilized along gender lines at the level of the community, in work groups, self-help groups, credit associations and rural cooperatives. Historically, women have organized on terms that are obligatory rather than voluntary. In addition, some African societies form gender-based and age-based kin and nonkin groups, secret societies and religious associations that can be effective power bases for women combating oppressive patriarchal structures and practices. I do not discuss these kinds of movement here, however, except when they engage the state (Amadiume 1987; Mba 1989; Kabira, Odoul and Nzomo 1993; Abdalla 1995).

Movements can seize or create political opportunities through continuous consciousness-raising efforts and responses to specific events. Events that threaten women's livelihood or that of their families, such as a steep rise in the cost of living, structural adjustment conditionality, armed conflict and oppressive governments, have had the most galvanizing effect. In recent years, women have been mobilizing at the regional level and with international women's movements against the negative consequences of globalization.

The strategies used by African women's movements have included empowering themselves for nation building, economic development and fostering institutional change. For example, they often lobby for changes in national policies and for legal reforms to end gender-based discrimination in education, employment and political participation. They are less often seen in protest activities aimed at ensuring reproductive rights, ending domestic violence, rape and sexual harassment, or securing child-care facilities and maternity benefits. The feminist agenda in many African countries is economic development for all and freedom from dependency and foreign domination.

Factors promoting women's egalitarian movements

Over the past two decades, four major forces have galvanized African women for egalitarian purposes:

1. the direct or indirect struggle against the political economy of globalization and the unequal world economic system;
2. the legacies of colonialism, apartheid, and postcolonial authoritarianism;

3. the impact of the international women's movement and the UN Decade for Women;
4. the new wave of democratization following the end of the Cold War.

Globalization

The political economy of globalization, debt, and structural adjustment has further marginalized Africa. Of the poorest 50 countries in the world, 33 are in Africa (UNDP 1996, 1997). Promoting equity in Africa means not only combating inequality and the poverty of people but also inequality and the poverty of nations. Most African states are weak and have been further weakened by globalization. Many are incapable of making the interventions in the market that would halt the spread of poverty among their populations (Deng, Kostner and Young 1991; Gibbon, Bangura and Ofstad 1992; Dembele 1998, 6).

Privatization has undermined Africa's comparative advantage and increased foreign investors' and multilateral financial institutions' control over African resources. Privatization has not promoted domestic economic growth, competitiveness or a rise in the overall standard of living. Liberalization and deregulation have had negative consequences for industrialization; they threaten African infant industries. As one scholar has observed, 'The rise of market values may tear apart Africa's social fabric by spreading poverty and economic hardship for the large majority of its citizens, notably women' (Dembele 1998, 9).

SAPs, the multilateral financial institutions' answer to the economic crisis that has plagued Africa since the late 1970s, have failed. Real per capita GDP declined by an average of 0.7 per cent between 1981 and 1990 and grew by only 1.6 per cent in 1990–94. The number of Africans living in absolute poverty (that is, on less than $1 per day) increased from 180 million to 220 million between 1987 and 1993 (UN Economic Commission for Africa, or ECA 1998). SAPs have failed to alleviate Africa's debt burden, which stood at $235 billion in 1996 compared with $80 billion in 1980. Debt servicing absorbs a large part of African government revenues, twice the amount spent on health care. Debt forgiveness has been minimal, and resource flows from Africa to more affluent nations to repay mounting debts continue to grow at alarming rates. Neoliberal development theory held that SAPs would empower market-oriented groups to eventually enforce macroeconomic stability through new rules of behavior in the state and in society. But after more than a decade of adjustment in Africa, not one clear case of success can be produced (Sarris and Shams 1991).

To understand Africa's current marginalization, it is important to realize that globalization in one form or another is not new to the continent. The integration of precapitalist systems into the global economy distorted Africa's development and resulted in the underdevelopment of Africa, a condition from which Africa has never recovered (Rodney 1981).

The current phase of globalization continues to forestall Africa's recovery. According to the 1998 *African Economic Report*, 'Africa's economic performance in 1997 demonstrated once again the fragility of the recovery and underscored the predominance of exogenous factors in the determination of the outturn' (UN ECA 1998). Growth declined. Commodity prices and real incomes continued to stagnate. And, despite the universal adoption of export-oriented policies, Africa's proportion of world trade fell to under 2 per cent, which is much lower than it had been before 1980.

African women have been particularly marginalized within the emerging international division of labor. Africa, unlike many other regions of the world, is witnessing increasing labor market segmentation by gender. The wage employment picture may have improved for women in other parts of the world, but there has been little change in Africa. Women remain concentrated in the informal labor markets and more vulnerable to increasing poverty. Although poverty affects both genders, disparities can be observed for women as a result of cutbacks in social services for education, health and welfare, and the privatization of these services.

Despite women's preponderant economic and social contributions and their numerical superiority, the statistics are discouraging. The majority live in rural areas and perform 60–80 per cent of the agricultural and domestic tasks under conditions of extreme poverty. In 1995, more than half of African women were illiterate and their life expectancy rate was 54 years, the lowest in the world. Many African women have no access to clean water and can spend as many as 28 hours a week during the dry season simply going from pump to house (UN 1989; Boserup 1995; UNDP 1995). Female-headed households in rural areas and urban slums of Africa have been growing steadily. In some countries, such as Malawi, Zambia and Botswana, women head at least one-third of the households. At the same time, the economic base of these households is eroding. Problems of landlessness and environmental degradation are worsening under the weight of policies that stress export production and the use of more intensive and environmentally unsound production methods (UN 1989; UN Environmental Program 1991).

Based on these realities, women's movements have gone beyond the usual quest for gender equality to press for liberation from economic dependency and democratization. As will be seen later, their contributions as grassroots activists, researchers and academics have influenced (and been influenced by) the international agenda for development, the international women's movement, and many policy decisions at the UN.

The colonial legacy and postcolonial authoritarianism

In many African countries, the quest for nationalism and independence from colonial rule opened political spaces for women that led to the emergence of a nationalistic feminist consciousness. Colonialism was recognized as rooted in patriarchal ideology and rigid hierarchies that favored men and disregarded women's economic and political contributions. No wonder women experienced differential access and control over productive resources, low investments in their education, inadequate social services and an increasing workload (Sen and Grown 1987; Boserup 1995).

In addition to being authoritarian, undemocratic and racist, colonial regimes promoted a robust form of capitalism backed by military might and economic advantage. This undermined many indigenous institutions in which women had political power. Finally, colonial law introduced gender hierarchies in terms of inheritance and land rights (Hoffer 1973; Okonjo 1981; Amadiume 1987).

Not surprisingly, some of the earliest egalitarian movements took the form of resistance to colonial policies that threatened women's economic well-being and objections to colonial rule in Nigeria, Kenya, Cameroon and Tanzania, to name a few. Women were also active in the women's organizations of nationalist movements for independence in several countries, such as Ghana and Sierra Leone (Steady 1975; O'Barr 1976).

After decolonization, egalitarian values – especially gender equality – were more apparent in the socialist ideologies of former Portuguese colonies and in other socialist leaning states, such as Tanzania. But most postcolonial states continued to maintain the authoritarian and gendered character of their colonial predecessors. Until the pressure to democratize grew following the end of the Cold War, the political emphasis in Africa had been on centralization. One-party regimes replaced the two-party system, and men dominated both the government and the single party. In many instances, the state became privatized, with political leaders acting as the main entrepreneurs

(Mugyeni 1988). In this atmosphere of privatized statecraft and male-dominated governance, women were further marginalized. They could participate only as members of women's wings of ruling parties or as tokens in a few ministerial and administrative posts. Moreover, African nations have been plagued with military coups since the early 1960s. Military rule, almost by definition, excludes women.

The International Women's Decade and beyond

Egalitarian movements took on an international dimension with the declaration in 1975 of the first International Decade for Women. The decade ended with the World Conference on Women held in Nairobi in 1985, an event of particular importance in Africa. Following that conference, many African countries signed the Convention on the Elimination of All Forms of Discrimination against Women (CEDAW) and some governments – including Kenya, Tanzania, Mozambique and Nigeria – have translated the articles of the convention into domestic legislation. Most African countries have set up government institutions responsible for the advancement of women, and these institutions became important targets for women's activism.

The 1985 UN review of the achievements of the decade noted that the economic crisis that emerged in the 1970s had undermined the proposals made in 1975. It had particularly affected developing countries and, most acutely, the women of these countries. The 1985 Nairobi conference called for increased commitment by the international community to establish a new international economic order founded on equality, sovereign equality, interdependence and common interest. Ten years later, little progress had been made. The 1995 Beijing Fourth World Conference on Women therefore called for 'analysis from a gender perspective of policies and programs, including those related to macro-economic stability, Structural Adjustment Programs, external debt problems, taxation, investments, employment, markets and all relevant sectors of the economy ... with respect to their impact on poverty, on inequality and particularly on women' (Beijing Platform for Action 1995, par. 58). Thus, the international articulation of goals especially relevant to African women continues.

The new wave of democratization following the end of the Cold War

In the current wave of democratization, women have actively championed the minimal requirements – multiple parties and elections – now achieved in so many African states. Yet these minimal changes do not guarantee democracy, economic development or gender equality. In fact, women have tended to become marginalized in the new structures. Feminists have criticized the liberal democratic tradition for failing to recognize the needs of women, who constitute the majority but remain poorly represented within patriarchal governments. In general, women's political participation in Africa has been largely confined to what Milbraith (1965) has termed 'spectator' voting activities rather than to the high levels of 'gladiatorial'.

Women's political participation at the high levels continues to be constrained by limited resources for campaigning, limited education, heavy workloads and domestic obligations, in addition to cultural restrictions on interacting with men. Nevertheless, some recent political activities by women have been spectacular and successful. In the 1996 elections in Sierra Leone, women's groups – represented by the Women's Forum – lobbied for an end to military rule. In Zambia, women pressured Parliament for the abolition of all discriminatory laws against women. In Uganda, where the vice-president is a woman, women have participated actively in constitutional reform.

Case studies of women's activism for equality

The recent history of three large and geographically representative countries illustrates these conclusions. Case studies follow of women's activism in Kenya, Nigeria and South Africa.

Kenya

In view of the large number of women's groups and the long history of mobilization for collective work and self-help activities, the women's movement in Kenya is sometimes referred to as 'the women's groups movement'. Women's groups have been important agents for development as well as for democratization. There are over 100 women's groups in Kenya today working for equality and the advancement of women. The oldest and largest is Maendeleo Ya Wanawake, founded in 1952.[1]

With independence and the adoption of the Harambe self-help spirit, women's groups became a vital component of the mobilization of the population's potential for rapid development. Yet by the 1980s, the oldest groups had become closely associated with the Kenya African National Union (KANU) ruling party and dominated by women of the political ruling elite. The state undermined women's efforts by manipulating those in leadership positions and interfering with their autonomy. Donor communities that claimed to be interested in supporting women's self-help efforts did little to overcome these problems. They may have helped fund some other organizations, but they also undermined women by stressing welfare-type programs, implementing poorly planned and inadequately funded programs, and importing the patriarchal biases of the international development community (Rogers 1980).

The new wave of democratization and the re-emergence of multiparty politics in the 1990s led to a proliferation of women's groups with a focus on democratization and development. Many of these groups are involved in business activities, community projects and revolving loan agreements. The National Council of Women of Kenya and the League of Women Voters organized voter education throughout the country. In addition, the league produced and widely disseminated a booklet on women's rights and democracy. In 1992, a national women's convention was held in Nairobi. It convinced most political parties to include women's issues in their constitutions and platforms.

Previously, women's participation in politics and public decision-making had been very low. In the 1991 elections, women won only two out of 200 seats. In local government, the situation was similar. Despite women's active involvement in mobilization campaigns for the elections, their gains were marginal. According to the *Daily Nation*, 21 January 1992, the results of the elections were shocking, given the extensive democratic fervor and the participation of women, and reaffirmed the belief that Parliament remained a bastion of male dominance and privilege.

Nevertheless, women are still involved in legislative campaigns for gender equality and have been pressuring for a constitutional amendment that would enforce women's rights and outlaw sex discrimination. Women's groups are also demanding that the government become more committed to affirmative action, discipline public officials that make derogatory remarks against women, and include women in appointed decision-making positions. Another important demand is that women's issues be treated separately from issues of youth and children.

Kenyan women regard some political parties as more gender-sensitive than others, which may improve the situation both for women in general, and for those parties in future elections. The Democratic Party has women represented in all party offices in a meaningful way. It takes a strong stand against gender-based discrimination and has made commitment to gender-equity issues one of the criteria for party leadership.

Gender disparities remain not only in political participation but also in education and employment. In education, despite basic structural changes and changes in the curriculum and an increase in school enrollment of girls inspired by the UN Decade for Women, major gender gaps remain. Since 1991, there has been a steady decline in the proportion of girls entering universities, leveling off at 27 per cent in 1993. In science and technology institutions, female enrollment ranges from 3 per cent to 6 per cent. No improvement has been noted for female participation in male-dominated subject areas. After more than 30 years of independence, young women continue to be overwhelmingly enrolled in secretarial and nursing courses.

In the case of employment, although women have been entering wage employment in large numbers in recent years and now stand at 21 per cent of the formal labor force, they are concentrated in lower levels of agriculture and forestry and the services. In the informal sector, about 78 per cent of the enterprises are owned by men and 22 per cent by women. Yet progress has been made in reducing gender disparities in the civil service, and women now have greater access to credit. Women's access to land has been expanded, so that at least 40 per cent of Kenyan smallholdings are controlled by women and almost all rural women have access to land. The formation of women's groups is also improving the situation of land ownership and tenancy in urban areas where women and children comprise the majority of slum dwellers.

The UN Decade for Women helped promote the women's agenda in Kenya. A UN Women's Bureau has been operating in Kenya since 1976, and its programs have been successful. Kenya ratified CEDAW in 1984. In 1993, the government established a task force to review all laws that conflict with the fundamental rights of women; and in the 1994–96 National Development Plan, the government established Women's Desks in all ministries.

Nevertheless, major problems for Kenyan women remain in the country's marginalization by processes of globalization, in the debt burden, and in the conditionalities of SAPs. Liberalization and privatization have led to increasing ownership of vital natural resources by non-Kenyans and Kenyan elites, and capital flight remains a major problem. The country's per capita income, $250, is one of the lowest in the world. The incidence of absolute poverty in Kenya is 47 per cent, and the percentage of female-headed households in poverty continues to grow (UN ECA 1998).

Nigeria

Africa's largest country, with a population that will reach 150 million by 2010, is also one of the most inegalitarian. Poverty is endemic and gender-inequality ubiquitous. The Nigerian economy is based primarily on the export of agricultural products and oil, both of which have suffered falling prices throughout the 1980s and 1990s. In this economic crisis, women face the hardest constraints in terms of access to resources, education, training and technology.[2]

Nigeria has a long history of female mobilization, however. The Igbo Women's War is one of the most celebrated instances of female resistance to colonial rule. Women are also active in nationalist movements. The mobilization of market women was key to one party's domination of about one-third of the country. Market women's groups, especially in Western Nigeria, are widely regarded as the oldest, largest, and most effectively organized of all Nigerian women's associations.

Yet not even market women were initially prepared to understand and respond to the SAPs designed to help promote recovery, economic restructuring and growth. In Nigeria, as in many other parts of Africa, SAPs reinforced the suffering of the economically disadvantaged population. Recession has seriously affected the country's ability to finance development activities that would benefit women. In fact, Nigerian women's mobilization in response to globalization began, to a large extent, in the 1980s when the country's military rulers started to involve women farmers in export production as a way to increase foreign exchange earnings and the debt repayment required by the SAPs.

To understand the conditions Nigeria's newly mobilized movements faced in the 1980s, it is important to remember the legacy of postcolonial gender inequality. Nigeria's history of military governments has almost completely excluded women from political life. Even when Nigeria experiences one of its experiments with democracy, as in 1998 and 1999, most women who aspire to political positions run as independent candidates, because male-dominated parties tend to choose men as candidates. The 1976 Constitution Drafting Committee included no women members, but this was 'rectified' by the 1989 Constitution Review Committee, which had 13 per cent women members. In the 1988–89 Constitutional Assembly, there were 14 women and 565 men. Between 1987 and 1994, eight women had been appointed as ambassadors; another headed the foreign service from 1987 to 1991. In the Muslim north, women received the franchise only in 1978 and only one regional party, the People's Redemption Party, has regularly appealed to women and included women among its candidates.

The new momentum provided by the democratization movement of the 1990s has served to open the political space for women in Nigeria. The sudden death of Sani Abacha, the military dictator, in 1998 and the succession of a pro-democracy military ruler and then a freely elected former general provided an opportunity for women to mobilize for electoral office. But even under a liberal constitution, women will face serious obstacles including their relative poverty (combined with the relative importance of money in Nigerian politics) and the ambivalence of the ruling class, both civilian and military, toward women's active political participation.

Gender inequality is also apparent in other areas. In education, women are poorly represented at the tertiary levels, although enrollments continue to increase at the primary and secondary levels. Women are to be found in all key areas of science and technology as well as in polytechnic and research institutes, but their numbers remain small. The number of female teachers is increasing, as is the number of professors. Two women have become vice-chancellors of universities. Equality in education for women has been given priority by the government, but economic recession has affected the degree to which female equality in education can be achieved.

Although Nigeria has some prominent women in top professional positions, at the bottom of the economy the picture is quite different. Mass unemployment has resulted from the combined effects of SAPs, neglect of agriculture and reliance on oil exports. The situation is worst for women. The informal sector is weak and unorganized and dominated by women with little education, and few financial resources or skills for urban living. Traditional land ownership remains under the guardianship of men with usufruct rights available to members of the ethnic group. Through this scheme, most women have access to land use for agricultural purposes, but private and commercial ownership of land is available only to women who have the resources and a few women who are land owners and property developers.

In 1989, the National Commission of Women was established as one of the national responses to the UN Women's Decade. The commission was inspired by the Better Life Program, an NGO established in 1985 by the controversial first lady at that time, Miriam Babangida. The commission's objectives were to enhance women's participation in social development and eliminate all social and cultural practices that tended to discriminate against women. It drafted a National Policy on Women, an important milestone for Nigerian women.

Another major group, the Women in Nigeria, established in 1982 with a membership of both women and men, aims to combat discrimination and sexist practices in the family and in the workplace. Equally important is the Federation of Muslim Women's Associations in Nigeria

(FOMWAN) founded in 1985. It emphasizes education and skills acquisition and conducts classes in adult literacy and primary education. It also runs nursing schools and vocational education centers. Its 'each one teach one' methodology has been effective.

Less effective has been the National Committee on Women and Development (NCWD), established in 1982. The committee was meant to act as a liaison between women's local NGOs, which number over 300, and the government. It aims to coordinate activities relating to women, to advise the government on women's issues, and to design programs to help women's integration into the development process. But the class and urban biases of this committee rendered it ineffective in addressing the needs of 90 per cent of the Nigerian women who live in rural areas.

Another state-sponsored group, the National Council of Women's Societies (NCWS), promotes a vision of economic independence, self-reliance, gender equality and sustainable development for women but has little to say about feminist issues such as reproductive rights or sexual harassment. Its administrative policy requires that its head should be the first lady of Nigeria. Other leadership positions tend to be confined to other wives of politicians and bureaucrats and high-ranking women. This has created many conflicts within the group as well as with other women's groups, such as the Women in Nigeria (WIN), a group established in 1982 by radical scholars and activists.

WIN promotes sexual and reproductive rights and works for the elimination of sexual harassment and violence against women. State officials see many of its views and its consciousness-raising activities as radical and threatening. They have tried to pressure WIN into an alliance with the pro-government NCWS, refused to grant WIN legal status, and threatened some of its members with imprisonment.

Other groups that have operated independently of the state and allied themselves with other progressive movements working toward democratic transformation of the society include the Country-Women Association of Nigeria (COWAN). It has also experienced pressures of cooptation by the government and pro-government women's associations. COWAN promotes rural development and provides services to grassroots women. Because of COWAN's advocacy, the government established the Directorate of Foods, Roads and Rural Infrastructure.

Observers agree that issues of concern to women now regularly receive the attention of the Nigerian government as a result of the work of women's organizations. Differences based on class, ethnicity, religion and interorganizational conflicts have not stopped the women's movement from having an impact. In fact, some scholars argue that the movements have become too closely tied to the state; they have come to facilitate the state's goal of the further integration of the Nigerian economy into the new system propelled by globalization. Abdalla (1995) argues that a better way forward would be through collaboration with trade unions, human rights groups and democratization movements that work toward transformation of all oppressive structures within society.

South Africa

In South Africa, women were among the most victimized individuals under the apartheid system and were relegated to the status of minors by law. Unsurprisingly, they were among the most active participants in the resistance to apartheid. In the early 1920s, the trade unions were the first organizations where women in the laundry, clothing, furniture and baking industries achieved leadership roles. In 1913, the African National Congress (ANC), the main opponent to the apartheid regime and now the country's ruling party, established the ANC Women's League.[3]

Women became active members of other groups fighting against apartheid, such as the Pan African Congress (PAC), the Communist Party of South Africa, the Campaign for Defiance Against Unjust Laws, the Black Women's Federation, the Federation of South African Women and the Black Consciousness Movement. Women's political efforts included campaigns against Bantu education, the pass laws and forced removals. Women were actively involved in the Cato Manor uprisings, the Crossroads protests, the Soweto uprisings, and numerous other protests.

In the 1980s, some women's grassroots organizations affiliated with the United Democratic Front began to organize women around consumer issues, the standard of living, poor housing, and poor education, as well as labor issues and oppression by the state. Foremost among these organizations were the Federation of Transvaal Women, the United Women's Congress in Western Cape, and the National Organization for Women. Another important movement of the 1980s was the Rural Women's Movement, a grassroots organization whose main objectives included resistance to policies of forced removals and resistance to the Bantustans, which deprived blacks of South African citizenship. The movement consisted mainly of poor women who depended on irregular remittances from male family members working as migrant laborers in South Africa's mines.

In 1990, the apartheid regime lifted the ban on liberation movements and entered an era of negotiations aimed at dismantling
apartheid. This opened a new political space for African women. The
burgeoning women's movement was able to insist on putting gender
issues on the national agenda for the new South Africa. In his address
to Parliament in 1994 (the year that marked the end of *de jure*
apartheid), President Nelson Mandela stated:

> The objectives of the Reconstruction and Development Program will
> not have been realized unless we see in visible and practical terms
> that the condition of women has radically changed for the better
> and that they have been empowered to intervene in all aspects of
> life as equal members of our society.

Mandela's speech represented a historic transformation in the
rhetoric of the unusually patriarchal South African state. But women,
especially black women, remain among the most politically, socially
and economically marginalized members of society. Since the first
postapartheid election in 1994, women's representation in Parliament
has shown a dramatic increase, but their numbers remain small. They
make up 25 per cent of the National Assembly, 17 per cent of the Sen-
ate, 20 per cent of the ministers and about 1 per cent of the provincial
premiers under a constitution that deliberately places a great deal of
power at the regional level. They are underrepresented in all sectors of
society, including in political parties such as the ANC, which continues
to be male-dominated.

The end of apartheid coincided with the era of globalization, with its
tendency to reinforce poverty and its propensity to generate inequality
among social groups and between men and women throughout Africa.
South Africa has an unusually high rate of poverty, especially among
the black female population in the rural areas. They often exist without
enough food, land, health care, schools, clean water or reliable sources
of energy. The informal labor sector, 60 per cent of whose workers are
women, is nevertheless expanding. Women are finding more opportunities as domestics, casual agricultural workers, and even in marginal
positions within South Africa's export-oriented factories.

Yet wage differentials based on gender and gender exclusion from
the most lucrative work continues to affect women in all parts of the
country. Although women comprise 36 per cent of the workforce, they
fill only 13 per cent of management positions. They are systematically
disadvantaged in hiring, pay, promotions and training. In full-time

unskilled employment, their wages are, on average, less than half of the wages earned by men. Despite high-level pronouncements on gender equality, progress has been limited. Most ministries have neither the staff nor the skill to deal with gender issues. No effective monitoring machinery exists, and there is little legislative oversight, largely because the women in Parliament who might be interested in providing such oversight do not have the time. Most carry out two full-time jobs, one in the home. And even within Parliament, they are required to play a more active role than men, if only to provide token female representation in every meeting on every subject.

Despite these obstacles, women in Parliament started the women's budget initiative in March 1996. It focuses on the needs for social services, education, housing and work of the poorest and most disadvantaged members of society. The initiative has had demonstrable impact at the national level but has yet to percolate down to the provincial level, where so many fewer women are part of government. Frene Ginwala, a feminist and Speaker of the House, has cautioned against the possible loss of autonomy by women's groups that are too closely linked to the political parties. Similarly, Lindiwe Zulu (1998, 156) summarizes the situation at the end of the 1990s this way:

> The task facing women in South Africa today is enormous. Nevertheless, a solid foundation has been established. It remains our task to mobilize more women into a united front, encourage debate on the formation of a women's movement, especially now that the Women's National Coalition [an organization of 90 women's groups established in 1992] has fulfilled its original mandate to draft a charter for women's rights. The majority of the women who were active before the formation of the National Women's Coalition are now all in parliament and this has left a gap. We almost have to start from scratch in making sure that we have other women taking the place of those women who are in parliament today. Many women now in parliament do not want to let go of the positions that they had when they were outside of government but it becomes difficult for them to split themselves into two and be able to run organizations outside of parliament.

In the new South Africa, feminist struggle is especially complicated by the challenge of bringing together women from diverse racial, class, ethnic and geographical backgrounds. For many black women, the struggle against racism is supreme because many institutionalized forms of apartheid remain intact. As Patricia de Lillie of the PAC puts it, 'I am an African before I am a woman' (Kemp *et al.* 1995, 148–9). Many black women rejected feminism as a white American import that would dilute the liberation struggle. After all, although apartheid has been legally abolished, South Africa remains a country of extreme contradictions. *De facto* and institutionalized apartheid still exists in terms of economic domination and widespread poverty among the African population in the townships and rural areas. The economy is still dominated by whites. Whites overwhelmingly own the land; and land redistribution to blacks, who make up more than 75 per cent of the rural population, is one of the major challenges for the government. Earlier, it was easier to equate international (and especially UN-based) support for South African women's organizations with the international support offered to the anti-apartheid movement, including the UN-based sanctions movement. By the late 1990s, the principles and strategies offered by a largely white and largely wealthy international women's movement have come to be seen as more problematic in a country where white privilege remains the gravest social issue.

African women and international alliance building

Egalitarian movements in Africa took on an international dimension with the first of the UN Women's Conferences. Some of these movements now transcend the continent, because globalization is increasingly perceived as one of the major sources of inequality. African women have joined other Third World women to struggle against the feminization of poverty brought about by global forces. For example, SAP conditionalities can force rural women to become cheap sources of labor for export-oriented development in agro-based and other labor-intensive industries (K. Ward 1990).

Many regional women's groups have sprung up in Africa over the last 20 years with agendas that focus on development, democratization and resistance to the negative consequences of globalization. Among these are FEMNET, a network of NGOs and women in the media who advocate the advancement of women and the elimination of all obstacles including obstacles to development. WILDAF (Women in Law and Development in Africa) promotes human rights for women and has developed programs for legal equality, legal literacy and civil and voters' rights education. ABANTU for Development and AKINA MAMA AFRICA, both based in London, promote capacity-building programs and leadership training institutes for women, especially young women.

Based in Dakar, AAWORD (Association of African Women Organized for Research and Development) promotes critical research on gender, development and democracy, and it has a major program aimed at challenging the negative economic impact of globalization on African countries and African women. It recently sponsored a major conference and research initiative on the subject. AAWORD also promotes democratization. The organization argues that women's political participation and influence can change the normative parameters that determine the exercise of power and reduce the centralization of power in male hands. According to AAWORD: 'Women are bound to change the nature of power and its management mode through the inclusion of their ideals of peace and justice. As active members of civil society, women are potential pillars for effective action-based solidarity in the building of democratic culture and practices in Africa' (Fall 1998). AAWORD also campaigns against the debt burden, urging African women to become actively involved in the assessment of the performance of highly indebted countries since it involves critical gender issues:

> It is … time for us to launch an African Women's movement that goes beyond monitoring the World Bank's commitment to women but engages itself with monitoring all the International Financial Institutions that are actively contributing to mortgaging women's well-being. In so doing, we may need to recall that the Bretton Woods Institutions – the World Bank, the IMF, and the GATT, founded in 1944, are indeed agencies of the United Nations. For that reason we would make them accountable to women's needs despite the fact that unlike the UN General Assembly they do not function on the principle of 'one country, one vote' but on the basis of 'one dollar, one vote'. (Fall 1998)

Other pan-African women's movements have also criticized the inimical consequences of globalization. In a statement issued at a regional meeting held in Cape Town in 1996, ABANTU called for joint campaigns against the World Bank and the IMF and other financial institutions 'to restructure their economically unsound, undemocratic and dehumanizing policies and programs' (1998).

Similarly, DAWN (Development Alternatives for Women in a New Era), an alliance of women activists, researchers and policy-makers from the Third World, challenges the unequal and antiwomen model of development (Sen and Grown 1987). African members of DAWN have helped develop a position that views existing global economic and political structures as producing inequalities between classes, genders and ethnic groups at both the macro- and microlevel in most societies. As researchers and activists, they seek to build alliances with women at the grassroots level.

Conclusion

The economic crisis in many African countries has severely constrained their ability to empower themselves despite the proliferation of women's egalitarian activities. Given the failures of development efforts in Africa during the last three decades, consumerist demands for goods and services and for jobs have been among the priorities of egalitarian movements of women.

Globalization, colonization, authoritarian regimes, the UN Decade for Women and democratization are major factors in promoting women's egalitarian movements. African women have seized the momentum of the current democratization movement to open the endangered and engendered political spaces. They have been active in multiparty activities, political campaigns, legal reforms and the promotion of equitable economic development. Nevertheless, the record of democratization has been generally disappointing. The cases of Nigeria, Kenya and South Africa show some limited, new opportunities for women in politics. In each country, at least one political party works to gain the votes of women. In South Africa the ruling party, the ANC, also presents women as candidates for elections and for high political positions, so that many women have actually entered government. Yet even in South Africa, much more remains to be done.

As a result of the International Women's Decade, CEDAW and the Beijing Conference, all African governments have made some changes designed to promote gender equality. The significance of these initiatives is open to question because governments have tried to coopt women's movements or influence priorities in ways that serve the state. In some cases, attempts have been made to subsume women's organizations within umbrella organizations affiliated to the government, such as in Nigeria and Kenya. Africa's more feminist-oriented and politically radical movements remain few. They include WIN in Nigeria, AAWORD's program in Kenya, and the Rural Women's Movement in South Africa. These movements share a vision that links struggles against external domination with a challenge to local patriarchal structures and ideologies. They also tend to take their agenda beyond the national level and building alliances with regional and international women's movements. The results so far, though preliminary, appear to be promising.

Women's groups, in conjunction with the international women's movement, especially Third World women, are increasingly mobilizing to protest and resist the dominant economic model connected with contemporary globalization. These alliances aim to study and analyze the range, strategies and impact of these negative processes on women. More studies are needed of the larger political and economic forces that reinforce North/South inequalities and inequalities within nations and thereby prohibit equitable economic development, gender equality and democracy. Significantly, we need to determine to what extent these movements can bring about social transformation in Africa. We also need to know whether, given their humanitarian thrust, they can help promote common egalitarian values within civil society as a whole. Given the hegemonic tendencies of globalization and the rate at which it reinforces inequality and the structural subordination of women, one is led to Manuel Castells's question (1983, 329): in the final analysis, are social movements more symptoms of resistance to social domination than agents of structural change?

Globalization as we know it today does not permit regulation of the market; and without such regulation, human equality will remain difficult. Even when we speak of democracy, we can hope to have only what some scholars call 'low-intensity democracy', and that only in some countries. For some others, various forms of fascism, fundamentalism and tribalism will probably prevail as a result of economic domination through globalization (Robinson 1996b; Amin 1998). For women in Africa as well as for most of humanity, the dream of equality will remain only a dream.

Notes

1. The Kenya case study relies on Kameri-Mbote and Kibwana (1993), Khasiani and Njiro (1993), Nkomo (1993) and UN documents.
2. The Nigeria case study relies on Abdalla (1995), Mba (1989) and UN documents.
3. The South Africa case study relies on Kemp *et al.* (1995) and Zulu (1998).

5

Egalitarian Responses in Postcommunist Russia

Jane Dawson

Postcommunist societies in Russia, the newly independent states of the former Soviet Union and Eastern Europe present a profound paradox. Although the collapse of communism has generally been accompanied by the rapid erosion of social welfare provisions and the retreat of the state from its protective and redistributionist role, postcommunist societies have shown little inclination toward the mobilization of egalitarian movements. While salaries have stagnated and income inequities and wage arrears have increased in leaps and bounds, state provision of health and child care, maternity benefits, pensions and higher education has plummeted in the postcommunist world. Paradoxically, those people most negatively affected by these changes have remained largely quiet and apparently quiescent. In postcommunist Russia and Eastern Europe, labor movements are typically weak, fragmented and disorganized, women's movements barely discernible, and human rights movements all but dead. Given the immense erosion of the state's protective role and the obvious threat to egalitarian principles posed by postcommunist transitions, why have workers, women and other aggrieved groups failed to organize in opposition to the state?

The relative absence of egalitarian movements in postcommunist societies becomes even more puzzling when international economic integration is factored into the equation. Whereas the economies of the region were largely insulated from international economic pressures during the communist era, all of these countries have moved rapidly since the collapse of communism to integrate themselves into the global economy. In opening themselves to world economic forces, postcommunist societies have subjected their inefficient industrial and agricultural sectors to intense international competition, thus intensifying the economic threat to much of the population. One might expect that the multiple threats posed by international economic integration, globalization and postcommunist transition would provide more than ample stimulus for the mobilization of egalitarian social movements in these societies, yet these movements have largely failed to materialize.

The key to the puzzle lies in the legacy left behind by decades of communist rule (Jowitt 1992, 284–306; Chirot 1995; Bunche 1992; Jowitt 1998; Tismaneanu 1998) and the nature of the transitions from communist rule now under way in the postcommunist world. Unlike other cases in the developing world, postcommunist societies are not simply continuing along an evolutionary path toward greater development and globalization; they are attempting a dramatic shift away from their previous economic, political and social institutions. The transitions from a state-owned command economy to a privatized, market economy – from an authoritarian party-state to a less hierarchic and more participatory political system, and from a mass society to one differentiated by interests and class – are immense and might typically be expected to dwarf the potential impact of growing globalization in the world economy.[1] The upheaval wrought by these difficult transitions from communist rule and the institutional and attitudinal legacy left behind by the communists have created a distinctive context for the mobilization of social movements. Given the uniqueness of the processes now under way in the postcommunist world and the enduring legacy of decades of communist rule, it is not surprising that patterns of mobilization in these societies differ substantially from those expected or observed in other parts of the world. I argue that although globalization plays a significant role in the erosion of egalitarian measures, it cannot be viewed separately from the overall postcommunist transition process.

I also argue that both the legacy of communist rule and the distinctive nature of the transition processes under way in postcommunist societies must be taken into account in order to understand the weakness of egalitarian social movements in the former Eastern Bloc. In particular, I contend that the nature of the communist legacy and postcommunist transition creates a situation of resource scarcity, in which both tangible and intangible mobilization resources are severely lacking among the most aggrieved groups in society. As predicted by resource mobilization theory (Jenkins 1983), the dearth of mobilization resources creates a substantial obstacle to successful social movement formation. In addition, the sense of group identity and solidarity that many theorists believe central to successful mobilization (Habermas 1981; Touraine 1981; Cohen 1985; Melucci 1985) is largely absent in postcommunist societies as a result of the legacy of the old regime. In sum, the relative absence of resources and viable group identities caused by the communist legacy and postcommunist transition processes creates an environment in which the mobilization of strong and organized egalitarian social movements is highly unlikely.

In yet another twist, the absence of egalitarian social movements in postcommunist societies has not meant complete government disregard for egalitarian principles. In fact, the governments of many of these societies appear committed to slowing or even reversing the erosion of social welfare provisions that have accompanied the transitions. This tendency again may be traced to the legacy of communist rule and the nature of the postcommunist transition. The tendency reflects the continued appeal of the socialist agenda of surviving communist parties and their socialist successor parties. It may be argued that the Russian Communist Party and socialist successor parties in other postcommunist countries represent an important egalitarian response to the pains of transition and globalization, but I focus specifically on social movements and the mobilization of the aggrieved groups themselves. Although an analysis from the perspective of political parties – their platforms and level of popular support – would provide additional insight into the issue of egalitarian responses, it is beyond my scope in this chapter.

Whereas the postcommunist societies of the former Soviet Union and Eastern Europe span a broad spectrum in terms of both commitment to and success in building capitalist economies and democratic institutions, all share a common legacy of communist rule and confront similar challenges in attempting a transition away from Soviet-style communism. I begin by considering the general legacy and transition problems likely to be common to all postcommunist societies. I then turn to the Russian case to demonstrate more concretely how legacy and transition have affected the mobilization of labor, women and human rights activists since the collapse of communism in 1991. In concluding, I return to the issue of variation within the postcommunist world and briefly address the question of whether the lessons derived from the Russian case study still apply to countries at the extreme ends of the transition spectrum.

Transitions from communist rule: the communist legacy and its impact on social movement formation

Some observers in the early 1990s predicted a rapid transition from communism to market capitalism and democracy in the newly independent states of the former Eastern Bloc (Schmitter and Carl 1991; Przeworski 1995), yet we have since discovered the immense obstacles that lie along this path. The transition process from communism mandates a change in every aspect of the system – economic, political and social – and is far more complex than many observers expected. Decades of communist rule left a legacy in each of these sectors that is difficult to erase. An immense challenge that so far has been achieved successfully by only a handful of countries is transforming a state-owned command economy to a privatized, market system; a hierarchic party-run system to an open, participatory democracy; and an undifferentiated and repressed society to one flowering with interest groups, social movements and strong political parties. In addition, it must be noted that although all of the countries of the former Eastern Bloc are attempting to make transitions away from Soviet-style communist rule, not all of these societies are either committed to, or making progress toward, capitalism and democracy.

Of the three aspects of transition (economic, political and social), the one creating by far the most turmoil and disruption in people's lives is the attempt to dismantle the old command economies and move toward greater reliance on market forces. Some analysts initially envisioned this process taking place quickly, perhaps even over the space of a mere 500 days (Hewett 1991, 441–58). But the task of creating all aspects of a functioning market economy and eliminating residual elements of the old system has been slow and arduous. Transforming the economy implies massive privatization of state-owned enterprises and property, the introduction of unfamiliar market exchange mechanisms, and opening the economy to world economic forces. The by-products of this triple process of privatization, marketization and international integration may be even more difficult for postcommunist societies to handle. These by-products include growing income and wealth differentiation; loss of government subsidies to industry, agriculture and society; bankruptcy; unemployment; and the erosion of the total social safety net provided by the old regime.

In reality, the economic transition has presented extreme difficulties to all societies that have attempted it. In all postcommunist societies, movement away from command economic structures has initially implied a substantial drop in GNP and increased hardships to society (Wiener Institut 1995; World Bank 1996). Whereas some of these societies were able to reverse the process quickly and set out on the road to renewed economic growth, many have floundered, taking almost a decade to reverse this trend or even continuing the downward slide into the twenty-first century. In addition, the currency crisis in 1998 has negated almost all of the progress achieved in Russia in the 1990s and holds the potential to spread to other former Eastern Bloc countries as well. Such huge drops in GNP have generally been accompanied by falling standards of living for the bulk of society.

The economic transitions have not affected all members of society equally. Immense corruption in the privatization process and the fluidity of the economic system have allowed for the creation of vast differentials in income and wealth. While many in the new business elite bask in almost unimaginable wealth, the bulk of society struggles simply to survive and maintain an adequate standard of living. Poverty abounds, with many postcommunist societies reporting more than a quarter of their population currently living below the poverty line (Milanovic 1994, 1995; McAuley 1995). Given the egalitarian principles with which communist societies were raised, the appearance of huge inequities in income, accumulated wealth and standard of living might not be expected to sit well with much of society.

Added to the growing inequities in society is the severe impact of the transition on the government's ability and desire to provide a comprehensive social welfare net. First, falling GNP and huge government deficits have made the provision of a complete package of health care, child care, pension, education and employment benefits unrealistic for transitional societies. Second, the logic of the transition from a totally state-owned and subsidized economy to one based on private ownership and initiative and market forces is not generally viewed as compatible with large-scale state subsidization of society. The result has been the rapid dismantling of accustomed social welfare provisions and the somewhat tardy substitution of market-based alternatives. In the short run, the transition has brought about the collapse of access to health care, child care, higher education and adequate pensions for the bulk of these societies.

Finally, a key component of the economic transition in all postcommunist societies has been opening the economy to international competition. In removing restrictions on private foreign trade and shifting to convertible currencies, not only have these new economies created new opportunities to reap the benefits of international economic integration but they have also exposed inefficient economic sectors to highly competitive world markets. In fact, very few Soviet-era industries have been able to meet world production standards in quality and efficiency, thus leading to bankruptcies, layoffs and unemployment. And those workers who do not suffer loss of employment are nevertheless affected by the readjustment of domestic price structures to match international standards. No longer are prices determined by the state, based on social needs and state subsidization of necessity items; instead, the prices are set by the market, with consequent skyrocketing prices for housing, food, clothing, and other items long protected by state subsidies. Again, the transition has severely undermined the egalitarian cornerstone of the old system and threatened large sectors of the population with a falling standard of living (and, for those on state pensions, near starvation and penury).

In addition to moving from almost totally insulated economies to joining the international economic community, the postcommunist societies have chosen a particularly difficult time to open their economies. As globalization links the economies of the world ever closer together, economic shocks in one part of the world reverberate in the rest. During 1998, as the Asian economic crises deepened, many postcommunist societies – particularly Russia – found themselves suddenly jolted out of their hard-fought currency stability and plunged into an unexpected and severe currency crisis themselves. Assistance from the IMF and other international actors has been predicated on further reductions in state subsidies to inefficient industries, balanced budgets and increased tax collection. Thus the tightening monetary policy triggered by the Asian currency shock has further eroded the state's ability to prop up the egalitarian support structure of the old system. International economic integration in an era of increased globalization provides inauspicious conditions for costly social services and inefficient economic enterprises to be maintained.

In sum, the postcommunist economic transitions have had both macro- and microlevel effects on these societies. At the macrolevel, attempts to transform these command economies into market-driven systems have led to severe crises of economic growth and the almost complete erosion of the state's provision of social welfare. At the microlevel, some new business elites have become extremely wealthy, but most of the population in these postcommunist societies is struggling economically. Not only are jobs in danger but also the state has withdrawn its comprehensive social safety net, leaving those who flounder without even minimal unemployment subsidies and services and the accustomed state welfare system to protect them.

The implications of these difficult economic transitions for social mobilization are twofold. On the one hand, postcommunist societies are suffering a much greater erosion in accustomed state welfare provision than is observed in other parts of the world. These societies are moving from a comprehensive social safety net (complete with guaranteed employment, subsidized food and clothing, free health care and child care, extensive maternity benefits, free education, and more) to an almost total absence of any protection for society. Nowhere in the world has the retreat of the state from its redistributionist and egalitarian role been as rapid and complete as in the postcommunist world. Given the impact of this shift on the bulk of postcommunist societies, it is obvious that enough grievances exist to mobilize social actors; what is lacking are mobilization resources for the aggrieved groups in society. Although some members of society are prospering (and thus have plenty of tangible resources for mobilization), these are not the people who are suffering most from the retreat from egalitarianism in the postcommunist world. Those people most negatively affected by the transition possess few of the resources needed for effective mobilization: funds, communications technology and time are all in short supply among the most aggrieved groups in society.

Despite the low economic resources of aggrieved groups, we might still expect to see some popular mobilization based on the extreme nature of grievances and threats posed to some sectors in society. Given that these populations were raised on principles of egalitarianism and have never before experienced these extreme inequities in income, wealth and access to social services, an explosion of anger and rage in society would be quite unsurprising. Even poor groups can afford to carry out disruptive actions, such as protests and strikes. Throughout Russia and the former Eastern Bloc, however, workers, women and other aggrieved groups have remained largely unorganized and inactive.

The relative quiescence of society given the extreme nature of the threat becomes even more puzzling when the sociopolitical aspects of the postcommunist transitions are taken into account. The degree of openness and democracy that has been achieved in each society varies; but in most of the postcommunist countries, new opportunities for active social participation in the public realm and political decision-making have accompanied the economic transitions. No longer does the Communist Party monopolize all public discussion, association and politics; since the collapse of communism, new freedoms of speech, association and political participation have become commonplace in almost all postcommunist countries.

Aggrieved groups are free to speak out against the state or their employers; they are free to organize clubs, unions, and even political parties. Thus, structural opportunities for people hurt by the economic transition process to form social movements and demand greater egalitarian protections have vastly increased in most countries since the heyday of the communist era. Although many sectors of society took advantage of these growing opportunities during the late *perestroika* period (the final era of communist rule) since the demise of the communist regimes in 1989–91, social activism has plummeted.

We return to our initial paradox: despite immense grievances affecting the bulk of the population, as well as new structural opportunities to mobilize and protest against the government or enterprise policies, very little effective organization of labor, women or human rights groups has been observed in postcommunist societies. What has kept aggrieved sectors from uniting and organizing to demand redress? The answer may be found in the transition process and the legacy left behind by decades of communist rule. Whereas the transition has severely limited access to key tangible mobilization resources for these groups, the legacy of communist rule has further inhibited mobilization potentials by denying these groups access to important intangible resources and by leaving these societies with few viable group identities around which to unite and mobilize.[2]

As noted earlier in regard to tangible resources, the most aggrieved groups in postcommunist societies are those who are suffering economically and thus possess few resources to invest in social movement formation. With the constant struggle simply to put food on the table, these aggrieved groups lack not only funds but also the leisure time needed to join in social movement activities. Their lack of intangible resources also becomes obvious when we recall that the Communist Party completely monopolized all public activities and mobilization under the old regime. Those outside the party are thus unlikely to have developed the needed organizational skills, and neither are they likely to find many pre-existing networks of people outside the old party ranks to mobilize *en masse*. What tangible and intangible resources these aggrieved actors have may largely flow from outside sources, particularly transnational movement entrepreneurs. Excluding for the moment the potential impact of transnational actors, most sectors of postcommunist societies may be expected to suffer from a severe shortage of key mobilization resources.

Mobilization appeals are also enhanced by the pre-existence of strong group identities. When aggrieved populations also share a common sense of identity and group solidarity, the potential for a powerful social movement to emerge is greatly increased. One of the most enduring aspects of the communist legacy has been the fragmentation of these societies and lack of strong group identities on which to base mobilization appeals (Bonnell 1996). Throughout the communist era, little opportunity or incentive existed to reinforce class or gender identities. Although private property and freedom of association generally combine to produce many competing interest groups, in the absence of both elements, society is likely to remain undifferentiated by interests. When communism collapsed, few pre-existing group identities could be counted on to provide the basis for effective mobilization.

Ironically, the one group identity that was reinforced by communist institutions was ethnicity. National boundaries in Eastern Europe and republic boundaries within the USSR were based largely on ethnic identities. Reinforcement of these identities was strengthened inadvertently through affirmative action systems or promotion of the titular national group, constant reminders of one's ethnic identity through the passport system, and the so-called internationalist communist system (Lapidus 1989a; Roeder 1991; Suny 1995). This phenomenon became apparent during the late 1980s, when ethnic and nationalist groups became the dominant basis for social movement formation. Since the collapse of communism, the persistence of these ethnic identities has become increasingly obvious; the hardships of transitions are far more likely to trigger an ethnic response or interethnic hostilities than to mobilize movements based on class, gender, or abstract ideals such as democracy and human rights.

Whereas the legacy of communism and the nature of the transitions may be expected to impede the mobilization of egalitarian social movements in postcommunist societies, several factors may militate against this outcome. First, the legacy of communism cannot be expected to last forever. In societies that were under communism for a shorter period (such as the Eastern European countries) or where the transition process has already shown substantial positive results, the impact of the communist legacy would be expected to diminish rapidly over time. In particular, as a new generation raised under the ideology of capitalist democracy begins to play an ever-greater role in shaping policies and ideas, the legacy of the old regime will diminish in importance. Second, postcommunist societies do not exist in a vacuum; they are, in fact, in contact with a multitude of transnational and international actors and organizations.

How important are outside actors in shaping social movement formation in postcommunist societies? Obviously, their influence will vary across countries and movements. It should be expected that in a situation of resource scarcity and confusion of identities, international and transnational actors with resources to share and strong, established group identities would have the potential to play a substantial role in the mobilization of social movements in postcommunist societies. The extent of the role outside resources and groups have been able to play in the mobilization of labor, women and human rights groups in post-communist societies has been much more limited than might initially be expected.

Egalitarian social movements in postcommunist societies: labor, feminism and human rights

Much has been written during the past decade about the importance of civil society in promoting and sustaining democracy in postcommunist societies (Lapidus 1989b; Fish 1991). Although communist societies were well known for the absence of civil society and the party-state's total monopolization of the public realm, since the collapse of communism many political analysts have watched carefully for signs that a nascent civil society may be emerging that could support both continued progress toward democratization and the few democratic institutions that have already emerged. Building civil society from scratch – while plagued by all of the resource and identity problems discussed earlier – has turned out to be a slow and tortuous process. The weakness of labor, feminist and human rights movements in postcommunist societies should not be viewed as a unique phenomenon but rather as part of a broader pattern of the difficulties in creating strong interest groups, unified social movements and cohesive political parties upon the ruins left behind by the communist era.

New opportunities for activism and mobilization now exist, but the institutions of the old regime did not strengthen group solidarity and identity along class or gender lines. Workers and women have found themselves with almost no sense of solidarity and group identity, and unable to find a common language to unify an organized move-ment. The fluidity and hardships of the transition period have created unusual allies and cleavages in society that have made the formulation of a class or gender-based agenda all but impossible. At this point, common class and gender interests have yet to become apparent, and agenda confusion abounds. As for human rights mobilization, there appear to be almost no group identities (aside from ethnic) upon which to formulate a cohesive and unifying platform, leading to the almost total absence of organized movements.

To understand the agenda confusion that plagues all these nascent movements, consider the position of labor in Russia. Even the simplest questions, such as who should be mobilized, whom or what the labor unions should target, and what they should demand, cannot be answered simply. Should unions support reformist governments who may offer the promise of long-term economic survival; or should they consider the immediate interests of their working constituency and demand continued government subsidies, protection from bankruptcy, and more generally slow down the transition to a market economy? Should workers organize in opposition to management, or should they consider their common interests in the continued economic viability of their enterprise and work with management to achieve concessions from the state? Since the specter of unemployment is haunting all workers, would a union that targeted management be in the best interests of its members? Should workers organize by enterprise (thus focusing on their immediate interests) or focus more on building a long-term structure and organizing on the basis of occupational groups? Given the fluidity and economic instability of Russia's first nine years of attempted economic transition, there can be no obvious and consensual answers to any of these very basic questions.

Likewise, whereas postcommunist transitions have indisputably damaged the position of women in society – economically, politically and socially[3] – little consensus exists on how the agenda of a women's movement should look. In a male-dominated society in which being called a 'feminist' is almost universally viewed as an insult, the appropriate place of women in society, the economy and politics is an open question for men and women alike. Although some women may be willing to endure the derision of being associated with a Western feminist agenda and calling for greater economic and political equality, most either reject the calls for equality as ludicrous and unrealistic or take the other extreme, demanding the right to stay home and be full-time mothers and wives rather than being forced into the workforce, as they were during the communist era. As with workers, it is unclear whether women who have lost benefits for maternity, health care, abortion and child care through the reform process should organize in support of continued marketization or in opposition.

Finally, human rights activism presents the most confused picture of all. What is there to unite activists, and how should they establish which human rights violations to take on first? The crimes committed during the communist era may provide a unifying force for the victims of the repression and their relatives, but the crimes of the present are subtler and more difficult to unify around. At least these activists can agree on a common goal – moving forward with reform rather than backward – but they have no common group identity or sense of solidarity to mobilize an organized movement. In some cases, perceptions of ethnic discrimination may provide the basis for an ethnically organized human rights crusade, yet in almost all other cases the human rights cause is taken up by individuals in these societies rather than organized groups.

Assessing the labor, feminist and human rights movements in Russia

The question of why labor, feminist and human rights movements have failed to coalesce in postcommunist societies is not a novel one; nearly every scholar studying these movements has asked just this question. The absence of an organized social response to the erosion of egalitarianism in postcommunist societies has been widely noted, from Paul Christensen's (1997) 'Why Russia Lacks a Labor Movement' to Jeffrey Goldfarb's (1997) 'Why is there no Feminism after Communism?' To understand how the legacy of the old regime and the nature of postcommunist transitions have worked to obstruct the formation of organized egalitarian movements, it is useful to look more closely at the specific cases.

It is ironic that in the Soviet Union – a supposed 'workers' state' – there were no organizations that genuinely reflected the interests and demands of workers.[4] As with all other forms of public social organization, labor unions during the communist period were official organizations and completely under the control of the ruling party. In the USSR, the All-Union Central Council of Trade Unions formed the umbrella for the hierarchy of trade unions that stretched from the federal level down to the regional, finally ending at the enterprise level itself. Workers were not organized horizontally by occupation or skill but rather vertically by sectors, with each industrial sector (such as mining, metallurgy, and so on) having its own union structure and each enterprise branch incorporating all members of the enterprise, from the workers on up through management.

The goal of the enterprise-level union was not to improve worker conditions *vis-à-vis* management but rather to ensure adequate provision and distribution of social services for the entire enterprise cadre. Rather than representing the interests of the workers, the trade union officials worked in an administrative capacity to oversee the social infrastructure – such as housing, schools, children's camps, and so on – associated with the enterprise employees' daily lives. In doing so, the trade union officials worked very closely with management and even assisted management in such labor-related issues as maintaining worker discipline and pushing the workers harder to meet production targets.

During *perestroika*, as Mikhail Gorbachev created new opportunities for independent initiatives and public activism, signs of growing worker assertiveness emerged. In some industries, particularly among miners, new independent workers' committees were formed to promote worker interests. Worker actions, such as demonstrations and strikes, during the last years of the Gorbachev period seemed to presage growing worker activism and the likely coalescence of strong worker-oriented labor unions in the postcommunist period.

Since the collapse of communism, the organization of labor has not proceeded as rapidly or successfully as anticipated. Since 1991, two separate tendencies have been observed in the mobilization of labor: (1) the continuation of the pre-existing communist-era union structures, and (2) the emergence of new competing independent trade unions. Contrary to expectations, the former trend has tended to dominate in postcommunist Russia. Attempts to mobilize workers in independent, occupation-based unions that might represent the genuine interests of the workers have been observed, but the independent union movement has remained largely weak and ineffectual while the successor unions to the old official trade union structure have continued to maintain the largest membership and influence. Neither type of organization has yet managed to fulfill the function of adequately representing worker interests in postcommunist societies.

On the part of the successor to the Soviet official trade union organization, the Federation of Independent Trade Unions of Russia (FNPR) has found it extremely difficult to define its task and place in the new political and economic setting. With control over local social services, such as housing, day care and so on gradually being transferred from enterprise to local or regional authorities, the successor unions are faced with the difficult task of redefining their function. Yet having always worked closely with management, the successor unions have found it difficult to reorient their mission toward the achievement of workers' interests. For the most part, these successor unions have maintained their traditional sectoral structure, incorporating entire enterprises rather than particular groups of workers, and have found it extremely difficult to disassociate themselves from management.

Given the postcommunist economic situation in Russia the question also arises whether the new unions should attempt to define themselves as spokespersons for the workers and loosen their connections to management. Moreover, with enterprises collapsing left and right, are the workers' interests really in opposition to those of management? Or – given the immense state role that continues to persist in industry (be it through state ownership, state subsidization, or large stockholdings by the state) – would it make more sense for these successor unions to continue to represent the entire enterprise in its confrontation with the state? The tendency to favor the latter approach has promoted an image of stagnation among the successor unions that has clearly undermined worker support for the FNPR. The strategy followed by the newly created independent competitor unions has made them even less popular with the workforce.

Since their emergence in the late *perestroika* period, the new independent labor unions in Russia have attempted to model themselves upon Western unions. Rather than organizing sectorally, the new unions most often organize by occupation or skills and attempt to set up horizontal networks. In addition, the new unions have tended to try to distance themselves from management and focus on mobilizing workers in opposition to both management and state. In attempting to model themselves along Western lines, the independent trade unions have received some assistance from the AFL–CIO. Shortly after Russia achieved its independence, the AFL–CIO established the Free Trade Union Institute (FTUI) in Moscow to assist in the establishment of new, independent trade unions. Many local union organizers regarded FTUI as Western intervention that was incompatible with the formation of indigenous trade unions and also as a source of unnecessary competition and confusion in the independent trade union movement. Since this issue came to a head in 1994, the AFL–CIO has scaled back its involvement significantly, recognizing differences in the context and necessary characteristics of trade unions in the postcommunist context. The organization remains both interested and marginally involved in the independent trade union movement. Overall, the pattern of craft-based union organization, which has dominated the independent trade union movement, has been both ineffective and unpopular under the unusual conditions of the postcommunist economic transition.

First, as noted earlier, workers' interests tend to align themselves with that of management in the current context; both workers and management want the continued survival of the enterprise, state subsidies and tax breaks, and overall protection from the vicissitudes of the market. Second, even when workers' interests clearly oppose those of management (for example, when improved efficiency means cutbacks in employment and worker benefits), in a situation of intense employment scarcity and limited worker mobility, few workers are interested in confronting management and endangering their continued employment at the enterprise. Even those workers who have been unpaid for months or years but remain on the employment books are hesitant to challenge management. Why? Because continued official employment with the enterprise provides many perquisites in housing, health care, pensions and other social services that would be lost if the worker were to be laid off.

Although membership in the new unions is officially legal and protected, harassment by management is common and activists often suffer loss of employment and severe difficulties in obtaining other jobs. The dearth of both tangible resources (funds, communications technology, and so on) and intangible resources (genuine legal protection, organizational skills, strong pre-existing networks, and so on) has played an important role in undermining the appeal and effectiveness of these new unions.

Another reason for the low membership of the new unions lies in the continued role of the successor unions in the administration of enterprise social services. Anyone who leaves the successor union in favor of the new independent union is likely to find himself or herself at the bottom of the list for a myriad of social benefits, including housing, summer camps and so on. In addition, the new unions have found it difficult to mobilize workers on the basis of horizontal linkages (whereas it may make sense for occupational groups in the West to stand together). In a situation of high unemployment and limited state resources, workers' interests tend to lie more with their regional or sectoral affiliation rather than with their widely dispersed occupational group. The old system did not foster the creation of strong professional identities, thus leaving workers unprepared to mobilize themselves horizontally. Finally, as with all other emerging social organizations in postcommunist societies, the new unions have been plagued by leadership competition and personal rivalries that have significantly weakened their effectiveness.

Although the successor unions appear to be winning in the competition for members, neither of these two categories of unions has been particularly successful in defining a new role in postcommunist societies and devising a strategy that will truly support the interests of the workers. In a time of immense political fluidity and instability, the influence and effectiveness of both types of unions have been greatly hindered by their common inability to take a political stand. Not only do postcommunist unions tend to shy away from any kind of political

involvement (because of the negative connotations of union politicization under the communists), but they also have found it extremely difficult to determine where they should place themselves along the
political spectrum.

In the West, labor unions tend to be aligned with leftist platforms;
but in Russia, the successor Communist Party has yet to come up with
a coherent platform or one that clearly incorporates the protection of
workers' rights. Thus, the unions are reluctant to ally themselves with
leftist forces but also extremely wary of the dangers to worker security
associated with the liberal platforms of privatization and marketization. Given the quandary, both the successor unions and new independent unions have chosen simply to distance themselves from the
political playing field. Without any linkage to the political arena, their
potential to achieve significant improvements in workers' rights and
benefits remains slim.

Although workers remain poorly organized, with no strong unions
that can effectively protect them during this period of economic turmoil,
this does not mean that they are necessarily apathetic and quiescent. In
fact, their insecurity and declining standard of living appears to be generating substantial anger among the workforce, as may be seen most
clearly in the case of the long-unpaid miners who have waged strikes
and demonstrations periodically over the last decade. Pockets of mobilization do exist, particularly among the miners. In explaining these
anomalous pockets, Stephen Crowley (1995) has argued that paternalistic enterprise policies that provide workers with payment in kind –
food, clothing, vacations, and so on – rather than just monetary
salaries, tend to discourage workers from mobilizing strikes. The mining sector has long tended to rely on higher salaries but fewer side benefits, thus making it a much less paternalistic employer. This lack of
paternalism, accompanied by a 'tradition of labor militancy throughout the world' (Crowley 1995, 51), has been a major factor in the
unusual frequency and strength of miners' strikes since the late 1980s.

Whereas the legacy of the old regime and peculiarities of the transition process have generally obstructed the emergence of an organized
egalitarian response by the workers, the unorganized and unfocused
rage growing among the labor force in postcommunist Russia should
not be underestimated. Workers lack organization, yet they nevertheless may pose a severe threat to government stability (a point that I
return to in the next section).

Turning to the women's movement, similarities to the experiences of
labor are immediately apparent. Women (like workers in general) have

seen the postcommunist transition greatly erode their economic, political and social position in society, and the situation has led them to undertake certain organizational responses. Their response to the erosion of egalitarianism in postcommunist societies has been extremely weak and, as in the case of labor unions, has suffered from organizational fragmentation and low membership.[5] In contrast to labor, there are few signs of rage among this constituency. Whereas women have been hurt by the transition, they do not form a coherent voter bloc, and neither do they appear to threaten the stability of postcommunist governments. It is fair to say that prospects for this constituency waging any kind of effective battle for a reinstitution of egalitarian protections in postcommunist societies is extremely low.

The status of women's movements in these societies may be viewed as either a case of a glass half empty or half full, depending on one's perspective. Most observers focus on the weakness of women's movements in postcommunist societies, but others start with the assumption that mobilization will be low and marvel at the presence of even a minimal organized response (for example, Azhgikhina 1995). None of the observers is able to point to a strong, vibrant and influential movement anywhere in the former Eastern Bloc. As in the case of workers, the legacy of the communist experience and the nature of the contemporary transition process play a central role in explaining the difficulties in mobilizing a strong and influential women's movement in Russia and other postcommunist societies.

Before 1991, the Soviet state prided itself in its egalitarian principles, and particularly the full incorporation of women into the workforce. Women were portrayed as both mothers and laborers, working alongside men in the heroic construction of the communist society. Supporting this notion of equality between the sexes was the state's provision of critical social services for women, including guaranteed employment, easy access to abortion, generous maternity leave policies and child care. In addition, women were guaranteed their fair share of representatives in state bodies, such as the USSR Supreme Soviet. From the outside, the communists' commitment to equality for women appears impressive.

The reality of women's situation under communism was quite different. Although women had been drafted into the labor force and worked alongside men at construction sites and heavy manual labor, they were in fact not equals in the labor force. Women were consistently channeled into the lowest status jobs and earned less than men working in similar positions. For women, there was little hope of advancement or job satisfaction. In addition, despite the social services provided, women still carried an extremely heavy burden in terms of their household and child-care duties. Few men in Soviet society felt any obligation to assist in household chores and child care, leaving women working an exhausting 'double shift'. The plight of women was made even more difficult by the state's economic agenda, which placed little emphasis on consumer goods, thus leaving women to carry out their household duties in a situation of intense shortage. As to their political role, it was symbolic only. The real power lay not in the Supreme Soviet but in the top echelons of the Communist Party, a realm rarely penetrated by women. In sum, despite their success in mobilizing women into the workforce, Soviet society was pervaded by an overwhelming sexism that ensured women had the lowliest jobs, the added burden of an extremely demanding double shift, and literally no role in the political process.

Since the collapse of communism, the position of women in society has eroded even further. In a situation of employment scarcity, women are the first to lose their jobs (based on the explicit explanation that the male breadwinners need the jobs more). The career options that have opened to women as a result of the transition are also frightening; the new entrepreneurs and business owners are largely uninterested in hiring competent women as associates; instead, they blatantly advertise for attractive young women who will act as receptionists and more. There are no laws to protect women from unfair job loss, discrimination or sexual harassment. In fact, most women seem to see the contemporary treatment of women in the labor force as completely natural. The idea of sexual harassment is not a concept that resonates with (or even makes sense to) most men and women in Russia today.

Further erosion of women's position in society may be seen in the elimination of key social services and women's ever-diminishing role in the political realm. Free health care, easy access to abortion, maternity leave, state-provided child care and other social services supporting women's role in the family have all been drastically reduced. And in the political realm, the elimination of quotas for women has led to elected bodies dominated heavily by men. Within the government itself, men hold almost all the top-echelon positions.

Given the assault on women's rights and equality that has taken place since the collapse of communism, one might expect a vibrant women's movement to emerge. As in the case of workers, women have been plagued by a lack of a strong group identity and common agenda. With few pre-existing networks of women to mobilize and little agreement on the demands to be made, the women's movement in Russia has remained fragmented and weak. A state-sponsored Soviet Women's Committee (SWC) existed under the old regime; but its agenda was set by the party-state, and the organization did not operate as a genuine forum for women's concerns. Valerie Sperling's in-depth research (1999) has also indicated that the SWC did not provide the primary network for the mobilization of women after 1991. Instead, 'women's groups formed mostly on the basis of friendship networks, acquaintanceship through the workplace ... or work-related professional activity ... as well as through participation in Soviet-era organizations related to the state or Communist Party' (Sperling 1999, 1).

Although women's clubs are springing up all over Russia today, each club tends to be driven by its own local concerns and agenda; and the dominant trait of the Russian women's movement is its severe fragmentation. These groups (particularly in Moscow) have attempted to shape themselves into umbrella groups for nationwide organizations, yet the connection between the 'national' organization in Moscow and its regional chapters remains extremely weak. In addition, the various umbrella organizations that have formed in Moscow have found it extremely difficult to coordinate their activities, but competition rather than cooperation is the dominant trend among them. Will any of these separate strands become dominant and succeed in forging bonds across regions to form a genuine nationwide women's movement (Sperling 1999)?

Probably the most interesting fact in the mobilization of women in postcommunist societies is the immense disjuncture between the goals of highly developed feminist movements in the West and the aspirations of women facing the realities of the postcommunist world (Holmgren 1995). Whereas Western feminists have focused largely on professional goals – ensuring equal employment opportunities, job status, pay, and prospects for advancement and reinforcing new familial attitudes based on a more equitable division of household duties – women in postcommunist societies are largely uninterested in pursuing this agenda.

Emerging out of years of required labor, which offered almost no opportunities for job satisfaction, postcommunist women are fleeing the labor force in droves. For many of these women, the privilege and right to stay home and devote all of their energies to their family life is one they have dreamed of for years. In the highly chauvinistic world of Russian society, professional advancement is not even viewed as a realistic goal by most. From women's experiences in the workforce, there is little benefit to be gained through labor. Staying home with their family while maintaining access to health and pension benefits is the first priority of these long downtrodden women.

Even those women focusing on professional advancement generally view the attainment of a much-coveted secretarial job with a prosperous (male) business owner as the pinnacle of success. The goal of entering the professional world on an equal footing with men is so far removed from their lives as to seem utterly ludicrous and ridiculous for most women.

Given the experience of communism from which Russian women have emerged, it is not surprising that few women's groups even seem to speak the same language as Western feminists. In fact, many Western feminists who have attempted to step in and assist in the organization of an effective women's movement in Russia have been appalled and discouraged by what they have found. Few Russian women find the Western feminist agenda at all appropriate to their contemporary situation and most attempts at cross-national linkages have ended in mutual anger and frustration.

As stated earlier, numerous women's clubs have sprung up across Russia to campaign for the local interests of women: better schools, more subsidization of healthy foods, protection of children from local environmental contamination, and so on. Yet most of the clubs (particularly those outside Moscow) have no interest in what might be called a feminist agenda. In addition, with their local emphasis and focus on their role within the family, these groups have not managed to translate their demands into a coherent and effective political force. At present, there is no evidence of a voting bloc of women, thus leaving the male-dominated legislature to continue to pursue its own agenda.

Finally, concerning human rights, there is little to be said. The severe repression of the communist era produced heroic dissident activities before the communist collapse. Since then, this repression has provided the focal point for activists and organizations that demand redress from the crimes of the past (Adler 1993; Rosenburg 1995; Smith 1996; Gibney 1997), yet there are few activities focusing on the human rights abuses of contemporary postcommunist regimes. In general, with the crimes of the past looming so large, the human rights abuses that may currently be cited pale in comparison. Whereas prison conditions continue to be terrible, legal protections for the accused are minimal and discrimination against nonindigenous ethnic groups are rampant, none of these issues has resonated much with a society deeply engrossed in simply surviving. Addressing this kind of human rights violation may seem a luxury item to many who are struggling simply to maintain employment and put food on the table. In addition, individuals and intellectuals interested in promoting greater human rights have tended to act on their own; no common agenda has yet emerged that might pull these activists together into an organized mobilization force.

Probably the most influential human rights organizations in Russia are those based outside the country. Organizations such as Amnesty International, Human Rights Watch and International Physicians for the Prevention of Nuclear War have played an important role in publicizing continued human rights problems in postcommunist Russia. They have encountered little success in organizing branches within Russia itself. At best, they have been able to forge important personal and individual contacts that have assisted them in their crusades.

In summary, the unique legacy of the communist experience and the difficulties posed by the daunting and difficult postcommunist transitions now under way have greatly impeded the organization of coherent egalitarian movements in Russia. Grievances may abound, but potential activists suffer from a lack of a coherent and consensual group identity and agenda and the absence of tangible and intangible resources needed to organize an effective movement. Although the lack of a common agenda and group identity has stymied the mobilization of organized egalitarian movements in Russia, this does not necessarily imply an apathetic and quiescent society. The population may not break cleanly into such identity groups as workers, women and human rights advocates, but it is nevertheless teeming with angry citizens, resentful of the state's retreat from its redistributionist role and former commitment to egalitarianism. This rage has played a significant role in shaping government policy, despite the lack of an organized egalitarian social response.

Egalitarian policy responses in the postcommunist world

The postcommunist context may not encourage the emergence of well-organized social movements based on strongly held consensual identities, yet this has not meant that the new governments have been free to ax egalitarian measures with impunity. In fact, with the opening of the political process and new influence of the electorate, political actors in postcommunist societies have quickly learned that they must tread carefully in transforming their economies, reducing welfare support and slashing subsidization to ailing sectors of the economy. Across most of the postcommunist world, attempts at rapid marketization and dismantling of the old welfare structure have led to a popular backlash supporting antireform forces and a resurgence of former communist political elites. In Poland, Hungary and Lithuania, initial reformist attempts to move quickly toward greater marketization and diminished state subsidization led to a reversal in governments, with the former communists returning to power on the platform of egalitarianism and greater social protection from the state. In many other newly independent states of the former USSR, the old communist elites have never left and are moving only hesitantly toward a free market economy, while recognizing the volatility and simmering discontent in their populations. And in Russia, the dominant power in the region, reformists have surged forward one day, only to retreat the next.

With the IMF demanding bolder steps toward marketization but much of the population angry and impoverished by progress to date, the Russian government has dashed back and forth between promises of radical 'shock therapy' and continued subsidization of ailing industries and their workforce. Throughout the entire post-1991 period, the government of Boris Yeltsin faced continuous challenges from antireformist forces, both from the nationalist and the communist camps. In such a volatile political setting, the continuation of accustomed egalitarian supports has been deemed by many to be essential to the continued stability of the postcommunist Russian government.

A brief review of the ebbs and flows of market reforms in Russia provides more insight into the logic of egalitarian policy responses in postcommunist societies. When Russia assumed its independence in late 1991, Yeltsin had already been chosen as president of the Russian Federation through direct elections and had established his reputation as a bold reformer.

In the 1990–1 confrontation between the USSR (Gorbachev) and Russia (Yeltsin), President Yeltsin had made clear to all that his hands were not tied by Gorbachev; Yeltsin had already embarked on an ambitious '500 Days' program of marketization and privatization. In the political realm, he had established his credentials as a staunch democrat through his high-profile role in defending Russian democracy against the attempted communist *putsch* in August 1991. In addition, throughout his entire *perestroika*-era career, he had continuously attacked and exposed the privileges of the Communist Party's elite and demanded the elimination of this privileged class. When he finally shook off the conservative influence of the USSR and embarked on his own program of reform, many observers both at home and abroad expected him to move quickly in transforming the economy and cementing democratic institutions in place. But Yeltsin's progress in implementing reforms was disappointing, and at times it was difficult to even recognize the bold pre-1991 reformer in the somewhat authoritarian, corrupt Yeltsin presidency.

As elsewhere, the Yeltsin government was quick to accept the advice of Western economists (such as Jeffrey Sachs) and in 1992 embarked on what was often referred to as a program of 'shock therapy'. Unlike in Poland, where shock therapy produced a rapid economic transformation, in huge, unwieldy Russia the reforms encountered obstacles at every turn and their results were much less dramatic than anticipated. On the one hand, with a conservatively oriented Parliament and a Soviet-era constitution, which did not clearly delineate the balance of power between presidential and legislative branches, many elements of the reform package were simply blocked by the Parliament. On the other hand, in such a vast country with so many regional components, the power of Moscow to enforce implementation of unpleasant reforms outside the city turned out to be minimal at best. The result of the 1992–93 efforts to move quickly forward in transforming the old system was a virtual stalemate between the reformist president and the conservative Parliament, with very little change in economic structures. Meanwhile, in the absence of bold reforms, the old command economy continued to deteriorate, GNP contracted sharply, and standards of living fell across the entire country (Ericson 1995).

In October 1993, the stalemate was broken by a decree of highly questionable legality from President Yeltsin, dissolving the Parliament that he believed played such a central role in obstructing the reform process. In the aftermath of the confrontation between Yeltsin and the Parliament, the President was able to usher in a new constitution that shifted the balance of power toward the presidency and to bring about new parliamentary elections that he hoped would introduce a stronger reformist element into the legislature. After two years of high inflation and economic collapse, the population proved to be angrier and less reformist-minded. Much to the shock and dismay of President Yeltsin, as well as Western observers, the ultranationalist Liberal Democratic Party of Vladimir Zhirinovsky garnered the largest share of the party list vote. In marked contrast, the multitude of tiny democratic parties running in the election fared poorly, and the final composition of the new legislature was even more conservative than its predecessor (Remington 1999, 115).

Following the December 1993 elections, President Yeltsin appeared to recognize the current of popular opinion and began moving more cautiously toward economic reform. Following a strategy of gradual movement toward currency stabilization, market liberalization and privatization, the Yeltsin government was able to make significant – if slow – progress in economic restructuring in the period 1994–8. Throughout this period, he was never permitted to forget the strength of conservative political forces and the potential for social instability to erupt if they were pushed too far. These lessons were impressed upon him even more clearly in 1995 when the resurgent Communist Party became the largest parliamentary bloc, and in 1996 when he encountered a serious challenge to his presidency from communist contender Gennady Zyuganov. Throughout the 1996 presidential campaign, Zyuganov and Yeltsin were running neck and neck, and Yeltsin just barely eked out a victory in the two rounds of elections held during the summer of 1996 (Remington 1999, 118).

The population's tolerance for continued suffering in the name of reform was growing slim. Following the presidential elections, Yeltsin cast off the compromise cabinet advisers that had been forced on him following the 1993 and 1995 elections and attempted once again to jump-start the reform process. As he brought in a team of bold economic reformers throughout the 1996–7 period, reform appeared to be resurgent; and many observers believed that Russia was finally making it through the worst of the transition process and now would be on the road to economic recovery.

Unfortunately, the world held yet another surprise for Yeltsin in the form of the global currency crisis of 1998 and the new vulnerability of the postcommunist system to shocks from the global economy. His resignation, and the rise of his unproven successor, Vladimir Putin, followed. Since 1991, the Russian Federation had been gradually integrating its economy into the global economy, hoping to gain the benefits of foreign investment and free trade. Russia had taken a beating in terms of the competitiveness of its domestically produced goods, but it was expected that the competition would eventually lead to improved efficiency, quality and, in the long term, growth. It was not expected that integration into the world economy would leave Russia open to a market contagion that they would be powerless to halt.

There is no indication of how Putin can dig Russia out of its current crisis. What is clear is that the economic collapse has pushed the long-suffering Russian population almost to its limits, and that both Yeltsin and Putin were aware that steps needed to be taken to prop up the state's role in welfare provision and industrial subsidization. One of Yeltsin's short-lived prime ministers had proposed paying the back wages of the many angry miners and other long-unpaid state employees through the mass printing of currency, a strategy that would have marked an immense retreat toward a redistributionist state and away from the free market capitalist principles espoused earlier. In keeping with a retreat toward egalitarianism, the government hinted at measures to reverse the privatization of certain industrial sectors (for example, alcohol production and sales) and thereby rein in some of the Mafia activities and corruption that currently plague the system as well as enrage the impoverished person in the street.

In Russia (as elsewhere in much of the postcommunist bloc), the unprecedented attack on long-held egalitarian principles and policies has threatened the population with much more radical and abrupt cuts in the state's provision of welfare and social support than anywhere else in the world. With the threefold impact of the domestic transition toward a capitalist economy, increased competition through international economic integration, and the final blow of the global currency contagion, the people of Russia have encountered a much more direct and accelerated attack on their accustomed way of life than has occurred in other parts of the world, so it is not surprising that the population is angered and has taken that anger to the voting booth. Ironically, as the legacy of communism throws up immense obstacles to the mobilization of social movements, it simultaneously creates an even greater tension between accustomed egalitarian policies and the movement away from egalitarianism occasioned by the multifaceted postcommunist transitions. It is not surprising that even in the absence of organized opposition, politicians who want to survive the political fray find it necessary to consider public opinion and retain or reinstate egalitarian policies to which the public is strongly attached.

Conclusion

This review of egalitarian movements and policy responses in postcommunist Russia has revealed several important lessons:

1. Although the threat to egalitarianism posed by growing economic integration into an ever more globalized economy was a factor in the erosion of state social services and redistributionist policies, it was only one component of a much more dramatic and all-encompassing process of political, economic and social transition from communist rule.
2. Although the erosion of the social welfare net is both substantial and real in Russia, it has not been met with an effective organized

social response. Moreover, although workers and others suffering severe repercussions of the transition process have in some cases exhibited signs of anger and discontent, the legacy of the old regime and nature of the transition process has effectively impeded the formation of organized social movements. With deficits in tangible and intangible resources and lack of strong group identities, movements based on the protection of workers, women and broader human rights objectives have remained fragmented and weak all across Russia.

3. Finally, despite the obstacles to effective movement formation, the postcommunist government in Russia has learned quite quickly that political survival depends on maintaining support at the ballot box. Thus, while attempting to move forward with free market reforms and dismantling the all-encompassing social safety net of the old regime, the new democratic institutions have forced the government to retreat frequently and maintain social supports that counter the overall goals and logic of the transition process.

In putting the Russian case into a broader postcommunist context, it appears to fall almost precisely in the middle of the spectrum of postcommunist transitional success. Do these findings also hold relevant lessons for the more successful transition countries (such as Poland, Hungary and the Czech Republic) and for those still mired in economic stagnation and the institutions of the old regime (such as Belarus, Romania, Albania, Bulgaria and all of Central Asia)? A quick survey of the status of labor unions, women's movements and human rights organizations in the so-called success stories reveals patterns similar to those observed in Russia (Jones 1992; Marciniak 1992; Ostrovska 1994; Pollert and Hradecka 1994; Holmgren 1995; Molyneux 1995; Rosenburg 1995; Upchurch 1995; Heitlinger 1996; Sawa-Czajka 1996; Kamenitsa 1997; Frege 1997). The transition process cuts deeply into egalitarian support systems. Labor, women's and human rights movements are generally as fragmented and alienated from the West as are their Russian counterparts, and political pressures to maintain social supports play an important role in shaping policy and electoral outcomes (particularly the return to power of former communist elites in both Poland and Hungary in the mid-1990s).

If we look at the other end of the spectrum, we also see movement fragmentation, but both the government's level of commitment to moving away from an entirely socialized system and the mechanism through which a disgruntled population may pressure political elites to retain popular support differ significantly from the Russian and success-story cases. At this far and dismal end of the spectrum, the government's commitment to marketization, privatization and capitalist institutions is highly questionable. In addition, their progress toward the institutional-ization of genuine democracy is problematic. In these cases, the dynamic of government initiated market reforms restrained by a discon-tented electorate is largely absent. Although egalitarian supports often are maintained in these troubled postcommunist countries, the mecha-nism that supports them is quite different from that which we have observed in countries that have seriously committed themselves to transforming their systems into capitalist democracies. In these cases, leadership concerns about political stability and maintenance of their own personal power are likely to be the primary factors in decisions to retain aspects of the old regime's social welfare system.

In returning to the center of the transition spectrum, it is worth pro-jecting the implications of these findings for the future of egalitarian movements and policies in Russia. Given the obstacles to movement formation in transitional societies, the likelihood of strong egalitarian movements emerging in Russia within the next decade appears low. This leaves open the question of how the rage that is clearly building in Russian society is most likely to be vented. Will workers continue to put up with growing impoverishment and the withdrawal of the social safety net? Will women continue to accept their subservient position in society? And will the broader population continue to put up with obvious violations of human rights that still occur daily across Russia? I do not believe the latter two forces present a significant threat to these governments, but the extreme discontent of workers holds the potential for an explosion of some kind. Perhaps it will simply mean electing politicians committed to reversing the reform process, or perhaps it will lead to sporadic demonstrations and violence. Most worrying is the pos-sibility that this discontent may be scapegoated on to some minority groups and lead to ethnic hostilities and violence.[6]

Thus, the legacy of communism and nature of the transitions toward capitalist democracy have played a far greater role in shaping both egalitarian mobilization efforts and redistributionist policy responses in Russia than has the impact of globalization. Although integration into an increasingly global economic system has certainly played a role in this story, its relevance has been greatly overshadowed by the all-encompassing transition now being attempted in postcommunist Russia.

Notes

1. This generalization might be expected to hold true under all but the most extreme conditions. Integration into the world economy under the conditions of growing globalization is but one aspect of the immense transition process now under way in postcommunist societies. The importance of this factor may be greater under the extremely negative conditions of a global currency crisis. Thus, the global contagion that engulfed first Asia and then Russia in 1998 represents a somewhat anomalous situation in which the impact of globalization may temporarily become a dominant factor.
2. This interpretation builds on a synthetic approach to the study of social movements, which incorporates aspects of both resource mobilization and new social movement theories. Examples of this synthetic approach may be found in Dalton (1994), Dawson (1996) and Morris and Mueller (1992).
3. Just a small sampling of the immense literature on this includes Zdravomyslova (1995), Fodor (1997), Heitlinger (1993) and Rueschemeyer (1994).
4. The following discussion on Russian labor unions is based on excellent analyses provided by: Christensen (1997), Cook (1995), Crowley (1994, 1995), Jones (1995), Borisov, Clarke and Fairbrother (1994), Borisov, Fairbrother and Clarke (1994), Rutland (1990), Fairbrother and Ilyn (1996), Baglione and Clark (1998), Volkov (1992), L. Gordon and Klopov (1992) and Ashwin (1995).
5. In my brief survey of the status of the women's movement in Russia and Eastern Europe, I have relied heavily on Goldfarb (1997), Sperling (1999), articles by Penny Morvant, Martha Bohachevsky-Chomiak and Judith Acsady in the special issue 'Women: Changing Roles', *Transition* (1995), Holmgren (1995), Heitlinger (1996), Hallas (1994), Siklova (1998), Hunt (1997), Young (1996) and Azhgikhina (1995).
6. A rise in anti-Semitism has already been noted in Russia over the past several years. See, for example, *New York Times*, 8 November 1998 and 9 March 1999.

6
Nonsocial Movements and Social Nonmovements in China

Marc Blecher

The Dengist regime has transformed China's politics, economy and society since its inception in 1978. The Leninist one-party state-monopolizing political organization has remained the central political ingredient, with a bitter dash of Stalinistic repression added to the mix. But the state has also engineered significant reductions in the previously high Maoist levels of politicization of economic and social life, mass mobilization and ideological interpellation, while also elaborating new developmental, regulatory and entrepreneurial apparatus. Economic restructuring and the development of new economic institutions have proceeded rapidly though spasmodically, as have growth and inequality. New classes and strata have formed, and society has become far more diverse and fragmented. The country has been opened to the outside world, with significant (though uneven) effects on all these levels. In the first section of this chapter, I adumbrate these transformations.

China has so far defied the liberal model according to which rapid economic modernization leads to the development of civil society and some form of institutionalized representative politics. But society has not been politically dormant in the face of these transformations. In the second section of the chapter, I begin to develop two concepts for describing and explaining society's political responses to the stresses and strains occasioned by China's profound and mercuric changes. 'Nonsocial movements' refers to the activities of nonstate elites – intellectuals and renowned or well-placed citizens who are not themselves leading Communist Party figures – who engage with state institutions, sometimes as individuals, and sometimes by forming informal, temporary, *ad hoc* alliances and contacts. 'Nonsocial' connotes their elite provenance, and they can be called 'movements' because they involve purposive and, sometimes, organized political activity. 'Social nonmovements' refers to spontaneous popular protests that lack leadership and organization. 'Social' refers to their popular base, whereas 'nonmovement' denotes their fragmented and fleeting quality and their consequent lack of leadership, program and coordination. In looking specifically at egalitarian issues, societal (that is, non-state) politics around gender has taken the form of a nonsocial movement, whereas those affecting farmers and workers have involved social nonmovements.

In a concluding section, I evaluate the effects on equality of China's feminist nonsocial movement and its farmer- and worker-based social nonmovements. While not utterly lacking in consequences, their effects have been negligible at best. More surprising, the workers' nonmovement, which was, apparently, most feared by the Party throughout the 1980s, has in the end accomplished the least. I offer some possible explanations and questions for further research.

The Dengist regime

Popular politics and the state

In the Leninist mold, state power is still monopolized by the Chinese Communist Party, whose organizations permeate all important government institutions. The party-state strenuously forbids the formation of any alternative party or independent political organizations.[1] Citizens may form organizations around apolitical issues, but even these must be registered with the Ministry of Civil Affairs and allow close supervision by the security apparatus. Dissidents who have tried, cleverly, to establish such organizations around what they thought were safe issues such as corruption, environmental protection or economic development found their efforts frustrated by harassment, arrests, and confiscation of files and materials. Headlines on items distributed by *Agence France-Presse* (*AFP*) reflect the situation: on 15 October 1998, 'Chinese Police Detain Corruption-Watch Leader'; on 26 October 1998, 'Beijing Police Briefly Detain Environment and Development Activists'. *China News Digest* (*CND*) carried similar stories (4 November 1998).

Yet what the state does with its ongoing political monopoly has also changed from its Maoist origins. Elite conflict has moderated, which has encouraged the expansion of bureaucratic pluralism and gone far toward creating a more relaxed political atmosphere within the state as well as in society. In Tang Tsou's terms (1986, xxiv), the state's 'zone of indifference' has widened considerably. Ideological transformation of the masses into new socialist men and women is also off the agenda. The state's active commitment to class struggle has now been shelved indefinitely as being inappropriate to the present 'primary stage of socialism'. Law has undergone a renaissance, in part to help depoliticize and in part as a functional necessity of the economic reforms, which require contracts and clear property rights. The judiciary still lacks independence, and laws are still passed by party-dominated people's congresses. But the existence of law has emboldened a growing number of people, from China's handful of dissidents to many ordinary citizens who feel they have been wronged by a government official or fellow citizen.

The range of permissible speech for ordinary Chinese as well as prominent elites has widened astonishingly over the past two decades. People on the streets, in factories and on farms feel free to criticize government policies and even particular top leaders by name in conversations, even when they are with or within earshot of strangers who may, they know, be plainclothes security personnel or ordinary citizens who will report to them. Official government newspapers carry lively debates, sometimes in the form of signed letters from readers that are obstreperous in expressing their displeasure with present policies. An example of the genre, published in *Gongren ribao* (*Workers' Daily*), 10 July 1997, asks *Jiuye nan zai nali?*: what's the problem with employment? Citizens concerned about issues such as corruption, inequality, or the potentially devastating effects of the Three Gorges Dam publish articles and books on these subjects and have even gone so far as to engage in direct and open policy debates about them with the leadership, a phenomenon I term a 'nonsocial movement' and which I explore further in the case of gender politics. Such speakers, writers and activists know they are safe so long as they do not try to organize a formal group, hold a public meeting, or publicly insult or embarrass a top leader. In some but not all of these respects, China today is moving tentatively away from Leninist and Stalinist politics in the direction of Franco's Spain or even Perón's Argentina (Linz 1964).

Yet there still looms a Stalinist element in Chinese politics today, and one, moreover, that was not present in Maoist days. The 1989 protests were drawn to a violent close by the armed forces against unarmed citizens. The post-Dengist leadership has so far refused to revisit the 'correct verdict', issued under Deng, that the violence, though regrettable, was justified because China faced a counterrevolutionary threat at the time. It is impossible to determine the extent to which repression is a factor, compared with myriad hegemonic elements, in accounting for the political quiescence that prevails in China today. But it certainly cannot be counted out. In the 1990s the Chinese state pursued a 'market Stalinist' strategy. In the 1980s, the state – fearing popular protests – had failed to pursue unpopular economic policies, such as price reform and industrial restructuring, even though they were fundamental prerequisites for economic reform. In the wake of the 1989 crackdown, however, it felt emboldened enough do so (Blecher 1997, 114–15). Yet today, fear of violent repression is not strong enough to deter the legion spontaneous protesters who participate in China's social nonmovements, some of whom we meet later in this chapter.

Economic reform

The Dengist reforms began quickly in the countryside where, by 1983, decollectivization was complete. Although farmers have gained some latitude to make cropping decisions, marketization of grain production and distribution has been slower in coming and is still far from complete. In the cities, private markets and petty enterprise boomed soon after 1979. But the urban industrial economy proved much more difficult to reform than the rural economy, because of popular and bureaucratic opposition to price, enterprise and labor reforms. Only in the repressive post-1989 political atmosphere could these obstacles be overcome. By the mid-1990s, prices had largely been deregulated, state enterprise reform began to get under way, and significant layoffs from money-losing firms led to rapidly rising unemployment.

The reformist state has been relying for its political legitimacy (or at least its longevity) on the performance of the economy. In important respects, it has been able to do so. The Chinese agricultural economy achieved very strong economic results from 1979 to 1984 but then stagnated; after 1985, rural income managed to grow, albeit slowly, mainly because of rural industrial and commercial growth. In the cities, industry grew moderately faster in the 1980s than in the 1970s but really took off only after 1992, when the deadlock on price reform was broken, state industrial and labor reform began, and privatization was seriously encouraged. Still, losses continued to pile up in the large state-owned sector, where perhaps as many as half of the state indus- trial and commercial enterprises remained in the red in the late 1990s. Nevertheless, the boom in collective and other enterprises as well as in commerce and services drove up average urban incomes. This has gone far toward helping the state weather the political challenges it has faced from price reform and increased unemployment.

However, farmers remain under intense economic pressure; as we see later, their fury has sometimes boiled over. Costs of industrial inputs to agriculture, such as diesel fuel, machinery, chemical fertilizer and plastic sheeting, have been rising far faster than crop prices. Cash-starved and corrupt local governments have been levying all manner of *ad hoc* fees and taxes. Farmers face ongoing demands to plant unprofitable staple crops. Worse yet, because of the state's financial crisis, it often has lacked the money to pay for these crops and has had to distribute IOUs instead. In the cities, workers are chafing under the profound employment and wage squeeze resulting from industrial restructuring. Layoffs and wage arrears have become pandemic.

Increased economic inequality was nothing less than an explicit objective of the rural reforms, which sought to allow 'some to get rich first'. Rural household inequality, which had reached extremely low levels by the end of the Maoist period, began to rise after 1978. In 1988, the poorest 40 per cent of people in the Chinese countryside received 20 per cent of the income, while the richest 10 per cent received 26 per cent. The Gini coefficient of total rural household income rose further, from 0.116 in 1988 to 0.192 in 1995. In 1995, roughly 10 per cent of rural Chinese lived below the government-set poverty line, itself set at only 17 per cent of average rural income. For urban household income, the Gini coefficient increased from 0.233 in 1988 to 0.332 in 1995. Rural–urban inequality also rose starting in the late 1980s.[2]

Social fragmentation

The structural accompaniment to all this burgeoning inequality is aggravated social fragmentation. Existentially, people are no longer organized into the coherent and often all-encompassing 'units' (*danwei*) of the Maoist days. In the rural areas, several new classes have emerged: a petit bourgeoisie comprised of self-employed service providers and producers, a bourgeoisie of rural private entrepreneurs, and a rural proletariat of those who work for them. In the cities and towns too, the homogeneous working class of Maoist days has given way to one that is highly stratified along several dimensions: the employed, laid-off and unemployed; those with various categories of contracts; rural migrants versus urban dwellers; and those working in state, collective, private and foreign joint-venture firms. Alongside the urban working class is a new urban petit bourgeoisie of self-employed workers, a bourgeoisie that itself can range from owners of small workshops to huge private entrepreneurs, and a growing lumpenproletariat of beggars, prostitutes and criminals.

In the countryside, the collapse of collectives restored the dominant authority of the male household head and permitted the return of all manner of traditional patriarchal practices, such as wedding ceremonies that are demeaning to women. Women have been hit particularly hard by the decline of collectively funded education.[3] With the decline of local government capacity and its reorientation to a more exclusive concern with the economy rather than social and political transformation, it is probably more difficult for women to get protection against or redress for sexist discrimination and crimes. In the urban areas, overt sexism in employment persists and in some ways has worsened over Maoist days. On a more positive note, more women have begun to take up more positions in their own right in urban, regional and national government. A growing problem in both urban and rural areas is violence against women, including wife battery, rape, kidnapping for sale (to labor gangs, prostitution rings or marriage brokers), and female infanticide and abandonment.

'Opening up' to globalization

The Dengist leadership decided early and emphatically to 'open up' (*kaifang*) to the outside world. The decision has proven one of its most broadly popular ones among elites and ordinarly Chinese, although actual policy has moved forward in a spiral pattern – haltingly but, with each setback, even faster at the next expansion – with the vicissitudes of China's economic and political business cycles (J. Howell 1993). In the 1980s and early 1990s, the state attempted to concentrate foreign investment mainly in 'special economic zones' established along the coast. But by the mid-1990s, regions and localities gained a great deal of latitude to make their own deals. Moreover, property rights, taxation and profit remission issues had been significantly clarified and codified. By 1997, when I conducted interviews on the subject in Beijing, foreign capitalists were beginning to regard China as an environment that was as normal and predictable for investment as any in the late industrializing world.

Data reflect both China's general openness in the 1980s and early 1990s and the further rapid developments since then.[4] In 1985, the total volume of international trade reached 7.8 per cent; in 1995, it grew 18.7 per cent over the previous year. Direct foreign investment rose steadily 1978–88, plateaued in the retrenchment of 1989–91, and climbed vertiginously in the early 1990s, from $11.5 billion in 1991 to $48 billion in 1995. Wholly foreign-owned enterprises employed 60 000 workers in 1985, a figure that rose to 3 000 000 in 1997, and that in any event does not count the tens of millions employed in foreign joint-venture firms. My interviews during the period 1996–98 in Tianjin reveal that workers laid off by ailing enterprises often long for the arrival of a foreign investor.

Globalization has also profoundly affected China's way of life. Even in the early 1980s, farmers could take in free screenings of Western B-movies such as *Zorro* (Hinton 1986). By the latter 1980s, black-and-white televisions had become ubiquitous except in the most dirt-poor villages and by the mid-1990s most had been replaced by color sets. The majority of programming is Chinese, but there is a generous share of Western movies, has-been television dramas and sports. For the reading public, bookshops are awash in translations of popular Western (mostly English-language) novels and especially nonfiction works (such as history, biography and pop sociology). Urban consumption patterns have been reshaped by Western fashions, from fast food to clothing to hairstyles to beepers and cell phones. Opportunities to travel, or even better to live, study and work abroad, are treasured, and enormous sacrifices are made to undertake such ventures. For elites, the Internet provides a ready conduit for global information and communication and one, moreover, that is becoming a source of grave concern to the government because of its capacity to disseminate subversive information and to provide a tool for embryonic organizing against the state.

Society's response: social nonmovements and nonsocial movements

Chinese society has not responded to the stresses, strains, and political opportunities of the past two decades by developing a civil society: it lacks even a dysfunctional one such as the civil society that has appeared, for example, in Russia. Western scholars, who began to deploy the concept actively in the 1980s to describe China's growing political ferment, gradually began to appreciate its fundamental limitations in both the practice of and theory about the Chinese case. There are at least five interrelated reasons for the failure of civil society as a concept and as real politics to date in China. First, China lacks a historical tradition of a private organizational sphere juxtaposed to the state. Historically, merchant guilds and gentry organizations tended to develop organic connections with officials and often functioned as auxiliary arms of the state, a pattern that continued through the first decades of China's modernization and reform early this century.

Even the Nationalist Party, the dominant political force before 1949, developed an organic conception of the state as its creature, organized itself along Leninist principles even as it passed through liberal and then reactionary phases, and did not permit alternative political parties. Second, the superstructural concomitant of this historical pattern of organization is a political culture (at the levels of both elite and popular traditions) that has not drawn a clear distinction between public and private spheres, emphasizing instead their organic unity. Third, China never had a bourgeois revolution, which in Western Europe and North America founded polities based on liberal concepts of protected spheres of private property and individual rights.

Fourth, in Dengist China marketization has occurred through the state rather than distinct from (much less in opposition to) the state. In the liberal model of political modernization, capitalist development naturally promotes individual rights, civil society and democracy. But in China, the Dengist state led the way to marketization. This meant, first and foremost, that the kinds of political struggles against Western precapitalist states, which established private political and economic spheres, did not have to be fought. The Dengist state granted and, indeed, encouraged marketization while blocking the development of political rights and civil society. Replicating China's ancient pattern even on the terrain of modern capitalism, emergent economic and social classes and groups have found it best to pursue their interests by working through the state rather than separate from or against it (Nevitt 1996).

Fifth, the development of civil society clearly continues to be impeded by the continuing steadfast determination of the state to maintain its monopoly of political organization. The Chinese Communist Party may have adopted capitalism, but it has not given up on political Leninism and even some Stalinism. It permits society to be organized only by or through the state, never apart from it. In the Dengist period, it has adopted three broad approaches to society's political activity and organization:

1. It has tried to reinvigorate some of its own 'mass organizations', such as the labor unions and women's associations, granting them some limited space for advocacy of sectoral interests.
2. It closely monitors other organizational impulses emanating from society, requiring new groups to register and report on their activities.
3. Where absolutely necessary and where all else has failed, it has shown its willingness to use repression: for instance, to arrest dissidents and

to crack down on particularly threatening popular movements (such as minority nationalist organizations, clandestine religious outfits, and the 1989 demonstrations).

If civil society has fallen short both as a political form and an analytical concept, that does not mean that Chinese society has been dormant in responding to the profound pressures produced by the Dengist regime. Two kinds of reflexes have appeared. In one, intellectuals and what could be called social elites – people who have achieved some stature outside the political realm – have become politically active, attempting to influence specific policies, general policy directions, or the political agenda. Their activities have included writing for public media, drafting memos and reports to state officials, and working directly to influence decision-makers, often quietly behind the scenes but sometimes openly yet legally (for example, in efforts to lobby delegates to people's congresses). Indeed, these efforts focus directly on political elites, eschewing efforts at popular organization or mobilization. I have coined the term 'nonsocial movement' for this sort of activity to indicate (1) that it lacks a broad social base but is nevertheless directed at purposive political change, and (2) that it attains a level of organizational coherence, either informally outside the state or by working within and through formal state channels.

A second kind of social response has been spontaneous, *ad hoc* political demonstrations that lack leadership and organization. They have run the gamut from the 1986 student demonstrations and the 1989 mass demonstrations – which were neither produced by nor able to produce a coherent program or robust leadership or organization, although they did achieve a definite level of temporary coordination across and within localities – to the wildcat strikes, sit-ins, riots and rural uprisings that have become ubiquitous in the past few years. I call them 'social nonmovements': social because they are genuine popular political endeavors, but nonmovements because they do not attain a significant level of coordination, leadership and organization.

An egalitarian nonsocial movement: the case of gender

China developed a vibrant feminist movement in the early part of this century. The May 4 Movement of 1919, a modernist political awakening that could be compared to the ferment of the 1960s in the West, involved an active role for women as women. Campaigns took place to attack Confucian patriarchal ideology, to militate in favor of education and political rights for women, and to end barbaric traditional practices such as foot-binding and minor marriage. Female intellectuals and students were active participants in the Chinese Revolution of 1949. In this context, it may be more surprising that in the Dengist period Chinese women have not mobilized politically as women. In the 1986 and 1989 demonstrations, feminist issues did not surface on the burgeoning agendas of mass politics, and women did not demonstrate as women but rather, like men, as members of their neighborhood or work units. The contrast with the social nonmovement politics of farmers and workers, with their active mass bases (discussed in the following sections), is striking.

During the Maoist period, a great deal of progress was made on gender equality. But most of it was the indirect result of the transition to socialism and, to a lesser extent, the concomitant state attacks on traditional society which was highly patriarchal, rather than the expression of a pronounced feminist impulse (Blecher 1997, 151–6). Insofar as they existed at all, feminist politics consisted of the controlled and circumscribed activities of the state-run Chinese Women's Federation, which was made responsible for the mobilization of women to carry out the goals of the state, including population control and occasional stints of labor outside the home (especially during the Great Leap Forward). Under the Dengist regime, by contrast, a more genuinely feminist politics has begun to emerge around issues including divorce rights, crimes against women (such as female infanticide and sales of kidnapped women), employment discrimination and superexploitation, and prostitution.

It began among the intelligentsia, as young scholars began to pursue and publish research on these and other issues. As the reforms began to take hold, many of the gains achieved by women in the Maoist period evaporated surprisingly quickly. In the mid-1980s, a group of independent researchers began to raise serious questions about the obvious failure of the Women's Federation to get to the roots of gender oppression in the Maoist period, a time when the state was attacking so many social ills. The Women's Federation was thus put on the defensive. This occurred at a time when it, like many other organs of the state, was being asked to justify itself and to provide more fully for its own existence. The state was also depoliticizing and beginning to withdraw from strict control of many aspects of Chinese life. It was therefore content to permit the Women's Federation a more autonomous role in militating in favor of women. The federation decided to take more seriously its official role, submerged in the Maoist period, of representing and campaigning for the interests of women. It would use its newfound latitude to take on its newfound legitimacy and identity crises. The federation began to make common cause with its academic critics, by sponsoring their research, using that to publicize women's problems and to try to place them on the political agenda, and very gradually but nevertheless measurably becoming a livelier advocate for women within the state. For their part, many Chinese feminists began to see their best hope in working through a slowly reinvigorating Women's Federation (Wang 1997).

This elite-level ferment did not produce any effort to mobilize popular support even when the moment presented itself in the first half of 1989. The meteoric rise of Chai Ling to the top rank of student leaders in Tiananmen Square shows that sexism in the movement was not a serious obstacle. Chai – a daring, demagogic, narcissistic, and opportunistic young woman who now supplements her income as a US-based business consultant with stints as a pundit for American media whenever they have a big China story – was cut from different (and far less resilient and practical) cloth than the intellectual feminists and the Women's Federation cadres with whom they had begun to ally. For its part, however, the women's association did not become prominent in pressing women's issues, despite the fact that many 1989 protesters marched under the banners of their government organs and raised issues arising from their professional concerns. This new generation of middle-class Chinese feminists was more materially and culturally prone to work as writers and political activists operating within and through the state, not on the streets.

The year 1989 brought a crackdown that put statist-oriented leaders back in the driver's seat, sidelining political initiatives from society. But, ironically, the state's need to legitimate itself after 4 June soon presented Chinese feminists with a precious opportunity. In early 1991, thinking women's issues safe and the state's record on them comparatively positive, the leadership decided to go ahead with plans to host the 1995 Fourth World Conference on Women as a way to show the world a different China. After Li Peng was heckled by a group of German feminists during a visit to Germany in July 1999, however, the government decided that the NGO forum associated with the conference could get out of control. The government eventually relegated it to the remote town of Huairou on the lame excuse that appropriate facilities could not be found in Beijing. But even then, dispirited Chinese feminists within and outside the Women's Federation decided to make the best of the opportunity presented to them by the conference. They would use it to express themselves, make foreign contacts, and wait for a day when the repression would lift and they would once again regain some latitude to promote issues of concern to them (Wang 1997), some of which they might even share with the state.

With the successful conclusion of the conference and the gradual opening of some limited political space in the wake of the smooth succession to the post-Deng leadership and the reabsorption of Hong Kong in 1997, that day should not be too long in coming. In the past few years, the Women's Federation has become a lively public advocate for the interests of Chinese women. In the run-up to International Women's Day in early March 1997, it sponsored a series of articles in major newspapers – including decidedly unfeminist media such as the *Economic Information Daily* – attacking sexism in television advertising. Reflecting the orientation to feminist research that formed the basis of the alliance between China's independent feminists and the Women's Federation, the articles were based on a survey of 1200 popular advertisements: 'Women seldom appear in authority roles and are routinely portrayed as housewives, secretaries and sex objects.' The advertisements also 'suggest male intellectual superiority', they argued (United Press International, or UPI, 5 March 1997; Reuters, 30 April 1997). The federation has also been involved in public criticisms of bigamy, concubinage, slave trade in women and child neglect (Reuters, 2 April 1997; UPI, 20 September 1996).

The Women's Federation has sought to work with Chinese citizens who are concerned about women's problems. An item ran on the Reuters wire on 28 April 1997 concerning the Federation's campaign to raise private donations to fight female illiteracy. In Shanghai, the Federation accepted a donation of a half-million yuan from a wealthy businessman to build a battered women's shelter. Reuters reported:

> The Shanghai shelter, in a two-story building in the southwest of the city, is the brainchild of Zhang Zhiqin, 43, president of a restaurant, transport, and food firm which pays for the shelter's entire annual cost of $60,000 [¥500 000]. 'Last year, I read in a newspaper that two-thirds of those who committed suicide by throwing themselves in the Huangpu River were female victims of domestic violence,' he said. 'I also read of a 16-year-old girl who had run away from home and gone missing because of violence at home.' Moved by this and wanting to follow the US example of providing shelters for women in distress, he told the local Women's Federation of his idea. With their support, he opened the shelter in a building owned by his company, with a staff of 12. (11 March 1996)

Finally, the Women's Federation has recently become involved in legislative politics that turned public. Concerned about a rising divorce rate propelled in part by men seeking to 'trade in' their used wives for newer models, the federation became involved in drafting an updated family and marriage law that would make it more difficult for philanderers to walk away from their marital vows and family responsibilities. The draft circulated behind closed doors, and finally a public meeting was held to air it. Feminist critics soon lined up against the proposal, on the grounds that it represented warmed-over state paternalism and intrusion into private life, and that women can often benefit from liberal divorce policy (Eckholm 1998). As fascinating and portentous as the substance of the debate itself is what it indicates about the broadening sphere of feminist politics in China and the role of a formerly statist 'mass organization' in sparking and presiding over genuine public political debate. By 1997, a Chinese feminist scholar with long experience in the West could write that:

> The Women's Federation is no longer simply an organ of the government that only serves to make Chinese women statist subjects, as many believe it was in the Maoist era. Rather, the Women's Federation consciously explored strategies to work for women's interests. To be sure, carrying out state policies and demands is still a major part of 'women work' (*funu gongzuo*) of the Women's Federation. Nevertheless, the new dimension of the Women's Federation's 'women work', that is, studying and solving women's problems, helps place the Women's Federation in a mediator position between women and the state in the reform era. (Wang 1997, 131)

The characterization is apt. The Chinese Women's Federation is still formally a 'mass organization' under the leadership of the Chinese Communist Party. The state maintains a firm monopoly on political organization, which means that the Federation is the only game in town for Chinese feminists. That is surely one reason why there has been little if any noticeable effort by Chinese women to establish their own social movement. But the state's organizational monopoly (backed by its coercive power) cannot be the only reason; if it were, it would be difficult to explain the much higher level of extra- and, indeed, antistate organization and activity by workers and farmers, to which we turn below.

How might it be explained that feminists have reached more accommodation with the state than farmers and workers? Two theses can be advanced. First, the federation has been skillful in making itself something of a magnet for independent feminists and their male supporters. It has proved willing to seek them out, to open its ranks to them, to foster and publicize their research, to campaign on the basis of it, and to work with them on specific social projects. Perhaps another reason is the middle-class basis of contemporary Chinese feminism. The protagonists in feminist politics have been scholars, social service workers, government officials and philanthropists; by and large not the sorts whose class backgrounds incline them to attend clandestine meetings, to take to the barricades, or to try to mobilize their working sisters for political action. Moreover, working-class Chinese women have not been prominent in fashioning their own, potentially more mobilized, feminist politics. They have not created a radical push from below that could have radicalized some middle-class women, or put middle-class, intellectually rooted, accommodationist feminism on the defensive. In the end, then, Chinese feminism in the Dengist period has been a nonsocial movement, a fact that may help account both for its successes in achieving a limited measure of autonomy and in opening space for genuine debate, and also for its limitations.

Egalitarian social nonmovements of farmers and workers

As we have seen, the first decade of the Dengist period saw only the most dilatory efforts at reform of the urban economy. The hardest steps – price, labor and structural enterprise reforms – were put off. Although the reasons were complex (having to do with the high stakes, the lack of a viable model and serious disagreement over how and how much to reform) the leadership's concern about political instability growing out of working-class protest was a major factor. The government was not just projecting idly, based on having been burned by radical workers during the Cultural Revolution. Even at a time when the government was handling the working class with kid gloves, workers were protesting. Items in the *Foreign Broadcast Information Service's China Daily Report* (*FBIS*) chronicled the unrest. In 1986 and 1987, the much-vaunted Shenzhen Special Economic Zone just across the border from Hong Kong experienced 21 strikes. Some 70 per cent of the strikes arose from pay disputes and 20 per cent from 'encroachments on workers' interests', including hours so long that many workers were dropping from exhaustion (*FBIS*, 2 August 1988). Far away in China's northwest, 1100 workers in a state-run medical appliance factory struck for three months starting in late 1987 over what even the official trade union admitted were violations of workers' rights (*FBIS*, 25 October 1988; 1 February 1989).

The official press reported almost 100 strikes in 1987, over 100 in 1988, over 700 in the second half of 1989, and over 1600 in 1990 (*FBIS*, 6 September 1988; 1 February 1989; 29 August 1991). The vertiginous rise of labor protest after the June 1989 crackdown is stunning, especially in view of the severe punishment meted out to workers during it: punished more swiftly and more harshly than the students or intellectuals, workers alone among the protesters faced execution.

With the onset of price reform in the early 1990s and labor reform a few years later, labor protest has become pandemic. Strikes, demonstrations and violent outbursts against hated factory managers are a daily fact of life. The Ministry of Labor reported 33 000 labor disputes in 1995, a 73 per cent increase over the previous year. The increase in 1996 was of similar magnitude (Forney 1997). The typical pattern is that a group of workers – ranging from the dozens to several thousand – sit-in at a government office, close down a factory, or block a major transport artery. Their demands often center on egregious wage or benefit arrears, especially when these occur in the face of what they regard as particularly corrupt or incompetent leadership. In some cases, the workers seize the factory, its manager, or both. The government then sends in officials to try to mediate and often to distribute funds to meet workers' demands. If necessary, police are sent in, and some ringleaders may be arrested. The incident is thus brought to an end, but soon enough another occurs and the pattern is repeated. Such protests have become commonplace in many Chinese cities in the past two or three years, yet they have not led to any coordinated social movement.

Wildcat strikes have been particularly prominent in factories run by Hong Kong, Japanese, South Korean and Taiwanese capitalists. Interestingly, women have often been at the forefront of these strikes, where employment discrimination and sexual harassment have been prominent issues. More significant, although these strikes have elicited some limited support from China's trade union federation – which, by flogging foreigners, can try to increase its legitimacy and that of the state among workers and patriots – the Women's Federation and independent feminists have not made the plight of these abused women workers a serious focus of their efforts.

In the countryside, too, many farmers have been politically active, often in novel and creative ways (Blecher 1997). In some cases, they respond to *ad hoc* exactions or other impositions by informing themselves about state policies; then, armed with documents that clearly support their case, they remonstrate in a number of ways. They may first protest to village officials and, if they are not successful, then on up the ladder to the township and the county authorities. Many stage peaceful sit-ins in front of government offices. Thousands upon thousands have written letters (or hired scribes to do so) telling their stories to newspapers and magazines. In many cases, these letters attract the attention of editors and investigative journalists interested in publishing exposés. Some farmers even go to court seeking redress against local officials whom they accuse of acting improperly. These peaceful, legal and legalistic forms of protest may portend a new form of political participation in China (O'Brien 1994; O'Brien and Li 1995). One question is whether they can transcend their parochial concern with individualistic complaints by contributing to civic organizations that engage in advocacy on policy formation rather than just implementation.

To these peaceful forms of rural protest can be added the violent rural uprisings by peasants caught in a tightening economic vise between higher input costs and rising government exactions on the one hand, and stagnant or declining crop revenues on the other. These became increasingly common starting in the late 1980s and, like the urban protests, continued past the 1989 crackdown. In one example that became prominent in the Chinese press, in June 1993 spontaneous protests by farmers in Renshou County (Sichuan Province) against road construction levies led to 'beating, smashing and looting ... [in which] some people ... stormed the district and township governments and schools, beat up cadres and teachers, smashed public and private property, and illegally detained grass-roots cadres and public security personnel'. When police responded with tear gas, some were taken hostage by the angry crowd, and police cars were set on fire (*BBC Daily Report*, 14 June 1993). An effort in July 1993 by a county government in Hunan to requisition land along a railway line prompted farmers to seize weapons, including semi-automatic rifles, from the local armory; several hundred troops and armed police were drawn into a battle in which 35 people were wounded (*BBC Daily Report*, 6 July 1993). Farmers have been slaughtering and maiming tax collectors: in 1989 in Shandong Province alone, five were killed and over 3000 wounded, 353 permanently (*CND*, 6 October 1990). During 1991 flooding, farmers were enraged by what they perceived to be the state's insufficient attention to water conservancy work and its mismanagement of relief efforts. They engaged in over 100 incidents, including mass rallies, looting of state warehouses, armed clashes, and even efforts to set prisoners free in four provinces. In Guizhou alone, 30 people were killed (*CND*, 8 August 1991). Even routine work by local officials – in land reallocation, population control, dispute mediation and public welfare work – is often met with reprisals from farmers, including vandalism and beatings. Battles have broken out between villages over property rights and access to water. Secret societies are making a comeback, which ought to frighten the leadership most of all, because they portend a possibility of organized protest.[5] By 1997, the numbers involved were staggering. Details published 1 August 1997 in *Zheng Ming* illustrate the scope of the protests:

> Between 17 and 22 May, nearly 200,000 peasants in over 80 townships and villages in Lixian, Linli, Nanxian, Anhua, Ningxiang and other counties in Yiyang and Changde prefectures, Hunan Province, assembled, staged parades and demonstrations, and filed petitions on more than 80 occasions. Between mid-May and mid-June, more than 100,000 peasants in over 70 townships and villages in Xiushui, Yifeng, Anfu, Wanan, Xingguo, and other counties in Jiujiang, Yichun, and Jian prefectures in Jiangxi Province assembled, staged parades and demonstrations, and filed petitions on more than 100 occasions. Incidents of peasants seizing the county party and government buildings, and attacking supply and marketing cooperatives for chemical fertilizer and cement were reported in Xiushui, Anfu, Wanan, and other counties. Over 800 peasants assaulted the public security bureau in Yifeng County and confronted the soldiers and policemen for more than 70 hours. More than 130 peasants were arrested in a clash. (19–21)

Workers' and farmers' protests appear so far to have been spontaneous, unorganized, and lacking in leadership and coordination. Recently there are signs – no doubt ominous ones from the state's point of view – of efforts to provide some direction. Leaked internal government documents about the May–June 1999 outbursts were published in *Zheng Ming* (1 August 1997: 19–21). The documents reported:

> Rural party and government cadres at the township and village levels also encouraged peasants to demonstrate and personally participated in the procession, and put forward the slogans such as, 'Down with the urban bureaucratic exploiting class and share the wealth of new local overlords in the countryside' and 'Establish peasants' own political power.'

In 1998, democracy activists began to try to forge linkages with striking and protesting workers.

Chinese dissident Lin Xinshu has written an open letter to Communist Party Central Committee, adding his voice to a rising chorus calling for free trade unions in the country ... [H]is letter aimed to follow the lead of Wuhan-based dissident Qin Yongmin, who last week issued a similar nationwide call for independent trade unions, prompting public statements of support from other dissidents throughout China. (*AFP*, 1 January 1998)

Predictably, Qin promptly attracted the close attention of the security apparatus and was ordered to leave the country (*AFP*, 26 January 1998). Repression may not be at the forefront of the state's approach to dealing with protesting workers, and it certainly has not been effective in intimidating them into quiescence. But in preventing a linkage between intellectuals and workers, it has been absolutely crucial so far. Such a linkage is not easy to forge in the first place, as the aborted popular Polish movements of 1968 and 1971 demonstrate all too clearly. The Chinese state is taking no chances, a wise move from its point of view in light not only of the subsequent Polish events of 1976 and 1980 but also of the pressures building up on the Chinese working class and the sheer temerity of both workers and dissidents.

To date, then, the very significant levels of self-mobilization among China's discontented farmers and workers have produced only a social nonmovement: that is, a series of outbursts that remain disconnected from each other and that lack a coherent political leadership or program.

Effects

China's middle-class feminist nonsocial movement has gone far toward airing the problems faced by Chinese women of all classes, setting public agendas for government action, and beginning to become an elite-level participant in legislative policy-making around some of the issues it has raised (such as divorce). It has also contributed to the broadening sphere of serious public debate, an important step in the direction of democratization. But it is difficult to point to a single major policy change resulting from initiatives or pressures from the Women's Federation or from feminists working with it or on their own. It is possible, and indeed likely, that some incremental changes have occurred in national or regional policy-making and implementation because of quiet, behind-the-scenes efforts of feminist scholars and government officials, both within and outside the Women's Federation. But overall China's feminist movement has not been able to do much to stem the rising tide of gender inequality, discrimination and abuse of women that has surged out of China's breathless marketization and opening to the West. Employment discrimination continues, not just among foreign-invested firms but also in Chinese enterprises and offices (including government-run ones), where women must often conform to sexist physical criteria to land a job and accept lower pay and inferior working conditions if they successfully obtain one. Prostitution still appears to be on the rise: by one account (which I obtained in a 1999 interview in Beijing), it employs five million Chinese women. It is fueled not just by marketization and the desire of some young women for Western-style goods, but also by unemployment. A Sichuan study found that 87 per cent of prostitutes were otherwise unemployed (*AFP*, 28 January 1998). There is no reason to think that wife battery, female infanticide and abandonment, and abduction of women for sale have declined, or that educational attainment has equalized.

The lack of progress can be attributed in part to the political shortcomings of the feminist movement, such as its relative de-emphasis on employment issues and its failure to attract a mass base. However, the Women's Federation is also short of the political and financial resources needed to tackle the problems facing Chinese women. Finally, the sheer magnitude of the asperities created for women by marketization and globalization would dwarf even far more heroic, single-minded and well-endowed efforts to fight them.

Farmers may be able to point to one positive outcome of their stirrings over the past several years. Starting in the late 1980s, cash-strapped village governments and grain bureau officials were issuing IOUs in payment for required grain sales to the state. When farmers vented their rage, the government became genuinely concerned about the threat of snowballing rural unrest. Premier Li Peng warned strenuously on more than one occasion that IOUs should no longer be issued, because they threatened both agricultural production and political instability. In response to the Jiangxi rioting mentioned earlier:

> On 19 May, the General Office of the State Council and the Ministry of Agriculture issued a circular: 'On Conscientiously and Firmly Carrying Out Work in Purchasing Agricultural Products and Protecting Peasants' Interests According to Policy'. This document warned local government departments against unhealthy practices which lead to peasants' defiance such as issuing IOUs, forcing purchasing prices down, giving short weight, refusing to purchase farm products,

imposing exorbitant new taxes and levies, imposing arbitrary charges, and offering gifts to cadres. (*Zheng Ming*, 1 August 1997: 19–21)

Reports of the problem are down in the past year or two. However, that may be illusory, or it may prove only temporary, especially if government deficits persist and if banking reform goes forward in a serious way (the Agricultural Bank of China has usually been called in to make much-needed loans to strapped purchasing agencies), or if corruption spirals further out of control.

Aside from this possibly ephemeral achievement, China's farmers can point to little gain from their political mobilization. Thus far, the outbursts have been infrequent and isolated enough for the state to be able to deal with them one by one, often with more stick than carrot. There has been no noticeable shift in China's urban-biased pattern of investment, development planning or social policy.

Most astonishing and puzzling is the ineffectiveness of the urban working-class social nonmovement. In the 1980s, as we have seen, the Chinese leadership was loath to pressure the working class with measures to reform urban industry. But the 1989 movement seems to have been a turning point that emboldened the state. Even though workers increased the frequency and severity of their protestations after the crackdown, urban economic reform in the 1990s finally moved into its most thoroughgoing phases of price and labor reform, which caused inflation and unemployment to gallop ahead. Today inflation is under control, but unemployment is proceeding apace. Parts of the working class have responded with ever more demonstrations and strikes, while others have evinced broad resignation and a flight into alternative employment or other coping strategies. The state, undeterred by the former and encouraged by the latter, has gone even further since the mid-1990s by pursuing structural enterprise reform more earnestly. It is reducing its support for unprofitable firms, many of which are sinking into bankruptcy and winding up their operations, propelling unemployment ever higher.

The level of worker unrest that the state can withstand now appears to be quite a bit higher than the level previously suspected by the state and many observers. Why this has proved to be so, why the working class's mobilization against the state has not been still greater, and under what conditions it might increase, are questions that form a complex puzzle requiring a great deal of timely research. Perhaps the proletarian volcano will soon erupt – especially if China were to experience an economic meltdown akin to the 1997–98 Asian economic flu – and then the picture would look very different. But as of this writing, the egalitarian movement, which seemed the most potentially dangerous of the three movements considered in this chapter and has been perhaps the most active among them, has also accomplished the least.

Notes

1. 'China Detains Two Dissidents Over Plans for Opposition Party', *Agence France-Presse (AFP)*, 18 September 1998; *China News Digest (CND)*, 28 October 1998; 2 November 1998; 'Chinese Authorities Will Not Permit Opposition Parties: Li Peng', *AFP*, 1 December, 1998; 'China Says Xu Wenli Held on Suspicion of Damaging State Security', *AFP*, 2 December 1998.
2. Blecher (1976); Rozelle (1988); Khan and Riskin (1988, 242, 247); *CND*, 9 December 1993.
3. *China Statistical Yearbook* (1995, 597); *China Quarterly* (1995, 136: 1048).
4. *China Statistical Abstract* (1996, 2, 110); *China Statistical Yearbook* (1998, 130). The foreign investment figures refer to actual investment. Planned investments in 1995 reached $103 billion in 1995.
5. *Inside China Mainland*, October 1990, 8–9; *BBC Daily Report*, 30 April 1991; *CND*, 26 January 1993.

7
Capital, Crisis and Chaos: Indonesia and Malaysia in a Globalizing Era

Christine B. N. Chin and Sylvia C. Tiwon

The phenomenon generally labeled 'globalization' has dominated discussions increasingly in academic journals, policy forums and the popular media, particularly over the last decade. Some of the proponents of the process insist that globalization is about the remaking of a new world, envisioned as a borderless world created with the help of new communications technology, in which all peoples will have unobstructed access to resources in a global marketplace (Ohmae 1990). Detractors warn that unless we question the process by which this borderless world is constructed, we risk socioeconomic disjunction, as the rich grow richer while new groups of the poor are left to languish in what may become uninhabitable areas of the globe (Bauman 1998).

Whether for or against globalization, such stances point to fundamental changes and ensuing consequences in the ways that we use existing symbolic and material resources, create new ones, or do both. At the core lie questions about the structures of political and economic governance and the manner in which these structures should be guided toward improving the human condition, and hence social life as a whole.

Late twentieth-century globalization appears simultaneously as the panacea to and the key cause of different forms of inequality and injustice. Concerted efforts to open up markets and to ensure unobstructed trade across the globe promise (or threaten) to level any and all differences in the ways that people live and interact with each other and their physical environment. But these efforts also promise (or threaten) to underscore such differences, if not make them immutable.

Developments during the latter half of the 1990s appear to highlight this paradox of globalization. As a result of decades-long efforts to liberalize financial sectors and to integrate national and regional economies within the global economy, the financial turmoil that began in Thailand in July 1997 quickly spread to the rest of Asia and then to Latin America and Russia (Greider 1997; Henderson 1998). Unprecedented levels of currency devaluation and ensuing economic and political instability point to a crisis in the globalization process itself. They also indicate that the 1997 crisis can no longer be understood as a limited, regional phenomenon, as the oft-used rationalization of the 'Asian Flu' or 'Asian Crisis' would lead us to think.

It is significant that in Asia the rapid rise and subsequent demise of what were earlier hailed as 'miracle economies' (World Bank 1993–94) elicited accusations of inequality and injustice from different parties operating on the global and regional levels as well as at the level of nation and community. Depending on the context, the villains were variously identified as the West, the IMF, global hedge funds and speculators, the state, the security apparatus, the landlords, shopkeepers, or even clerics. In the Asian countries that suffered the most severe financial meltdown, Gramscian-style 'national-popular' movements emerged to challenge the 'common sense' that had come to characterize state hegemony in a globalizing era (Chin and Mittelman 1997). Organized and spontaneous protests, boycotts and strikes succeeded in dislodging regimes in South Korea, Thailand and Indonesia, although their counterparts thus far appear to have failed in Malaysia. In 1999, Indonesians replaced the interim government of B. J. Habibie, a former vice-president and protégé of Suharto, through street protest and the ballot box. In the case of Malaysia, an argument can be made that it is but a matter of time before Dr Mahathir Mohamad transfers power to a successor. That successor, given the logic and force of global economic restructuring, will be compelled to relinquish capital controls and partake in the kind of liberal political and economic reforms necessary to reattract much-needed capital for economic recovery and industrialization.

Over time, the unfolding crisis of globalization in Asia might contribute to an increasing strength of movements demanding equality and justice, especially from the state, and perhaps even to their eventual success. The simple passage of time cannot in and of itself effect desired transformations, however, unless these movements begin to address the historical structural inequities and injustice built into and framing existing relations between social forces.

The crisis in Asia raises an important question: how has the phenomenon of globalization shaped state–society relations? More specifically, in what ways and with what consequences have notions of equality and justice between the state and social forces been framed and addressed, particularly in multiethnic and multireligious societies within the historical context of capitalist development?

In this chapter, we examine transformations of the state's relation to social forces in the Southeast Asian countries of Indonesia and Malaysia. At the outset, these two neighboring countries, marked by significant diversity in their populations, share the regional heritage of having been subject to one or another form of European colonial rule until the mid-twentieth century. After independence and a period of turmoil – including a brief time of 'confrontation' with each other in the mid-1960s – both countries began a course of rapid economic growth beginning in the early 1970s, and succumbed to rapid economic downturn toward the end of the twentieth century. Nevertheless, closer analysis demonstrates that the separate historical trajectories of state–society relations in the respective countries have brought about different ways of coping with challenges presented by the financial turmoil in the region.

Indonesia

Shortly after the devaluation of the Thai baht, the Indonesian rupiah and the Jakarta Stock Exchange began to fall uncontrollably. By mid-1998, the rupiah had lost over 80 per cent of its value against the US dollar as market capitalization of the bourse fell by 88 per cent, or $96 billion. The economy was plunged into a recession marked by extremely high rates of unemployment and inflation (*Asiaweek*, 23 July 1998).

The rapidity with which domestic and transnational capital left the country exposed and exaggerated existing fissures in the fabric of Indonesian society. The social chaos that ensued ultimately led to the resignation of President Suharto, one of the longest-serving leaders in the region. Since Suharto's downfall, a decades-long history of corruption and repression has surfaced, revealing the fault lines in the ways in which the New Order state governed the archipelago. Why was it that relative to the size and composition of the population there had been few outright rebellions, or even open resistance before 1998? What are some of the key political, economic and social consequences of Suharto's fall from power?

Shaping state power

State–society relations in Indonesia may be understood historically as part of the complex process of nation-building from a colonial past.

One of the most complicated issues facing the nation's independence leaders in the mid-1940s was the task of governing a territory comprising more than 13 000 islands inhabited by at least 300 ethnic groups with different religious backgrounds, of which Islam was practiced by the overwhelming majority.[1] From the Dutch, Indonesians inherited a centrally controlled state apparatus and a system of patronage, particularly in Java, that used traditional rulers to exercise control over a rural population. The colonial heritage had created a small urban, educated elite that tended to dominate what Benedict Anderson (1991) calls the imagined community of nation. The majority of this varied population, however, lived in rural areas and lacked access to education and to the horizontal and vertical mobility that Anderson identifies as the processes by which a nation is shaped.

The rapid political shifts that marked the period between 1945 and 1959 may be understood as having emerged out of competing ideas of appropriate democratic and economic processes, which turned on the interpretation of the role of the state in managing a large and diverse population and a wealth of natural resources. These tensions continue to shape the political, economic and social dynamics in Indonesia today.

Indonesian independence was achieved through a revolution that broke out as the Dutch attempted to reinstate control over the colony it had been forced to abandon in the face of the Japanese occupation during the Second World War. In 1945, Indonesians under Sukarno proclaimed a new secular republic comprising the territory that had once constituted the Dutch East Indies. The new state that came into being was based on a constitution that prominently included Sukarno's *Pancasila*, the five principles affirming belief in God, nationalism, humanitarianism, democracy and social justice.[2] The state retained an entrenched bureaucracy, however and a repressive colonial legal framework (particularly in the criminal code and in a variety of political regulatory laws).

Between 1945 and 1959, the Indonesian constitution was changed three times in response to shifting allocations of power between a presidential-authoritarian structure and a parliamentary-liberal structure of governance. In 1949, the executive-heavy Constitution of 1945 was replaced by a federalist constitution which, in turn, was quickly replaced by the provisional Constitution of 1950 reinstating the centrally governed unitary state, while retaining a parliamentary cabinet system. The 1955 elections, generally recognized as the most free and open elections in the history of the nation, formed a body called the Konstituante to draft what was envisioned as the country's final constitution. However, intense pressure – including political action from the army – was already building to move the nation away from what was perceived as a liberal democratic process, while the Indonesian Communist Party (PKI) – the largest communist party outside the communist world – demanded a shift away from an increasingly liberal economy. By 1959, the Konstituante had yet to resolve the issue of the ideological foundation of the state (articulated in religious versus secular debates) when President Sukarno decreed a return to the Constitution of 1945, characterized by 'Guided Democracy', which involved the restoration of a presidential cabinet. An important part of this new political package was the concept of a 'Guided Economy' as a move away from a liberal capitalist economy. The Guided Economy was based on Article 33 of the Constitution of 1945, which conceived of the state as the ultimate arbiter of social justice and granted it control over natural resources (that is, 'the land, water and all wealth contained therein') for the greater public welfare. These events followed in the wake of wholesale nationalization of industries, particularly Dutch and British concerns (see especially Nasution 1992).

The period of Guided Democracy saw a severe retardation in economic growth as the country entered a process of rapid political and economic alienation from the West (Nasution 1992; Poulgrain 1997). Hyperinflation and virtually zero growth in export and import volumes, coupled with the perceived threat of PKI influence over policy-making, eventually led to a particularly violent period in Indonesian history. Between 1965 and 1968, General Suharto and the Indonesian armed forces wrought Sukarno's downfall and the annihilation of the PKI, with the massacre of more than a half-million citizens, perhaps as many as a million. 'Leftists' and 'communist sympathizers', including intellectuals, artists, doctors, journalists and women leaders, were detained. And all left-leaning organizations, including peasants', workers' and women's organizations, were dismantled. The elimination of these organizations marked the official end of all social movements that publicly espoused the ideal of social justice. It also marked the beginning of the combination of an authoritarian regime with a liberal economic project that freed capital as it repressed social formations outside direct state control. Some of the most repressive facets of the so-called Old Order became the foundation for New Order governance (see especially Anderson 1991). Suharto retained the Pancasila and kept the Constitution of 1945 for the enormous powers it concentrated in the hands of the presidency and its weak articulation of representative democracy and human rights, while abandoning its principle of social justice for the sake of economic growth.[3]

Since its inception, the New Order state's twin goals were to enforce political stability and to foster economic development. Political stability was pursued in distinct ways. *Pancasila* remained the ideology for 'unity in diversity', even while Jakarta retained a colonial-style relationship with the resource-rich outer islands. The central government appointed provincial leaders and determined regional budgets and tax rates, while extracting most of the wealth from these areas. Javanese citizens were 'exported' to less densely-populated outer islands through an intensive transmigration program and were appointed to the most prestigious – and lucrative – administrative positions.

Political stability meant, as well, disarming all forms of opposition, especially through the 'streamlining' of the political party system that forced all existing political parties to coalesce into two major parties: the PPP (*Partai Persatuan Pembangunan*), for Muslim parties and the PDI (*Partai Demokrasi Indonesia*) for secular nationalists and non-Muslim parties. These two parties were subordinated to the Golkar (a united front of so-called functional or nonpartisan groups) which, in effect, was the state party. (All government employees had to vote for Golkar. All members of the administrative hierarchy that reached down to the village levels and all teachers and university professors at state educational institutions were also forced to declare loyalty to Golkar.) In addition, the New Order enforced a 'floating mass' policy that prohibited the activity of political parties at the village level. Because Golkar was not officially regarded as a political party, it was exempt from this prohibition. All this was achieved through legislative approval in a legislature dominated by Golkar and through reliance on the military to quell signs of opposition.

Economic development involved a series of policy packages, particularly in the financial and industrial sectors, to liberalize and 'modernize' the national economy (Papanek 1980). Initially, these policies did not end conflicts between (neoliberal) technocrats and economic nationalists in policy-making, but the mid-1980s collapse of oil prices and changing transnational capital flows strengthened technocratic control of macroeconomic policies. The implementation of managed currency devaluation and greater economic liberalization packages worked to sustain economic growth in the wake of declining oil revenues. Foreign direct investment in Indonesia surged, especially after the 1993–94 World Bank report. In 1993, total foreign direct investment was $8.1 billion; a year later it had climbed to $23.7 billion

(Bowie and Unger 1997, 61). Repressive labor legislation and the ever-constant threat of military force to suppress overt opposition succeeded in maintaining a relatively stable and cheap labor environment to attract and keep essentially mobile capital (Winters 1996).

This path of economic development produced a new generation of state-dependent urban middle classes because it strengthened the patronage system characterized by what Indonesians later would call *Nepotisme, Kolusi, dan Korupsi* (NKK): nepotism, collusion and corruption. Patron–client relationships were duplicated from the highest echelons (that is, Suharto's immediate family and their extensive corporate holdings) to the lowest (village-level) echelons of power. Yet despite the economic dominance of Suharto friends and family, provided that the economic pie continued to grow, critics of the system generally were unable to find strong allies among the new middle classes (Robison 1996).

The Indonesian armed forces had always been a major participant in what has become known as New Order crony capitalism. Until the separation of the military from the police force in 1999, the dual function (*dwi-fungsi*) of the armed forces enabled it to participate directly in political life and legitimized its dominance of the bureaucracy and its significant role in socioeconomic development. Its corporate investments had been significant in the provision of pensions for its retired officers (Crone 1991). Apart from its own complex investment systems, however, the dominant role lay in securing stability for investments (particularly foreign investments), often through direct military deployment, as seen in the cases of the Freeport gold and copper mine in West Papua and Arco Oil in Aceh. The military's participation in the economy, to be sure, involved economic partnerships with Chinese big business. Under the system of patronage, the client's relations to the state elite facilitated acquisition of permits, licenses and even protection, in return for the receipt of profits by the patron.

The growth and expansion of Chinese conglomerates under Suharto masked what had been a sanitization of Chinese culture in the country. Fears about the political ramifications of a vibrant Chinese identity with perceived links to the People's Republic of China led to legislation that stripped the community of outward symbols of Chinese culture. Ethnic Chinese were forced to take non-Chinese (*pribumi* or 'indigenous') names. The use of Chinese languages in public and the sale and distribution of literature in Chinese were prohibited. Efforts to render the Chinese more indigenous, however, posed a major challenge with regard to distinguishing them from the local peoples. Hence, symbols of differentiation on legal and formal documents (for example, birth certificates and identity cards) were used to mark them officially as 'nonnative' citizens (non-*pribumi*). Quotas were imposed on the number of ethnic Chinese students admitted to state-run universities and schools and the Chinese were discouraged from entering the civil service and the armed forces. In postcolonial Indonesia, as in the colonial era, the Chinese were to be restricted primarily to the role of the intermediary. Significantly, the similarity/difference approach constituted the Chinese as easy scapegoats to deflect 'social jealousy' from the state elite. This closely circumscribed role of the ethnic Chinese reduced any political influence they might have had.

The social engineering of the New Order state involved the construction of an administrative structure reaching down into the family (*rumah tangga*). This system required extensive paperwork and permits, especially the *kartu tanda penduduk* ('identity card') and *surat kelakuan baik* ('good behavior papers'), without which one would be unable to get a job or attend school. The administrative structure had the power to issue, deny or revoke *surat jalan* ('walking papers' or permission to travel), permits for visitors staying for more than one night, permits for public gatherings and so forth.

Through this administrative network, the New Order state apparatus controlled the vital underpinnings of social organization and identity formation further braced by a gender policy based on the interpretation of the so-called *kodrat* ('God-given essence') of women as wives and mothers responsible for the family and subordinate to the husband as head of the household.[4] The small nuclear family, ideally composed of two adults and two children, was expected to reside in separate housing, which enabled simpler bureaucratic administration and facilitated military surveillance while it undermined the potential support offered by the structure of the traditional extended family.

This holds true particularly in the islands beyond Java, for example, among the Dayak in Kalimantan, whose traditional long-houses have been largely demolished. The nuclear family structure was expected to diminish the power of primordial ties. Relocation into single-family housing units has also been under way in West Papua. It is significant that most of the measures taken to 'civilize' people branded 'primitives' have taken place in especially resource-rich areas.

The agrarian laws of 1960 – originally drafted as a means of land reform (promoted energetically by the PKI in rural areas) – were used by the New Order state to legitimize wholesale land appropriation for the extraction of natural resources (for example, mining and timber industries), the establishment of plantations and the development of industrial, commercial and residential zones. Coupled with this, the Uniform Village Administration Act of 1979 facilitated the disruption of traditional and local forms of community organization and leadership. The family planning program (that is, the 'small happy nuclear family'), marriage laws and other state legislative instruments, including taxation, thus undermined indigenous community structures in several ways. They imposed a model of civilization (*perbadaban*) intended to bring these communities closer to the needs of the pyramidal administrative structure, while simultaneously depriving them of access to resources within their traditional environment.

Emphasis on capitalist industrialization also saw the expansion of industrial estates around the major cities and a high level of labor recruitment from rural areas, where the Green Revolution had transformed traditional labor structures and relations in the wake of the aborted land reform program and the terror of 1965–8 (Hart *et al.* 1989). Highly repressive labor regulations undermined the labor laws of the Sukarno era that had been designed to protect workers. New labor regulations, largely imposed through ministerial decree, especially favored foreign capital and gave workers (particularly the large number of young women workers in the light manufacturing industries) no bargaining power. The only recognized 'labor union' was the SPSI (*Serikat Pekerja Seluruh Indonesia*), a state-supported organization that served to protect the interests more of capital than of labor. Military intervention in labor was widespread – for example, pensioned military personnel were often hired as personnel administrators – and the military often was deployed to break up labor strikes or to maintain labor acquiescence (in some cases, terrorizing labor activists by subjecting them to torture and death).

The extensive reach of the New Order state thus appeared to leave little room for the growth of nonstate institutions. Even as policies and legislation systematically fragmented subnational community identities, rigid control over the mass media and the educational system went far toward homogenizing the national community. The deployment of death squads (ostensibly to 'protect' society from unwanted elements) underlined the seriousness with which the New Order state undertook its mission of control in the name of law and order. The notorious *Petrus* (*Penembak Misterius*, or 'mystery snipers'), for example, supposedly went after recidivist criminals, in effect practicing extrajuridical executions sanctioned not only by the government but also and significantly, by the urban propertied elite, who saw these executions as a way of maintaining 'law and order'.

Distrust of nonstate formations extended to potentially powerful religious groups, particularly the Muslims. After forcing an uneasy alliance of various Muslim political parties under the PPP, the state elite undertook to coopt and domesticate Islam by appointing cabinet ministers and key army personnel who publicly espoused Muslim values, granting substantial funds to mosques and other Islamic institutions, and appointing the powerful Council of Ulama. The state also eventually formed the Muslim Intellectual Association under the aegis of B. J. Habibie, at that time the influential Minister of Research.

However, such tight control over the population and the contradictions it wrought would sow the seeds of the New Order's eventual dissolution. Already in the early 1970s, what could be called Polanyian double movements formed in response to New Order-style capitalist development, as protests were raised by the university community against corruption, mismanagement of resources and the injustices of the development program. Opposition to state control also emerged from under the banner of Islam, notably in protest against the 1974 Marriage Laws, which regulated polygamy. In the 1980s, Nahdlatul Ulama under its influential leader, Abdurrahman Wahid, announced its dissociation from party politics because of its opposition to state intervention in the expression of religious identity.

The rise of an emerging working-class consciousness could be seen in the increasingly frequent and vocal labor strikes and rallies. Such demonstrations were not restricted physically to the factories, as the workers carried their protests against exploitative industrial relations to the streets, to the Ministry of Manpower and to Parliament. During the 1980s, students and university graduates who began to form a number of NGOs were generally critical of and opposed to the social, political and economic inequalities cultivated by the New Order's specific mode of governance (Eldridge 1995). The New Order state clamped down quickly, often deploying the military to quell public expressions of protest and often with violence that led to bloodshed in a number of incidents.

By the early 1990s, resentment of state control had become widespread. The banning of three major publications, particularly the prestigious newsmagazine *TEMPO*, brought the middle classes to the streets in open protest. New labor unions were formed that declared their independence from the state (see especially Aspinall 1996; Heryanto 1996). When the state elite engineered the removal of Megawati Sukarnoputri as head of PDI, a vocal segment within the party refused to recognize the new party chair elected through a process manipulated by the state. This act of resistance eventually led to a severe crackdown by the military but, paradoxically, gave the public a high-profile opposition figure in the person of Megawati, daughter of deposed President Sukarno.

The 1998 'reformasi'

The financial turmoil of mid-1997 suddenly weakened state control over the economy and quickly transformed into a full-blown economic crisis that revealed the vast dimensions of a sociopolitical crisis manifested in mass protests by various social groupings. By early 1998, demonstrations and mass action in the streets had become almost daily events. Coverage of these events was broadcast over the entire region and the world via cable television networks CNBC Asia and CNN and throughout Indonesia via the nationwide satellite system, which brought television to the remotest islands. The Internet was instrumental in helping university protesters evade surveillance and distribute opposition material to the masses. Taxi drivers, for example, displayed downloaded Internet materials, which anyone could purchase from them on the streets at traffic intersections.

Global and domestic pressure eventually convinced Suharto to step down. He then transferred the presidency to his protégé and vice-president, B. J. Habibie, an engineer with little political experience, who professed a form of economic nationalism and who had a background of conflict with the military.

Two important points emerged from Habibie's first televised speech in his capacity as the self-declared 'reform' president: (1) development would continue to be controlled by the state; and (2) as president, he had taken over the position of commander-in-chief of the armed forces, suggesting that he had settled a perceived split within the military over his ascent to power and was now fully in charge. The message was that, with the exception of superficial changes, Habibie would govern in much the same way as had his mentor. The army was quick to fashion a role for itself in the reform movement, publicly declaring its support for Habibie in a move to divest itself of involvement with Suharto.

Nevertheless, mass protests continued with some quickly escalating into mini-popular revolts. Peasants who had been evicted from their land began to reclaim golf courses and fenced-off areas designated for development, particularly those linked to the Suharto family. Even

Suharto's showcase cattle ranch was invaded by locals, who staked out individual lots on which to plant their crops. The word *reformasi* began to show up, carved out in large letters across golfing greens, as peasants grasped the opportunity to define their own version of reform: that is, land reform necessary for subsistence rather than for the expansion of cash-crops for export or for the luxurious pastimes of the urban elite. Peasants also stormed plantations, hacking down palm-oil trees and replacing them with other crops. Entire villages arose to depose unpopular village leaders whom villagers perceived as allies of Golkar. Workers began to join forces with student and peasant protesters, demanding the repeal of the 1997 Manpower Laws that were slated to remove state intervention in industrial relations. Liberal in spirit, these laws would eliminate entirely any semblance of state protection of workers against exploitation and were an important spearhead of the move toward shrinking state power *vis-à-vis* capital.

An assault on Habibie's legitimacy claims to reform came from the Team of Volunteers for Humanitarian Causes, which began to issue reports on its investigation into the May riots. At least 1200 people had lost their lives in the conflagration and hundreds of ethnic Chinese women had been raped. Initial news reports had blamed the events on rioters and looters from among the urban poor. The reports, however, began to uncover evidence that the riots had been deliberately provoked by security forces and paid paramilitary squads. The Habibie cabinet initially questioned the veracity of the accounts. When the president was first asked to comment on the economic impact of the flight of ethnic Chinese capital and persons from Indonesia, he responded defiantly: 'Do you really think that we will then die[?] ... [Their] place will be taken over by others' (*Far Eastern Economic Review*, 30 July 1998: 13). Whatever the actual motivation of the provoked urban riots and anti-Chinese actions, they had a significant initial impact on the nascent social movement for reform.

The fear inspired by these chaotic incidents of what appeared to be the urban poor 'running amok' redrew the lines separating the middle classes from the *rakyat* ('the common people') and separating the campus from the *kampung* ('village', or settlements of the urban poor). Even when Habibie relented under pressure to hold general elections in 1999, the effort to divide and rule continued. Whereas student protesters were said to constitute a moral force as 'heroes of reform', for example, the masses were labeled *penjarah* ('looters and rioters') by the military and local media. The international media would follow suit in its broadcasting of what seemed to be growing anarchy in the archipelago.

Such divisive discursive tactics increasingly were seen to accompany, if not directly fuel, the spate of rioting. And the riots (which appeared to involve deep ethnic and religious animosities, especially in Ketapang, Jakarta, Maluku, Kalimantan and East Java) threatened to tear the country apart. In April 1999, Minister of Justice Muladi stated publicly on national television that the incidents led to the impression that Indonesia was an 'indigenous country'. He used the term 'indigenous' as a euphemism for 'primitive', thus implying that Indonesians could not possibly be ready for democratic governance in the multiethnic, multireligious country.

Threats of food shortages, runaway inflation and capital flight continue to be immediate concerns, as are the state's halfhearted efforts to locate and repatriate the Suharto family's purported wealth (*Time-Asia*, 24 May 1999). In the debates, the IMF has played the role of the villain, mainly because it had been extremely slow in disbursing aid even after Suharto's resignation. The overwhelming focus – at least among the urban elite – has been on efforts to regain economic ground. Little concern has been voiced for the possible impact of the structural adjustment (finance and economic reform) package itself on the lives of the working poor and on the natural environment, as the drive begins to secure capital investment and foreign exchange.

In the run-up to and the completion of the June 1999 general elections, the military became restrained in the use of repressive violence. Its restraint is best explained by two factors. The first is the existence of a large international presence in the country and the pressure it exerted. The second is the effect of evidence of military atrocities unearthed since the fall of Suharto. It severely undermined the military's public image as 'maintainer of law and order', even to the extent that it was forced to abolish military operations against separatists in Aceh, East Timor and Irian Jaya (Indonesia Labour Information Institute 1999).

The elections appear, on the surface, to be a victory for the people. The apolitical Muslim leader Wahid and long-time dissident Megawati serve as president and vice-president. Yet the international financial institutions remain the government's closest economic adviser, and there has been little open debate as yet on how to conceive the role of the state *vis-à-vis* its people, on the one hand and transnational capital, on the other. Futhermore, debate has not questioned whether freeing capital from the shackles of patronage and state intervention will secure social justice for the diverse population on the archipelago. The second half of a Polanyian double movement may have begun, but its institutional consequences have yet to emerge.

Malaysia

When Suharto stepped down as president of Indonesia on 21 May 1998, many observers of Southeast Asia also anticipated the resignation of Dr Mahathir Mohamad, the Malaysian prime minister since 1981. Political instability had begun to become apparent in Malaysia at a time in which the Malaysian ringgit had depreciated by at least 40 per cent of its value against the US dollar, while the local bourse gave up over 76 per cent of its value, or $216 billion (*Asiaweek*, 23 July 1998). However, the major political casualty was not Mahathir but his protégé Anwar Ibrahim. In September 1998, Anwar was unceremoniously relieved of his several positions as deputy prime minister, finance minister and deputy president of United Malays National Organization (UMNO). The arrest of Anwar, his physical abuse at the hands of the Inspector-General of Police, police harassment of his family and supporters and the conduct of his trial elicited mass demonstrations, protests, riots and the consequent formation of oppositional movements calling for various reforms in governance. Today, the movements necessarily must confront a long history of fragmented resistance because of the historical legacy of social relations that have shaped how inequality and injustice have been addressed in Malaysian society.

The New Economic Policy: legislating ethnic socioeconomic equality

When the Alliance Party assumed control of Malaya from the British in 1957, it did so under a multiethnic coalition of UMNO, the Malayan Chinese Association (MCA) and the Malayan Indian Congress (MIC). The nonviolent Bargain of '57 extended citizenship to non-Malays in return for their recognition of Malay Special Privileges (MSP) in the constitution. Among the privileges provided for were continuity of Malay reservation land and Malay royalty's symbolic role as protectors of Islam and leaders of the people (Milne and Mauzy 1978). The bargain implicitly apportioned political supremacy to Malays while it allowed non-Malays the enjoyment of unobstructed capital accumulation processes in the economy.

Until 1969, European capitalist pursuits – supplemented by a burgeoning Chinese capitalist class – continued relatively unencumbered as the Alliance Party managed the country. Commodity export-driven development during the 1960s, which maintained the colonial geo-ethnic division of labor (that is, rural areas dominated by Malay peasantry and urban areas characterized by the presence of Chinese and Indian professionals and proletariats), had masked growing economic gaps within each ethnic community. The perception that only a handful of the political and business elite from each ethnic community had been benefiting from the development path and that each ethnic group was losing ground in relation to the others culminated in the 13 May 1969 postelection riots between the two largest ethnic groups, Malays and Chinese. What had been economic inequalities between and within the ethnic communities were to be expressed solely along the ethnic divide created and nurtured by colonialism (Brennan 1982; Brown 1994).

The May 1969 riots, in effect, forced the postcolonial state elite to clarify and implement its practice of pursuing socioeconomic equality in Malaysian society. The neat delineation of who controlled which arena was dismantled when the country emerged from nearly two years of emergency rule. The Alliance Party was restructured into the larger *Barisan Nasional* (National Front) in which UMNO became the undisputed leader, as public discussion and parliamentary debates on MSP were strictly prohibited.

The mostly *laissez-faire* development path was replaced by the New Economic Policy 1971–90 (NEP), an affirmative action development program for Malays, the largest ethnic group, which constituted slightly over 50 per cent of the population (Lim 1985). The state apparatus, now irrefutably controlled by UMNO, was expanded and charged with leveling the socioeconomic playing field for Malays. Related policies and legislation encouraged Malay urban in-migration, imposed Malay quotas in the public and private sectors, established financial and nonfinancial public enterprises catering to the Malay community and redistributed corporate wealth from non-Malays to Malays. These measures were expected to facilitate the transformation of the predominantly rural Malay society into urban Malay professional and business communities.

Initially, the NEP was based on a 'redistribution first, growth later' philosophy. This specific path of development via state trusteeship was made possible by a changing international division of labor and by rises in commodity prices during the 1970s. Together, they created the perception of an ever-growing economic pie in which the Malay portion would be increased without either shrinking or seeming to shrink those of the non-Malay communities. In the aftermath of the May 13 riots, the politically weakened non-Malay parties within the National Front created investment arms to address economic issues of their respective communities without having to confront directly their lack of bargaining power *vis-à-vis* UMNO.

By the early 1980s, a capital-intensive heavy industrialization program that Prime Minister Mahathir launched in the early days of his
mandate proved to be ill-timed – coming in the midst of sharp declines
in oil and other commodity prices – and ultimately dictated the state's
retreat from the economy. State elites realized that economic recovery
from the mid-1980s recession would entail the pursuit of liberalization
and privatization projects aimed at attracting and retaining transnational capital. Yet the gradual privatization of key industries took the
form of transferring control and ownership of state enterprises to
investment companies that were linked to UMNO and, to a lesser
extent, MCA and MIC political-business elites (Gomez and Jomo 1997).

Postcolonial efforts were undertaken to redress the colonial legacy by
officially leveling the playing field for Malays in an era of the transnationalization of capital and production. Such efforts at redress had come
to mean much more than the provision of jobs and the redistribution
of wealth. Polanyian double movements developed, as seen in the
demands of a variety of social forces: for example, the alliance between
students and peasantry called for greater state subsidies. Organized
labor demanded the right to work protection. Environmentalists called
for the right to a toxin-free environment. Indigenous peoples demanded
the right to ancestral land. The Chinese community demanded the
right to cultural continuity. Islamicists called for the right to religious
lifestyles and governance (which included vocal critiques of the
conduct of young Malay women factory workers). And the opposition
parties called for the right to demand state accountability in economic
privatization processes and the oversight of financial institutions
(Committee Against Repression in the Pacific and Asia 1988). By 1987,
divisions within the rank and file of UMNO over control of policies for
the Malay community had resulted in a highly publicized legal battle
and temporarily threatened Mahathir's control over the party and the
state apparatus (Means 1991).

Under siege from several fronts, the state's repressive arm was
deployed in the October 1987 'Ops Lallang', as the police invoked
the Internal Security Act (ISA) to detain without trial 109 labor union
leaders, academics, politicians, lawyers, businesspeople and hawkers
from different ethnic communities. The ISA originated in colonial
anticommunist legislation and empowered authorities to detain any
person for a specified period without trial.

The official rationale for the 1987 police crackdown was to contain
the spread of 'racial and religious extremism' and 'communist' influence in society. State deployment of the ISA, among other repressive

legislation, reconfirmed that the demands of social forces could not be articulated by way of public discussion, protests or demonstrations.

As dissent was silenced, policy-makers continued to adjust quickly to the changing global and regional economic environment. Ongoing and proposed infrastructural projects, tax holidays and tariff reductions were some of the initiatives adopted to attract new flows in transnational capital redirected to Southeast Asia after the 1985 Plaza Accord, which realigned the Group of Seven currencies. Malaysia, with its improving transportation and communication networks and the presence of a relatively depoliticized labor force, quickly became an even bigger host to foreign direct investment in the region. State legislation, 'in-house' unions in the burgeoning electronics industries and the continued ethnically skewed union memberships in certain sectors converged to ensure labor acquiescence (Jomo and Todd 1994; Ramasamy 1994).

Since the UMNO-controlled state's existence and legitimacy were premised on the protection of Malay rights and welfare, the NEP's successor – the National Development Policy 1991–2000 – planned to continue to pursue wealth creation and equalization on behalf of Malays. However, it would do so in the context of an increasingly open economy. As the economy experienced sustained growth at roughly 8 per cent per annum, the entire country seemed immersed in helping to realize Mahathir's Vision 2020 of creating a modern, developed, technologically literate society and economy by that year. The constant inflow of long- and short-term capital provided a sense of unstoppable wealth creation that encouraged the expansion of the middle classes and new consumption-oriented lifestyles, the construction of massive infrastructural projects and the in-migration of low-wage workers from neighboring countries to address the economy's insatiable demands for domestic servants, waitresses and construction and agri-plantation workers (Chin 1998).

By the mid-1990s, the most visible threat to state legitimacy would not come from any particular constituency as distinguished in ethnicized, class-based, gendered or religious terms. Rather, the threat would be identified as having come from abroad.

Patriots and traitors

In the mid-1990s, the state elite announced that construction work would begin on the Bakun Dam in Sarawak. By creating a lake the size of Singapore, the dam would be a major source of hydroelectric power and national pride for Malaysia. The deputy director-general (sectoral) of the Economic Planning Unit said, 'Like the Petronas Twin Towers and the Kuala Lumpur Tower, the Bakun Hydroelectric Dam will be a symbol of our nation's ability to build world class structures. It is among a series of megaprojects ... [that] would put Malaysia prominently on the world map' (*Star [Malaysia]*, 15 March 1996).

The Bakun project did put Malaysia on the world map, but for reasons other than those foreseen by this official. Forty organizations from Peninsular and East Malaysia came together to form a coalition called *Gabungan*. It became the umbrella that encompassed several opposition political parties, together with NGOs that specialized in specific issues ranging from the environment, religion, trade, social justice and human rights to youth, indigenous peoples, women and migrant and plantation workers.

Gabungan scaled down and across to link with various community groups. It also scaled up to link with foreign powers and NGOs in order to publicize the issues involved and to gain support from the domestic and international public against the construction of the dam (see especially *Star*, 1 October 1996; 24 May 1997). The majority of participating organizations were skewed toward particular ethnic, class, gender and religious groups. But their ability to tease out the interrelated potential consequences of the Bakun project presented a significant collective threat to the state because it became extremely difficult for the authorities to revert to accusations of communist or extremist religious and racial influences.[5]

The coalition organized write-in campaigns and nonviolent demonstrations at public and private institutions that had direct and indirect interests in the project. State authorities responded by using the Police Act 1967 on several occasions to prohibit or to disperse public gatherings (*Sun [Malaysia]*, 23 May 1996). In response to a lawsuit won by the indigenous peoples to stop work on Bakun, the clearly irritated prime minister said, 'It is about time that our NGOs think of themselves as Malaysians. They are totally irresponsible. They do not love their country at all' (*Sun*, 28 June 1996; Heyzer 1995). Mahathir identified Western interests as responsible for inciting Malaysians to protest against what he considered necessary for the continued rapid industrialization of the economy and country. From his perspective, the activities of the Malaysian coalition threatened to betray over two decades' worth of efforts to move the status of the country from developing to developed. The federal government succeeded in having the verdict overturned in the court of appeals (*Star*, 20 June 1996). Nevertheless, the construction of the dam has been postponed indefinitely because of the financial turmoil.

The severe economic downturn that began in mid-1997 only sharpened Mahathir's public rhetoric on the 'threat of the West' toward stability and prosperity in Malaysia. He accused George Soros, manager of the global Quantum Fund, of being the party primarily responsible for the downward slide of the ringgit. In light of a series of currency devaluations and attempted currency devaluations from East to Southeast Asia, the prime minister's vociferous denunciations of currency speculators resonated well both within and beyond Malaysia. Even local opposition leaders voiced their support for his call to regulate foreign exchange transactions. Consumer International held a conference attended by NGOs throughout Asia and Australia in early 1998 that blamed the absence of international financial and monetary supervision for causing the crisis in the region, and hence hardship for the peoples (*Star*, 16 March 1998). The failure of the OECD to push through its unilaterally determined Multilateral Agreement on Investment (only later to have it resurrected in the IMF's proposal to place capital accounts under its jurisdiction) fueled a growing belief that international organizations controlled by advanced industrialized countries in the West were intent on removing all barriers to foreign exchange control and foreign ownership of national financial sectors (*Star*, 31 March 1998).

Under the prime minister's leadership, the state apparatus and political elite were mobilized – and, in turn, mobilized the people – to defend the economy and country. Public and private sector owned media consistently ran lead articles exhorting all Malaysians to be loyal to the country and to unite against unscrupulous foreigners, whose intention was to create chaos and underdevelop the country. Campaigns featuring mainstream politicians from all ethnic groups in Malaysia served two purposes: to reduce the outflow of currency (for example, the Love Malaysia, Buy Malaysian Products campaign); and to remind the populace to keep a constant vigil against the potentially disruptive effects of the situation on interethnic relations. News reports of the rapidly declining political, economic and social conditions in neighboring Indonesia could not but enhance the level of patriotism at home. Significantly, visual images of anti-Chinese riots in Indonesia were not broadcast, for fear of destabilizing Chinese–Malay relations in the country. Toward the end of 1998 and in the midst of mass demonstrations after Anwar's arrest, however, the media would begin broadcasting images of Indonesian ethnic and religious riots. The move may have been designed to counsel the Malaysian Chinese against any intent to participate *en masse* in pro-Anwar, or conversely anti-Mahathir, demonstrations (see especially *Far Eastern Economic Review*, 3 December 1998).

Extensive media coverage of the prime minister's explanations of the crisis in Asia, his call to regulate international currency speculation and capital flows and his criticism of IMF programs in the most severely affected Asian countries directed the public's attention and discourse to international rather than domestic causes of the economic downturn in the country. Daily reports of foreign interests – especially Western corporations purchasing the cheap assets of failed banks and finance companies from Tokyo to Bangkok – illustrated his argument that, at worst, the crisis in Asia was planned to facilitate Western recolonization of the country and region.

Although the crisis elicited consumer protests against the IMF in South Korea and Thailand and against the state in Indonesia, similar incidences did not exist in Malaysia. Indeed, the refusal to adopt an IMF-type measure eliminating public subsidies for basic food items was a major contributing factor to the absence of mass consumer protests in the country. More significant were the ways in which Malaysian women and labor unions became involved in keeping prices down.

Recognizing the gender traditionally responsible for managing the household, Minister of Transportation Ling Liong Sik said that women are the 'ministers of finance, tourism, home affairs, education and consumer affairs in a household because they are the ones who decide on daily matters. Men are considered foreign affairs ministers as they are not in the house most of the time and do not decide much on household matters' (*Star*, 4 February 1998). In a bold stroke, he validated (albeit under economic duress) what some scholars long had argued (that is, the welfare of the country and the welfare of the household are mutually dependent), while appealing to women's sense of patriotism. Campaigns for women (*wanita*) to come together and demonstrate their national love and pride were organized by *Wanita MCA* and witnessed the participation of 5000 to 10000 women in each state. *Wanita UMNO's Ehsan Wanita* Campaign encouraged women to save for the country (*Star*, 9 February 1998). Malay and non-Malay middle-class women in particular pledged to save as much as they could, to donate their jewelry as a way to increase the country's reserves and when possible, to buy only Malaysian-made products.

Meanwhile, the Ministry of Domestic Trade and Consumer Affairs made efforts to cap price increases of basic consumer items, such as sugar and oil and also capitalized on the activities of some unions to keep prices down. In early 1998, the Malaysian Trades Union Congress

(MTUC) and the Congress of Unions of Employees in the Public and Civil Services (CUEPACS) organized a boycott of chicken sellers to protest against price hikes that were considered to be unreasonable. Approximately one month later, the farmers' association reported that 30 per cent of chicken breeders had had to fold their operations temporarily, because they were unable to sell their stock even at discount prices (*Star*, 15 April 1998). State authorities chose to stay out of the boycott issue, relying instead on the unions to restrict price hikes in other items without having to issue further directives: producers or distributors then had to contend with MTUC and CUEPACS instead of the Ministry of Domestic Trade and Consumer Affairs.

Efforts by MTUC and CUEPACS to organize a boycott of fish, however, led to public criticism by the Federation of Malaysian Consumers' Associations (FOMCA). The latter argued that, in a period of economic crisis, boycotts of producers were counterproductive, given that the producers were Malaysians who also were affected by the depreciation of the currency. Instead, FOMCA suggested that the two other unions stick to their original missions: that is, to protect the rights of labor (*Star*, 10 March 1998). Despite attempts to connect the issue of labor to consumer rights, coalition building between MTUC, CUEPACS and FOMCA was mitigated by the latter's sense of preserving and appealing first and foremost to national unity.

The seemingly smooth path that patriotism took in suffusing the public arena soon became conflictual when state elites were faced with the need for effective policy responses to stabilize the economy. In his capacity as finance minister, Anwar Ibrahim introduced 'IMF measures without IMF assistance' to curtail sharply public expenditure and the growth of imports and credit (*Sun*, 13 January 1998). Not only did his mentor disagree with the measures, but Mahathir also argued that relaxation of the NEP's Malay corporate equity rule would be temporary (to allow non-Malays to buy into Malay-owned corporations), because he preferred to keep corporate control in Malaysian hands rather than foreign hands (*Star*, 26 February 1998). However, in order to maintain foreign investor confidence in the economy, Anwar insisted that the relaxation of the equity rule was a permanent policy, not a temporary one. Torn between the need to lure back investment capital to bolster a vulnerable economy and the need to protect specifically Malay interests, Anwar's choice of the former option projected him as being pro-IMF and pro-West, especially in light of the parameters of public discourse that already had been established by his mentor.

Salient policy differences between the prime minister and his deputy stoked rumors of a potential challenge to the presidency of UMNO, hence the stewardship of the country. (To add fuel to the fire, the Employees' Provident Fund had been used to bail out key corporations, among them one controlled by Mirzan Mahathir, the prime minister's son.) A public debate ensued about Western media reports of cronyism and nepotism in the management of Malaysia's economy. Implicit in the debate was the call for Mahathir's resignation. He retaliated by saying that such accusations were spoken by foreigners (read: Westerners), to be supported by certain Malaysians who sought to force him from power. At the UMNO General Assembly (in an indirect reference to his heir apparent, Anwar Ibrahim), Mahathir warned that whoever replaced him would 'submit to the wishes of foreign powers ... [and would be] prepared to have his country once again re-colonized' (*Asiaweek*, 3 July 1998). To prove that the accusations of cronyism and nepotism had no basis, he declassified a long list of individuals and corporations that had been awarded privatization contracts or equity (according to NEP rules) in public-listed corporations. The implication was that if crony-like behavior suffused the entire economy, then either it could not be labeled cronyism or every beneficiary (Malay and non-Malay) was his crony, including all Malays who had ever gained from education and employment quotas or from below market-interest rates for bank loans. Mahathir succeeded in linking the issue of cronyism to the very basis of the NEP: that is, affirmative action for Malays. According to an UMNO member, as soon as such a connection was made, all of Mahathir's UMNO critics and potential detractors 'had no other way but to defend the NEP' (*Asiaweek*, 3 July 1998).

Direct and indirect state control of the media aided in creating and enforcing the two categories of public voice: patriots and traitors. The construction and acceptance of this oppositional dyad in public discourse both anticipated and helped curtail criticisms and accusations of inequality and injustice that arose from the implementation of certain policies (including corporate bail-out policies) that had greatly benefited politically connected Malay, Chinese and Indian tycoons and their related complex web of corporate holdings (see especially Gomez and Jomo 1997).

Malaysian responses to the financial turmoil revealed how structural constraints continue to influence the expression of certain dimensions of identity over others. What appear as divided loyalties are the product of fragmented identities: that is, within the larger context of state manipulation of identities, the privileging of one dimension of identity may be read and has come to be read, as the subordination (and even betrayal) of others. At the height of the economic recession, the boundaries of what it meant to be a patriot or a traitor were tightened considerably in public discourse. In this way, dissent within and beyond the state apparatus could not but face either self-censorship and public humiliation at best or detention at worst.

By September 1998, the culmination of Mahathir's stance toward the alleged meddling of foreign influences in the domestic economy and politics took two forms. He imposed a series of capital control measures that would reverse the course of financial liberalization adopted by Anwar. (For example, the ringgit was completely withdrawn from international circulation and the flow of short-term capital was severely restricted.) He also purged the state apparatus and UMNO of all real and perceived dissenters. For at least three days after the announcement of capital controls, the Kuala Lumpur Stock Exchange indices appreciated sharply, by over 30 per cent. Malaysians appeared to affirm nationalist efforts to defend the currency and economy. Domestic opposition parties and even development-based NGOs initially lauded the prime minister's capital control measures (see *Star*, 3–6 September 1998).

The case of Deputy Prime Minister Anwar Ibrahim, however, soon changed the political landscape. Anwar's key supporters in the corporate, media, political, academic and bureaucratic worlds were either detained under the ISA or forced to resign their posts. Anwar was arrested, physically abused, made to stand trial and subsequently convicted of sexual misconduct and corruption. In 1998, Kampung Baru in Kuala Lumpur, which was the original site of the 13 May 1969 riots, once again became the first site of riots and protests. This time, however, the target of the unrest was not another ethnic group but unjust political and economic governance.

Three oppositional movements arose as Malaysians reacted to the manner in which Anwar was sacked and detained. Anwar's *Reformasi* movement, patterned after the successful Indonesian student-led reform movements and peopled by his Islamic constituency base (from his earlier years as the leader of ABIM, an Islamic youth movement), demonstrated for economic justice and for anticorruption and antidiscriminatory practices. *Gagasan* (the Coalition of People's Democracy), comprised mostly of the urban, multiethnic, professional middle classes, called for justice and freedom of expression. *Gerak* (Malaysian People's Movement), dominated by rural and working-class Malay-Muslims, demanded the abolition of the ISA. *Gagasan* and *Gerak* formed an alliance with one another, but not with *Reformasi*, arguing that 'it is not a campaign for Anwar' (*Asiaweek*, 30 October 1998). The common denominator for all three movements, however, was their collective demand for the abolition of the ISA.

In the face of direct and indirect state control over local media, Malaysians have relied on the Internet to exchange information. Over 50 websites were established for analysis, news and critique of the many different ways in which Mahathir and UMNO had become unaccountable in their control over the state apparatus and economy of the country (*Asian Wall Street Journal*, 30 March 1999). The state elite's responses have been to deploy riot-control police or the ISA to stem protests, to set up an official website on which to lodge public expressions of support for the prime minister and his policies and to investigate the possibility of censoring cyberspace.

Despite Mahathir's ability to win reelection in late 1999 against a fragmented opposition, his government is not completely secure. Anwar's case has politically fragmented Malaysian society, especially along specific ethnic, class and religious dimensions. UMNO's unofficial survey of the public revealed that seven out of ten Malays were unhappy with the stewardship of the country (*Far Eastern Economic Review*, 12 November 1998). The non-Malay middle classes are said to support demands for political reform but remain cautious of support for Anwar, because of his Islamic base and identity. Not surprisingly, the country's Malay, Chinese and Indian business elites continue openly to support Mahathir (*Asiaweek*, 30 October 1998; *Far Eastern Economic Review*, 12 November 1998).

In anticipation of the general elections in late 1999, Anwar's wife, Wan Azizah Wan Ismail, together with Chandra Muzaffar (a social activist and professor who was sacked from the Universiti Malaya) formed the National Justice Party (NJP) to cull votes from disaffected members of the public. In an interview published in *Asiaweek*, 16 April 1999, Azizah made it clear that NJP's social base was Malay, 'but we hope it will also be supported by non-Malays. Remember: this movement started from the Malays. It is natural for the leader to be of Malay ethnic origin.' When asked of her plan to continue or discontinue the spirit of the NEP, she responded, 'Justice for all would include moving toward a society that values ability and excellence. But the main goals of the policy [NEP] – the eradication of poverty and the stabilization of ethnic relations through economic justice – must remain.'

Malaysia's incorporation into the global capitalist order has elicited opportunities and setbacks for transcending social differences that have characterized the multiethnic society. Expressions of love for society and country can encourage and have encouraged incidences of coalition-building across ethnic, class, gender and religious dimensions. But such expressions are subverted by state manipulation of identities in the continued context of a specific path of public–private sector elite control over capital accumulation structures and processes. As of 2000, the result has been sharp political fragmentation manifested in the interlocking vertical and horizontal cleavages along the identity dimensions that characterize membership in the three movements and the NJP.

Conclusion

Discussion of the changing relationship between the state and social forces in Indonesia and Malaysia evinces two key interrelated themes: the state's role in dictating what could be considered equal and just in political, economic and social life; and the consequent conceptualization of nationalism in a globalizing era. Prior to the period of financial turmoil, the kind of common sense that undergirds state hegemony actively was affirmed and reaffirmed by a series of interdependent factors: the overt and covert manipulation of social identities and relations, the use of coercive force or legislation to silence dissent and the opening of national economies mediated through the respective and specific particularities of public–private sector alliances in Indonesia and Malaysia.

In Indonesia, state hegemony rested mostly on the use of coercive and repressive force that was ensured by (and ensured) the primacy of the military's role in the political, bureaucratic and economic arenas. In Malaysia, however, the relative absence of a historical role for the military did not make repressive governance ineffective. Rather, the 13 May 1969 riots became a memorialized weapon and the basis for an increasingly ethnicized, gendered and class-based state apparatus to insert itself into and dictate (via the NEP), the conduct of everyday life.

After about a decade of sustained economic growth, the immediate and massive outflow of transnational capital from both economies began to expose structural inequities and injustice that had come to characterize and support the path of rapid industrialization. Hence, the common sense that undergirds state hegemony began to unravel in the face of demands and accusations from and between, different sets of social forces. Although Indonesia's New Order state ultimately buckled under the pressure of student-led popular reform movements throughout the archipelago, state elites in Malaysia quickly moved to frame public discourse that initially mitigated oppositional action from society. It was only after Mahathir's removal of Anwar Ibrahim as finance minister, deputy prime minister and deputy president of UMNO that mass demonstrations, protests and riots erupted in the Malaysian capital. The catalyst then, was not the immediate responses of social forces to the negative economic effects of the financial turmoil, but the ways in which the second-highest-ranking political bureaucrat had been treated by his mentor, the police, the judiciary and UMNO.

Today, the continued insistence of transnational capital for greater economic reform as a prerequisite for its return to the region is echoed by peoples who call for accountability and transparency in state allocation of economic and financial resources. For protesters, especially those from the middle classes, the Internet became a medium (first in Indonesia, then in Malaysia) through which state-controlled information channels were bypassed to share knowledge within and beyond the country and through which to organize resistance against a repressive state apparatus. In this sense, infrastructural and seemingly ideological linkages (that is, the demands for accountability and transparency) evince a transnationalization of reform movements in both countries. It is evident as well from the Malaysian case that events in neighboring Indonesia can either help or undermine the state elite in its ability to manage dissent. Conversely, these events can embolden or discourage oppositional forces (for example, when convenient, visual images of riots in Indonesia were allowed to be broadcast in Malaysia to instill fear in the non-Malay communities).

Presently, the viability of reform movements in both countries rests on redefinitions of what can be considered equal and just in the construction of a new common sense as the foundation for the state and for whole ways of life. In different ways and to different degrees, what we continue to witness in post-Suharto Indonesia and in Malaysia is that the state elite in each country continues to draw on a history of manipulating social identities to frame public discourse that pits citizens against one another.

Given the specific historical trajectories and resultant social structures of Indonesian and Malaysian state–society relations, what is left unaddressed is the fundamental philosophical foundation of globalized neoliberal restructuring, an inescapable context that envelops and shapes any discussion and action toward reconstituting social identities, relations and structures characteristic of a shared sense of equality and justice. In both countries, the state elite's financial pact with their respective essential supporters greatly exaggerated what was already becoming a skewed relationship between capital and classes in rapid industrialization. Attempts to seize control of the state apparatus and to reform the dominant mode of governance without addressing the capital–class and state–capital relationships promise new tensions or affirmations (or both) of existing contestations between different social forces already fragmented by specific identity differences.

When national-popular movements in homogeneous societies capture the state, a key challenge will be dealing with class and gender disparities wrought by neoliberal restructuring. When national-popular movements in multiethnic and multireligious societies are able to capture the state, then the question of which ethnic or religious group assumes control of the state apparatus may, and probably will, become a major issue. In Malaysia, for example, its modern history allowed for one attempt at consociationalism that ultimately failed, resulting in a masking of class distinctions in favor of an emphasis (or a re-emphasis) on ethnicity. Ethnic identity is not primordial, but a long history of identity manipulation to justify particular state policies and legislation (whether in Indonesia or Malaysia) helps ensure its primacy in public discourse and consciousness. Such primacy greatly shapes what can be considered and accepted by the peoples as equal and just in the access to and allocation of resources.

Taken one step further, the unfolding of the crisis also highlights the pursuit of relatively different notions of nationalism. In Malaysia today, loyal citizens are considered to be those who would defend the state, economy and society against domestic traitors and foreign saboteurs. Those who dare to disagree are those who would betray what is considered the country's modern legacy of sociopolitical stability and economic growth. This 'outward' oriented dualistic conceptualization and this pursuit of a nationalism that sharply distinguishes between patriots and traitors sustains state legitimacy by containing the perceived damaging effects of the transnationalization of issues, discourse and action.

Across the Melaka Straits, loyal Indonesian citizens were those who demanded Suharto's return of the state, society and economy to the people. Those who dared to disagree were those who would betray the people's right to livelihood, freedom, protection and so forth. In the post-Suharto era, the conceptualization and pursuit of nationalism appears increasingly to be focused 'inward'. The potential of internal geofragmentation increased as Indonesians negotiated the granting of either independence or autonomy to the East Timorese. Since the former route has been taken, the potential may exist for Irian Jaya and Aceh to secede from the republic as well. The shape of the archipelago's future will depend on the ability to construct an Indonesian nation (to be decided partly by whether or not the military retreats to the barracks) that can effectively transcend what appear to be essentialized identities, from which the state elite continue to affirm and manipulate in the practice of divide and rule.

World Bank President James Wolfensohn said in March 1998 that he expected 'a new miracle in Asia' to be possible within a few years. He cautioned, however, that 'if it is a miracle, then it is likely to have a sounder base, more open, more transparent, more governed by international standards of finance' (*Star*, 30 March 1998). Wolfensohn expects the crisis to produce more democratic forms of governance in the fully liberalized Asian economic region. To be sure, Indonesians and Malaysians have entered a new era in the development of global capitalism that will exacerbate social differences as much as it purports to heal the rifts. Issues of determining the access to and the distribution and control of, material and symbolic resources in the diverse societies may well intensify as they become more vertically stratified because of economic restructuring. What remains unclear despite the movements for reform (and perhaps because of them) is whether the crisis in the region will usher in a new era of substantive democracy characterized by a consciousness of (and agreement about) the circumstances that guarantee respect for individual rights and expression. To be sure, the future will tell us if Wolfensohn's new miracle happens. Now however, capital, crisis and chaos warrant that states and social forces acknowledge and address the past even as they renegotiate an uncertain present and future in a globalizing world.

Notes

1. Despite this, other religions – particularly Christianity (both Protestant and Catholic Churches) – have wielded considerable influence in both the political and economic spheres. During the New Order's formative years in the 1970s, a significant proportion of the technocrats who shaped the country's development policy were Christian, as was General Benny Moerdani, a powerful force in the Indonesian army. The Center for Strategic and International Studies, an influential think-tank under General Ali Moertopo, Suharto's strategist during the 1970s, largely was dominated by Catholics. Further, a significant proportion of the wealthiest 'conglomerates' has been non-Muslims of ethnic Chinese backgrounds.
2. The drafting of the constitution was a contentious, if hurried, process. Dissension came mainly from the ranks of Muslim organizations that had

envisioned the creation of a Muslim state. Debates in the preparatory body focused in particular on a single phrase in the expression of the first principle: belief in God. The Muslim representatives insisted on including seven words (in Indonesian) in the first principle, which would then avow 'belief in God *with the obligation to practice Islamic Shariat for Muslims'*. It was mainly the adept mediation of Mohammad Hatta, who was to be the first vice-president, that broke through the stalemate on the role of religion in the new state.

3. Significantly, Article 33 of the Constitution of 1945 was not amended. It was, in fact, frequently invoked to justify wholesale appropriation by the state of land held under customary law (*adat* lands), particularly in such areas as West Papua (Irian Jaya, the Indonesian half of the island of New Guinea), Aceh and Kalimantan.

4. As legislated in the 1974 Marriage Laws, the *kodrat* is invoked as well in the General Outlines of State Policy, which is the foundation of the grand development scheme. For further analysis of the New Order's gender policy, see especially Suryakusuma (1996), and Tiwon (1996).

5. In Malaysia, non-Malay NGOs must devise strategies in addressing issues to avoid their being construed as 'against Malay'. An example of a successful strategy can be seen in the passage of the Domestic Violence Act (DVA). In 1994, Parliament passed the DVA, which criminalized violence against women. Lobbying by women's groups for the act began as early as 1985, when 20 women's organizations came together to form the Joint Action Group (JAG). JAG's strategy used three prongs. It engaged state agencies, such as the Police, Religious Affairs and Judiciary, in dialogue. It used the mass media to document different types of violence toward women. And it relied on Sisters-in-Islam (a professional Muslim women's group) to organize public forums and workshops on interpreting Islamic jurisprudence. The three-pronged strategy proved successful in ensuring a high degree of inclusiveness at the level of public discourse. JAG wisely handed responsibility for discussing domestic violence and Muslims to an essentially Muslim NGO. Despite the objections of a few Muslim clerics, Sisters-in-Islam played a key role in mobilizing Malay–Muslim support for the act (see especially Ng and Chee 1996).

8
Migrant Workers' Movements in Japan and South Korea

Katharine H. S. Moon

Migrant workers' movements (MWMs) in South Korea and Japan are newcomers to the world of social movements, and they are peculiar in that the Japanese and Korean nationals leading the movements are fighting to advance the rights and humane treatment of individuals inside their territorial borders but outside their national polities: foreign workers at the bottom of the economic ladder.[1] The notions of equality, fairness and justice that these groups raise incorporate dimensions or interpretations that are new and challenging to both societies. Both South Koreans and Japanese traditionally have understood equality as stemming from one's membership in the ethnonational collective. But the presence and difficult plight of migrant workers from poorer parts of Asia, Africa and Latin America challenge this basis for equality and force the liberal interpretation (that is, the idea of individual human rights) into social discourse more emphatically. Moreover, understanding how Japanese and Koreans address the new realities of discrimination and disenfranchisement may tell us something about their past and continuing treatment of those who have long been discriminated against and marginalized: for example, Korean minorities in Japan. MWMs also address new conflicts generated by economic globalization: the challenge to the integrity of national borders, the state's ability to define the rights and manage the welfare of its citizens, and the displacement and exploitation of the masses who do not direct the globalization project. Their work on behalf of migrant workers may give us a clue as to how contemporary, progressive social movements can challenge the aspects of globalization that abet further economic and social marginalization and powerlessness. Last, MWMs in Japan and Korea are transnational movements by membership, structure and strategy. Efforts to address nationally the issues involving migrant workers necessarily require international cooperation and transnational coordination. As such, they pose a challenge to the regional and international institutions that facilitate globalization to address the social relations of the process.

The Northeast Asian cases

Comparing MWMs in Japan and South Korea makes sense for several reasons. First, recent migration (1980s to now), mostly intra-Asian, is changing the face of both societies and challenging their long-held self-identities as homogeneous peoples in race, ethnicity, language and culture. Both are dealing with a historical first, the presence of hundreds of thousands of foreigners who not only seek a piece of the economic pie but also bring with them different skin color, languages, religions, education and skills, spices and lifestyles. Gary Freeman and Jongryn Mo (1996, 170) have deemed Japan and South Korea the most restrictionist in terms of migration/immigration policies among labor-importing Asian states. Both governments' objective has been to permit the entry of limited and controlled numbers of foreigners on a short-term basis in order to alleviate the labor shortage in particular economic sectors, namely construction and small businesses. The labor shortages and restrictive immigration policies together have given rise to hundreds of thousands of undocumented, or 'illegal', aliens among the migrant worker population. Because of their undocumented status, and hence little or no legal protection, they are particularly vulnerable to exploitation and abuse by business owners/managers and labor brokers, as well as to discrimination by the larger population. Unpaid and unequal wages (relative to Japanese or Korean nationals), inability to access accident insurance, arbitrary dismissals, withholding of travel documents by the boss or broker, sexual harassment and violence toward female workers, and discrimination in housing and social activities afflict migrant workers in both countries. Many who work in Korea have faced the additional problem of physical and verbal violence inflicted by their bosses. In both countries, activists and advocates have stepped in to address these and other problems that the foreign workers face. They have taken their cause for nondiscrimination, fair treatment, and legalized status and improved living conditions of migrant workers to the streets in demonstrations and rallies, submitted petitions to government ministries, and addressed the UN Commission on Human Rights through reports and rebuttals to their respective government's official reports. In addition, they have also forged and strengthened their links with regional and international NGOs and have publicized their issues and goals on the Internet.

However, the differences in the political and economic environments in which these social movements have emerged attract comparative analysis. First, Japan and Korea have contrasting legacies of state–society relations, particularly in reference to democratization. Chalmers Johnson (1987) has put it most succinctly in referring to Japan as 'soft authoritarianism' and South Korea as 'hard authoritarianism'. Japanese state–society relations have been less contentious than Korea's, mediated by the all-power bureaucracies and a corporate culture that took organized labor's interests under its wing for a large part of the post-Second World War period. Civic movements in Japan 'rationalized' much earlier than those in Korea, with issues and actors diversifying (for example, from agriculture and labor to consumer and environment) and transforming into interest groups throughout the 1970s. Korea, on the other hand, has a postwar history of violent confrontation and repression in state–society relations. Only with the recent change toward democratization have new civic actors and interests emerged, for example around the environment, aid to North Koreans, consumer rights, gender equality and political reform. Even in the traditional fight between labor and state, dissident labor unions (that is, independent of the state) achieved legalized status only in the mid-1990s. But as Sunhyuk Kim (1997, 1143) has noted, the first civilian-led government under Kim Young Sam continued to suppress and exclude the Federation of Democratic Trade Unions from debates and policies concerning labor. Although more 'moderate citizens' movement groups became dominant [in the 1990s], exponentially proliferating and impressively outperforming the radical people's movement groups [dominant in the 1970s and 1980s]', Kim notes that the old pattern of resistance and repression in state–society relations has not disappeared (1997, 1142). Inquiring into the impact of these respective legacies on the Japanese and Korean MWMs can help us understand their respective identities, strategies and effectiveness.

Second, South Korea and Japan face very different moments in the process of nation-state consolidation. For both the Korean government and people, the presence of foreign migrants and their demands for more equal treatment and legalized status raise the following difficult questions about the future of the Korean nation-state. What should be the basis for permanent residence, citizenship and civic rights: parentage, territory, ethnicity, or economic contribution? How permanent should foreign workers' residential status be, given the anxiety over a possible influx of refugees and migrants from North Korea in the near future? Might the rights and benefits conferred on foreigners today become undesirable precedents in the future, particularly with respect to individuals from North Korea? And should other ethnic Koreans, especially from China and the former Soviet Union, be granted special privileges? Because of the incomplete and fragile nature of (South) Korea as a nation-state, its relationship with the foreign migrants is particularly rife with ambiguity and conflict of interests.

Japan, on the other hand, is one of the strongest examples of a nation-state (Buzan 1991, 38). As Cornelius (1994, 375) notes, 'Since overrunning (but not completely exterminating) the indigenous Ainu and Okinawan cultures on the islands occupied by Japan, the Japanese have enjoyed centuries of ethnic and cultural stability.' Further, even the contemporary disputes over Sakhalin do not amount to the threat of territorial, national, and regime survival, as does the historical rivalry between the two Koreas. The second-class status and treatment of about 750 000 ethnic Koreans in Japan, most of whom are second- and third-generation Japanese-born, remains Japan's most widely acknowledged problem with ethnic/racial discrimination. But even this issue of who belongs to the Japanese nation does not threaten the integrity of Japan's national borders or the state's claim to legitimacy; rather, it is a question of how to treat and incorporate a small minority with several generations of history within one's borders, unlike Korea's question of whether to incorporate (and how to treat) millions of people outside its current borders.

Third, the Asian economic crisis and the related IMF bailout have sent shockwaves throughout Korean society, exposing the nation's economic vulnerability and reinforcing the power of external forces (foreign capital, governments and international organizations) on internal affairs. As many have observed, the shock recharged national-istic sentiments and political consciousness about winners and losers both inside and outside Korea. Even with a recession-ridden economy since 1992, Japan has not become a victim of the crisis afflicting much of East Asia. Such differences in economic strength and stability also affect public attitudes and governmental policies toward foreign migrant workers.

A micro-approach and the nature of the MWMs

Rather than focus on larger, structural changes and their effects on social movements, this chapter takes a 'micro' approach to understanding the

MWMs for the following reasons: First, most social movements today are not coherent entities and therefore do not respond reflexively to systemic changes. Second, relatedly, their opportunities, constraints, goals and strategies significantly depend on managing differences and conflicting priorities within the movement or coalition. Third, even if the formal rules and structures of the broader political and economic relations change, old habits and values continue to shape what social movements are and do. The following illustrates the organizational structure, goals and activities of the two Asian MWMs, and highlights the past legacies of social activism and the current trend toward the transnationalization of social movements as two factors that have been giving shape and momentum to the cause for migrant workers' rights and welfare.

Albert Melucci's most recent book (1996) on social movements notes two main orientations in the study of social movements: a focus on results, and a focus on social and cultural meaning. He argues that focusing solely on the political nature and relevance of movements leads:

> to the exclusive concentration on the visible and measurable features of collective action – such as their relationship with political systems and their effects on policies – at the expense of the production of cultural codes; but it is the latter which is the principal activity of the hidden networks of contemporary movements and the basis for their visible action. (Melucci 1996, 6)

His emphasis on the production of social meaning and cultural symbols stems from his observation that social movements in 'complex societies' (that is, in advanced industrialized nations) have moved away from focused political organization and action toward 'segmented, reticular, multi-faceted' (1996, 113, 115) collectivities that 'raise challenges to the dominant language, to the codes that organize information and shape social practices' (1996, 8).

The MWMs in Japan and South Korea also reflect such changes at work. For them, the 'visible and measurable features of collective action' – specifically, policy changes that legalize the status and recognize the rights of migrant workers, especially those of undocumented ('illegal') status – are currently the primary goals, but the long-term goal is to transform their respective society's 'cultural codes' around ethnicity, race, citizenship and rights toward inclusivity and universality. In this context, the MWMs are a blend of the old and the new, the traditional concerns of labor activism and the politicization of identity and culture.

Assessing the visible and measurable features of collective action requires an understanding of movements' specific goals. In general, the MWMs in Japan and Korea seek improved conditions in the workplace and the social environments of the foreign workers. But more specific goals and strategies differ depending on the particular 'member' of the movement because the MWMs are not clearly discernible and articulated entities from within or without, and the members' interests coincide or conflict at varying moments of movement activities. They accord with Melucci's characterization of contemporary social movements in complex societies (1996, 115):

> Individual cells operate on their own entirely independently of the rest of the movement, although they maintain links to it through the circulation of information and persons. These links become explicit only during the transient periods of collective mobilization over issues which bring the latent network to the surface and then allow it to submerge again in the fabric of daily life.

A lead or coordinating organization does exist within each movement – the National Network in Solidarity with Migrant Workers (NNSMW),[2] which is based in Tokyo, and the Joint Committee for Migrant Workers (JCMK) in Korea,[3] based in Seoul – but the 'affiliates' range from organized labor unions and unorganized labor sympathizers to religious institutions and groups, human rights organizations, women's rights and welfare groups, members of the legal profession, specific ethnic rights groups, and 'cosmopolitanists', to the foreign workers themselves who represent numerous nationalities, languages and religions.

In addition, the problem of organizational unity and coherence of goals is compounded by the fact that most of the disparate member groups themselves are not coherent entities and are riddled with a diversity of interests. For example, among the religious groups, there are those who employ secular means – through changes in immigration, labor and social welfare policy – to achieve better terms of work and living conditions for the foreigners and others who emphasize the importance of religious conversion and spiritual uplift as the primary means to improving one's situation as a foreigner.

Church leadership

This is particularly the case in Korea, where Christian groups and individuals dominate in numbers and motivation among those assisting migrant workers. For example, over 50 per cent of the JCMK affiliates are led by ministers, priests or Christian mission workers (Interviews with JCMK staff, Seoul, 24 March 1999).[4] With its history of radical Christian activists who had taken up labor's cause since the late 1960s through the Protestant Urban Industrial Mission and Young Catholic Workers, the religious affiliates that are led by traditionally left-leaning folks and those led by their conservative counterparts tend to be suspicious of one another. (The religious affiliates of the JCMK are recognized as more politically and socially progressive than the many evangelical churches in Korea that have developed programs for migrant workers as part of their missionary work.) Interviews with officials of the JCMK, the Association for Foreign Workers' Human Rights, and the Korean Confederation of Trade Unions (KCTU) underscore the difficulty of reconciling the interests of the secular organizations like theirs with the desire of some religious groups to Christianize the many Muslims, Buddhists and atheists (from China and formerly Communist countries) among the foreign worker population. The secular bodies emphasize the need to apply the Labor Standards Law to the migrant workers, to push the legal system to penalize brokers and business owners who abuse or exploit such labor, and to pass the Bill to Protect Foreign Workers. The religious groups emphasize church services, bible studies and revival meetings in their shelter or counseling work. Since 1994, several Buddhist organizations in Korea have also joined the tide of those reaching out to migrant workers, although in much smaller numbers than Christian groups. In order to maintain the movement's focus on political and legal change, an administrative committee of the JCMK evaluates a potential religious affiliate to make certain that the organization's main purpose is not religious proselytization or conversion (Interviews with JCMK staff, Seoul, 24 March 1999).

The tension between secular and religious approaches is not as significant in Japan. According to a staff member at the Catholic Tokyo International Center (CTIC), the main difference between the two types of movement groups is financial, with the religious organizations regularly receiving institutional support in terms of funds, office space and staff. Moreover, he noted that proselytization and conversion are not big issues for churches because about half of the migrant worker population (from the Philippines and Latin America) is Catholic. He and his colleagues at CTIC mentioned that it was not the Catholic Church in Japan that first reached out to migrant workers but rather the foreigners who came knocking on church doors, seeking material and spiritual succor. The churches 'were overwhelmed' by the newcomers; in Tokyo alone, the Catholic population among foreign workers was an estimated 70 000 in 1997, as compared with about 80 000 Japanese.[5] Urawa diocese, for example, is composed of 70 per cent migrant workers and only 30 per cent Japanese (Interview, staff of CTIC, Tokyo, 13 April 1999.)

The Catholic Church is the most prominent religious organization involved in the lives of foreign migrants partly because of pressure from the 'demand' side, the Catholic newcomers, but my interviews also reveal the importance of transnational missionary networks in facilitating a rather quick and constructive response to the presence of foreigners in Japan. The presence of Filipino priests and nuns working in Japan and the experience of Japanese laypersons who had participated in mission work in the Philippines and Latin America have allowed for better language communication and cultural understanding between Japanese and some foreign worker populations. The lack of emphasis on conversion is also due to the minority status and less aggressive style of Christians in Japan, who compose only about 1 per cent of the population, as compared with about 25 per cent in Korea (the growth of christianity and churches in Korea in the last two decades has also been one of the most explosive in the world). Apparently, Japanese Buddhists have not expressed an institutional response to the presence of migrant workers, many of whom hail from Buddhist Thailand.

Labor's involvement

In contrast to many of the religious activists, Japanese local unions that support the migrant workers' cause are motivated by ideological considerations as well, criticizing corporate–labor relations and seeking to strengthen labor's influence in society. Zentoitsu (All United Workers' Union), a 'general union' in Tokyo, is unique to Japanese society because 99 per cent of its members are undocumented foreign workers (about 1640 since 1992). The secretary-general of Zentoitsu emphasized that the struggle on behalf of the foreign workers is part of a larger mission to 'fight against the strong trend of neoliberalism in Japan, which is taking away rights already protected by law' (Interview, Tokyo, 14 April 1999). His long-term goal is not only to foster labor unions that serve and are led by migrant workers themselves but also to engender labor unions throughout Japan that do not require employment as a prerequisite, so as to protect people who are fired, laid off, day-workers, or in transit from one job to another. His rationale was that since the structure of labor is changing in Japan, with lifetime employment and job security becoming increasingly outdated, organizing must change to meet the growing instability of labor conditions (Interview, Tokyo, 14 April 1999).

In general, the labor unions in both Korea and Japan have had an uncomfortable relationship with the migrant workers' movements. In Japan, only the local and general unions, which are themselves on the margins of labor power, have paid some attention to migrant workers' needs. But the more influential enterprise unions, which tend only to members' issues, have all but ignored the call for the recognition of migrant workers' rights and have opposed large inflows of migrant workers. Rengo, Japan's largest labor organization (federation), voiced opposition to the growing influx of unskilled and low-skilled foreign workers in the late 1980s and 'requested that the government take legal action to punish employers who hire illegal immigrants' (Xinhua General Overseas News Service, 15 March 1988). The rationale is that 'inviting the unskilled only slows down a necessary shift from less advanced labor-intensive industries to high-tech industries that require fewer workers' (*Christian Science Monitor*, 21 December 1989). On the other hand, Rengo also accused Japanese employers of 'exploiting the Asian laborers, particularly in the construction industry' (*Christian Science Monitor*, 21 December 1989). Activists in local and general unions believe that the majority of Japanese union members simply do not consider the foreign workers as equals and therefore entitled to the same status and entitlements as Japanese workers. The secretary-general of Zentoitsu mentioned that Japanese labor unions are 'slowly beginning to accept' the foreign nationals as workers but that it is a gradual process. He noted that since 1993, when some of the labor communities began to take up the migrant workers' cause, even Rengo began to include statements of support for the foreigners' rights. When asked what accounts for the change, he commented that seven years of activism on this issue had an impact. The labor activists in the MWM tend not to deal directly with Rengo but have developed relationships with individual trade unions that are more progressive but within Rengo.[6]

The two main labor organizations in Korea have also had a prickly time with the migrant worker issue. Early on, like their Japanese neighbors, the Federation of Korean Trade Unions (FKTU) and the KCTU had viewed foreign workers as a possible threat to wage stability and the upgrading of technology and environment in workplaces. They had also opposed the rapid increase in the number of 'illegal' workers hired and preferred to see a limited but regulated importation of foreign labor. But the KCTU also extended some support to activists for the migrant workers' rights and to the establishment and leadership of the JCMK. It had helped coordinate demonstrations and sit-ins at Myongdong Cathedral with other human rights organizations. But again, the most difficult task has been to make Korean workers understand the situation of the migrant workers. To this end, the KCTU and JCMK have raised the problems and needs of migrant workers at Korean workers' rallies and meetings through presentations and cultural performances by foreign workers and their Korean advocates (Interviews with the Director, JCMK, and the Director of the Policy Bureau, KCTU, Seoul, 24 March 1999). But with the Asian financial crisis and the IMF regime, foreign labor's concerns have been pushed to the back of the bus. The dominant view of labor, society and state has been 'How can we help foreigners when our own people are suffering?' Nevertheless, the KCTU as an institution has not abandoned the migrant workers' cause. It continues to advocate the elimination of the industrial trainee system and 'to create an equal system for foreign workers and to include them into Korean workers' organizations in the long run' (Interview with the Director of the Policy Bureau, KCTU, Seoul, 24 March 1999). Although it serves a foreign labor population and is an autonomous labor rights organization, the JCMK office is housed in the headquarters of the KCTU.

Who are the migrants?

Additionally, the diversity of people within the foreign worker population makes agreement on priorities, goals and strategies difficult. For a start, there is the category of 'industrial trainees', who have entered the country legally and through the sponsorship of specific enterprises, business organizations or recognized labor brokerage firms since 1981 in Japan and 1991 in Korea. The Japanese government established programs to accept trainees in the 1960s, but the formal immigration status of 'trainee' was established in 1981 and then revised through the 1990 amendment of the Immigration Control Act. From the government's perspective, the ostensible purpose of the trainee program is to spread technical and managerial skills that would be useful in the local management of offices, factories and joint ventures of Japanese companies abroad, and relatedly to aid in the development of the foreign country. South Korea, Thailand and the Philippines had led the number of trainees working in Japan until the late 1980s, when China began its dramatic increase in exporting labor to Japan: numbers grew from 2688 in 1987 to 15 688 in 1993 (Mori 1997, 117). South Korea's program, which was modeled on Japan's and expanded in 1993, was also established ostensibly to offer skills training to foreign nationals already employed by Korean companies overseas. But both programs, despite the two governments' stipulations against the use of such foreigners as labor, have amounted in practice to what many observers call a 'side door' mechanism to alleviate the labor shortages in each country.

Critics have pointed out that the trainee system allows for the exploitation of all unskilled foreign workers because as trainees (as opposed to workers), individuals are not covered by each country's labor laws and because the existence of the system directly generates increasing populations of undocumented workers. The problem is that because of the numerous restrictions imposed on the mobility and the legal, work and wage status of trainees, many leave their designated training places and find work outside the system, which then immediately changes their status to 'illegal worker' But for the undocumented worker who entered Korea or Japan illegally or overstayed the (usually tourist) visa, the very existence of the trainee system, the side door, deters each government from addressing its need for imported labor more openly. In his comprehensive book on Japan's immigration policy and foreign workers, Hiromi Mori (1997, 98–9) points out that the 1990 revision of the Immigration Control Act was primarily intended to curb and tighten control over the growing number of illegal workers, especially from China, Pakistan and Bangladesh. The *Asahi News Service* (13 September 1991) put it more bluntly: the law was revised 'to severely restrict the number of foreigners with no Japanese blood'. To achieve that end, the law streamlined the limited legal means of entry and work, introduced legal sanctions on individuals who employed or assisted undocumented workers, and extended the imprisonment of persons illegally overstaying or 'engaging in activities beyond their assigned scope authorized by the law' to one year (Mori 1997, 99). In sum, the government's attempt 'to prevent illegal employment [and therefore exploitation] under the pretext of training' (Mori 1997, 118) by streamlining the trainee system involved harsher conditions for the undocumented workers in Japan. In Korea, the JCMK advocates the abolition of the trainee system and the establishment of work permits, but it is unclear whether the trainees already present in Korea would have the first claims on such permits, whether they would be repatriated, or whether they and the undocumented workers would all have equal access.

The portrait of foreign workers in the two countries is also complicated by the fact that some are ethnic descendants and either have special legal privileges or have easier access to language and culture. In Japan, since 1990, the *Nikkei* (Japanese descendants) from primarily Brazil, Peru and Argentina have composed the only unskilled category permitted into Japan and entitled to legal residence and work. About one year after the 1990 revisions, the Japanese Foreign Ministry estimated that about 150 000 *Nikkei* workers were residing in Japan (*Asahi News Service*, 13 September 1991). Most of them do not speak Japanese and are culturally not Japanese; many do not even look Japanese because of generations of intermarrying in Latin America. Yet their legal status places them in the upper ranks of foreign worker populations. The *Nikkei* are also the only migrant workers who are permitted to bring family members with them. Although the work of MWMs that emphasize multiculturalism and nondiscrimination benefits the *Nikkei*, priorities such as amnesty for visa overstayers and permanent residence status for long-term undocumented workers are irrelevant to them. But these priorities are the most urgent for the larger 'illegal' population.

Unlike the Japanese government, the South Korean government offers no preferential treatment toward the ethnic Koreans from China who constitute the largest ethnic group of undocumented workers. However, in the early stages of Korea's search for foreign workers, the government and employers favored the entry of Korean-Chinese because they would least disturb Korean homogeneity. For example, in 1992, the Korea Apparel Manufacturers' Association recommended to the Ministry of Trade and Industry that 'priority ... be given to ethnic Koreans from China and the Commonwealth of Independent States, in light of language problems [that nonethnic Koreans would face]' (*Korea Economic Daily*, 15 September 1992). Similarly, in Japan, Takashi Oka (1994, 43) found that 'employment brokers say they have been asked to supply Japanese-Brazilians who look as much like the Japanese as possible'. And the *Asahi News Service* reported that 'there is no question that the Japanese government decided to treat people of Japanese decent favorably because of the wishes of such businesses' (13 September 1991). The ethnically related migrants generally work in better paying, less dirty and less dangerous industries (Lee 1997, 353). For example, Korean-Chinese men tend to congregate in construction and higher forms of manufacturing work, whereas their South Asian counterparts tend to work in '3D' (dirty, dangerous, demanding) sweatshops. Similarly in Japan, the Japanese Overseas Association found in 1991 that 79.9 per cent of ethnic Japanese worked in factories and 7 per cent in offices, and 'only 5.3 per cent worked in construction, where so many illegal Asians work. In factories, 33.5 and 19.9 per cent worked in electric and electronics companies. Only 10 per cent were in the dirty metalworking industries' (Oka 1994, 44). But divisions exist even among the *Nikkei*, who fare better as a group than other migrant workers: 'Japanese-Peruvians, who tend to be more racially mixed than Japanese-Brazilians, complain of job discrimination, with some saying that they receive 30 per cent less pay than Japanese-Brazilians' (Oka 1994, 43).

Ethnic/racial segregation, whether officially or unofficially sponsored, appears to contribute to labor segmentation and hierarchy within the foreign worker populations. Moreover, the emphasis on ethnic and cultural homogeneity seems to foster in the ethnic-Japanese or ethnic-Korean migrants increased expectation of easier integration and better treatment in the ancestral homeland. Heh-Rahn Park (1996) offers poignant and compelling narratives of Korean-Chinese who had come to South Korea with high hopes, only to be disappointed and hurt by the lack of official preferences and the general discrimination by society. One of the saddest moments during my own field research in Korea involved a Korean-Chinese construction worker in his mid-30s who had come to a counseling center because his employers refused to pay him and the other Korean-Chinese in the construction crew: when I told him that I was also the descendant of emigrants, he looked at me with wide eyes in a gesture of familiarity and solidarity and softly muttered, 'An immigrant's existence here [in Korea], it's too lonesome ... too much pain' (Interview, Songnam City, Korea, 25 March 1999).

The possibility of massive refugee flows as a consequence of the collapse of the North Korean regime or reunification makes the government wary of extending rights and benefits to foreign workers. For a start, the North represents a large source of labor power; Park Young-bum (1996, 179) of the government-sponsored Korea Labor Institute recommended that 'Korea should not open its labour market on a large scale' and reasoned, in part, that because 'in North Korea, about 50 per cent of the labour force is still employed in the agricultural sector, it could be a major source of unskilled labour when Korean reunification occurs'. Relatedly, the Federation of Korean Industries, which represents big business interests, and the Korea Federation of Small Businesses together opposed the legalization of foreign workers through an employment-permit system (which the JCMK had been campaigning for) on the grounds that it would jeopardize the South's policy efforts toward the North. The *Korea Herald* (2 June 1997) reported the following statement of the business organizations:

> The guarantee of the same labor conditions for foreigners may also pose a burden on the government in its push for joint economic

projects with North Korea or after national reunification ... The employment permit system is expected to make it difficult for the government to send foreign workers back to their countries when there arises the need for Seoul to hire a massive number of North Korean after Korean reunification.

This is one of the reasons why the Korean government has not offered preferential treatment toward ethnic Koreans from China. To welcome such diasporic Koreans would be to set a precedent for other would-be entrants of Korean descent seeking economic and other benefits. Government policy toward migrant workers, then, is to some extent held hostage by the yet unfinished nation-state-building project on the Korean peninsula.

The movements' work

In addition to this politically charged context, the organizational and political identity and coherence of the MWMs suffer from the affiliates' role as caregiver to the migrant worker communities. The vast majority of MWM group affiliates and individual participants spend most of their time addressing the daily needs and crises of migrant workers and not the tasks of information gathering, goal setting, policy formulation, publicization of positions, and lobbying. The current head of the JCMK, for example, shuttles back and forth from managing and leading 20 affiliated groups, through her office in Seoul, to the shelter/counseling center for female migrant workers that she directs in Anyang, outside Seoul. Nearly every one of her JCMK predecessors also simultaneously directed his own shelter/counseling center for migrant workers.

A visit to such a center quickly reveals the moment-by-moment urgency of the problems migrant workers present for assistance. During my four-hour visit to the Migrant Workers' House/Korean-Chinese House in Songnam City, an hour-and-a-half's travel by public transportation from Seoul, the staff of about five Koreans, mostly volunteers, were pressed to take up the following cases: finding employment for the many jobless among the 80 or so people staying in the four-room shelter; getting medical help for a Korean-Chinese man whose teeth and jaws had been broken in a work accident; calling up the boss of a fan-production factory to verify the allegations of physical beating and verbal violence charged by three young Bangladeshi workers who were trying to hold back tears while communicating with great difficulty in

Korean; counseling a Korean woman whose Pakistani spouse (an undocumented worker) was facing visa problems; a Korean-Chinese worker whose entire face, hands and forearms had been badly burned in an explosion at work two months ago, who wished to know what further medical treatment he could get free of charge to improve his condition; a Korean-Chinese man who came to find out how he and his compatriots could get paid although their bosses at the construction sites refused; a Korean-Chinese woman seeking financial help for her Korean-Chinese husband who is in a coma, medical help for herself, and help in dealing with the travel brokers in China who demanded repayment for having arranged her and her husband's travel into Korea.

The Reverend Kim Haesong, the director, estimated that the center handles about 600 major cases a month, with countless numbers of queries for information and advice. In addition to these activities, Reverend Kim was guiding a group of 20 local pastors around the center to introduce them to the realities and needs of migrant workers in the community. And about 60–70 people who were present around lunchtime gathered to partake in a Bangladeshi meal as a gesture of cultural learning and sharing. In the midst of these activities, telephones rang off the hook, faxes were received and sent, Internet communication was conducted, position papers drafted, medical appointments and payments negotiated, while different staff members tended to my queries. Related work outside the center included making trips to the police station, hospitals and churches, getting legal assistance, fundraising, lecturing on the needs of migrant workers, giving newspaper interviews, and coordinating with other affiliates in the migrant workers' movement. And on top of all this, Reverend Kim pointed out, making sure that there is enough rice for everyone to eat is also a priority. This center also provides free Western-style medical examinations, offered once a week by volunteer physicians, and the services of a specialist in Chinese-style medicine (for the Korean-Chinese), as well as Korean-language classes and church services in several different languages. Further, staff members were concerned about the education prospects of two Mongolian children who had migrated with their parents – which is rare – and were living at the shelter, as well as the need to find a permanent place for the dozen or more funereal urns of deceased migrant workers, which had been stored (some for several years) in one of the closets. Moreover, maintaining the facilities and some kind of order among the different nationalities – from Bangladesh, China, Ghana, Indonesia, Kazakhstan, Mongolia, Pakistan and Korea – was also a never-ending task.

In the early stages of the MWMs, the Korean and Japanese advocates also had to build credibility and win the trust of the foreign workers. For example, even when informed of labor unions and other organizations that could help them claim their withheld wages, several Iranian men 'were interested but reserved' because they were 'distrustful of anyone who might report their real names to the authorities' (*Japan Times Weekly*, International Edition, 24 February–1 March 1992).

Staff members of CTIC in Tokyo also explained their organization's evolution from information provider about labor rights to facilitator/ provider of 'all-encompassing' life support on their behalf (Interviews with staff of CTIC, Tokyo, 13 April 1999). In the first four to five years since its inception in 1990, CTIC had offered mostly legal advice based on Japan's Labor Standards Law, but eventually came to realize that knowledge of legal rights without practical means to achieve them was useless to the mostly undocumented workers who came for help. Since the mid-1990s, CTIC has been concentrating on one-to-one, hands-on assistance to address the growing diversity of migrant workers' needs and concerns. Of the 340 major cases in 1998, 69 involved visa and passport problems, 56 labor relations, 46 marriage and divorce, 43 medical and health benefits, 23 police and immigration, 20 insurance, and others the education of children. Family needs have become increasingly central to the work of MWM affiliate groups since the early 1990s because of the tendency of the *Nikkei* to bring their families and the growing number of long-time visa-overstayers who take up residence and build their own families in Japan. Also, these welfare-related cases are usually time- and labor-intensive because they require consultations and negotiations with many different actors and bureaucracies as well as follow-up. Two of the staff members who guided me back to the subway station after my visit were themselves *en route* to a hospital to negotiate a reduction of fees incurred by an undocumented Colombian woman who had just given birth. Along with these daily duties, these organizations develop policy positions and network with others in the movement; in the case of CTIC, its primary policy goal is to get the government to grant amnesty visas to undocumented workers and legalize their status. The work of these MWM participants appears to reflect the following description of new social movements: 'Actors in conflicts recast the question of societal ends: they address the differences between the sexes, the ages, cultures; they probe into the nature and the limits of human intervention; they concern themselves with health, and illness, birth and death' (Melucci 1996, 9).

MWMs at the center of egalitarian social movement politics

If the nature of foreign workers' problems makes it difficult to label exactly what kind of a social movement the MWMs are, it also enables a wide variety of individuals and resources to come under the common umbrella. Because welfare, labor rights, racial/ethnic discrimination, citizenship and immigration rights, violence against women and human rights in general are all inherent concerns of the Korean and Japanese movements, they attract a broad base of participants among social sectors in Japan that do not directly or personally have a stake in how migrant workers fare. Also, the diversity of actors and resources helps compensate for weaknesses within one group or another. An attorney who specializes in cases dealing with migrant workers, including women who are trafficked into the Japanese sex industry, observed that grassroots NGOs and the legal community work 'hand in hand'; NGOs rely on lawyers to clarify and present legal violations or shortcomings suffered by migrant workers to businesses and government, and lawyers rely on the NGOs for actual information and experience (Interview, Tokyo, 12 April 1999). In 1990, 400 Japanese attorneys formed the Foreign Workers' Legal Aid in order to assist in the movement for the rights and protection of migrant workers. They have paid particular attention to putting pressure on the Ministries of Labor, Social Welfare, and Justice (Immigration), as well as local governments. For example, the Legal Aid group succeeded in lobbying numerous local governments to provide pamphlets on the rights of foreign workers, including *Nikkei* and 'illegals', and to establish local offices where they could go to get information on medical care, accident insurance and other benefits (Interview, Tokyo, 12 April 1999). Moreover, the Legal Aid (together with NGOs) lobbied the Labor Standards Office and Immigration services to change a practice that shortchanged the undocumented worker's right to accident insurance under the Labor Standards Law. Before 1992, when individuals applied to the Labor Standards Office to claim compensation for on-the-job accidents, claims processors would inform Immigration while simultaneously processing the application. Therefore, the tendency was to detain 'illegals' even before they had received medical treatment or had been financially compensated for the accident. But through the joint actions of the legal and NGO communities, this situation has gradually improved so that insurance claims and immigration status are not generally linked and, if the Labor Standards Office does notify

Immigration, it does so after the medical treatment is completed and insurance properly claimed (Interview, Tokyo, 12 April 1999).

Staff members of Zentoitsu also emphasized the importance of the division of labor among the different affiliates: 'No one group can specialize in everything, but all have expertise in something; so, cooperation is vital.' Before 1993, when labor groups first joined forces to address the problems migrant workers were facing, NGOs had less power to confront company owners and managers directly to negotiate wages, accident insurance, and other issues migrant workers presented as a problem. Zentoitsu leaders believe that because NGOs were advocating for 'illegal' workers, their case was compromised by the fear that the company/shop boss could easily call in the police and immigration authorities and get the foreign workers detained or deported. According to several case workers for the foreigners, bosses tended to demand that if the NGO wanted the company to address the complaint, the worker should present himself or herself in person. However, the head of Zentoitsu emphasized that because labor unions are legal entities in Japan, they cannot be challenged or refused by a company when they bring up matters that are covered under the Labor Standards Law. He noted that Japanese labor laws exceed international standards but that the problem lies in inadequate understanding by the foreign workers and their employees, systematic application to all workers, and the society's general discrimination that undermines the foreigners' rights.

In contrast, Korea's labor laws and social welfare entitlements are still below international standards and continue to be a focus of organized labor's activism (Korea Labor and Society Institute, 1998). Although the written laws themselves have progressed in the last decade, business and government still are not accustomed to treating labor as an equal and legitimate player in industrial relations and politics. By the same token, Korean organized labor is still in the midst of a decades-long struggle to establish itself as a legitimate social force in society and – with the IMF crisis – considers itself even more besieged, because international capital has weighed in against organized labor by advocating layoffs and the worker dispatch system (temporary workers on contract with labor brokerage firms). Even though the labor unions welcome economic reform, especially the restructuring and disciplining of the *chaebol* conglomerates, they view with cynicism the application of such reforms to Korea: 'The agenda of "reform" of Korean economy raised at the outset of the crisis was distorted to meaning nothing more than the resoluteness to sack workers' (KCTU 1998a). For example, the

KCTU vigorously supported the protest strike of about 10 000 Hyundai Motors (Ulsan plant) workers against the management's unilateral decision to fire about 2500 workers in mid-July 1998. It interpreted the act as a direct assault on labor unions, because most of the active members of the Hyundai Motors Workers' Union were on the termination list (KCTU 1998a), and deemed President Kim Dae Jung a dictator for allowing police and public security agents to round up and arrest several dozen union and 'democratic movement activists' (KCTU 1998b). The KCTU Ulsan Regional Council and the Ulsan Alliance of the National Alliance for Democracy and Reunification in Korea publicly stated:

> The swooping arrest of trade union leaders and democracy activists by the Kim Dae Jung government revives the spectre of military dictatorships which has [*sic*] used the malicious National Security Law as a weapon to repress workers and people's movements. The government is using the same techniques the past military regimes have used when they faced popular opposition. It is deceiving people's eyes and ears by staging [a] violent, illegal and false case in order to protect the ruling elite. (KCTU 1998c)

If Korean labor does not have faith in laws and rights to protect Korean workers, how much less can foreign workers rely on them?

Rather than stand on as yet shaky and contentious legal and political ground, the Korean MWM activists have relied on familiar territory in staging their fight for the rights and better treatment of foreign workers: public confrontation. For example, the JCMK itself is the offspring of the first public demonstration (called a strike by the *Far Eastern Economic Review*) by foreign workers, which lasted for nine days in January 1995. What started as a protest by 13 Nepalese industrial trainees against deplorable labor conditions, the withholding of their passports by their bosses and exploitation by labor brokers led to a confederation of more than 38 grassroots and labor organizations, which forced some changes from the Korean government and the Small Business Federation: the trainees' right to keep their passports, direct payment of wages, and access to overtime pay (*Far Eastern Economic Review*, 2 February 1995, 37). Consistent government oversight, however, has been lacking. During my meeting in March 1999 with about 20 young Indonesian workers in Ansan (many of whom had come as industrial trainees), the most common grievance was the continued practice of indirect payment through the brokers. In some of their cases, the brokers systematically deducted about half of their monthly wages for miscellaneous management fees and alleged that the rest would be kept in an account on their behalf until they were ready to return to Indonesia. In short, the trainees had no access to their own earnings.

Many other public demonstrations, including rallies, pickets and sit-ins, have continued to take place, and they reflect the symbolism, 'personnel' and rhetoric of the Korean labor, student and democracy movements of the 1970s and 1980s. For example, many of the protests, including the one by Nepalese trainees, have taken place in front of Myongdong Cathedral in Seoul, the traditional stage and refuge of antigovernment protesters in the era of military rule. And for many of the leading Korean activists, both secular and clerical, their current struggle on behalf of the migrant workers is an extension of their participation in the labor and democracy movements of earlier decades. For example, those heading the Association for Foreign Workers' Human Rights (the first secular advocacy group for migrant workers) and the Songnam Migrant Workers' House and the Ansan Migrant Workers' Center (the two largest and most active counseling/ advocacy centers near Seoul) had all been outspoken critics of military rule and labor repression in the 1970s and 1980s and had been jailed for their then antigovernment activism. The director of the Foreign Workers' Labor Counseling Office of the Catholic Archdiocese of Seoul, although not as politically radical in background as the leaders of the other three organizations, also has consistently worked in the Catholic Church's labor advocacy/ministry programs since the 1970s (Interview, Seoul, 23 March 1999). And many of the key younger leaders (in their 20s and 30s) began their political coming of age as university student protesters. Kim Misun, for example, who coordinates the Korean advocacy groups with regional and international NGOs through the Hong Kong-based Asian Migrants' Centre and the National Council of Churches in Korea, mentioned that as soon as she had registered as a first-year student in the early 1980s, she took to the streets to fight (Interview, Seoul, 23 March 1999).

Indeed, during its early years, the Korean MWM perceived the government's treatment of the migrant workers and their movement as a form of political authoritarianism. For example, their depiction of the government crackdowns on escaped trainees and undocumented workers recalls the violence by the police and military against dissident activists in the democracy movements of the 1970s and 1980s. In a statement entitled 'Our Position on the Police Intrusion on a Migrant Workers' Counseling Office', the activists claim:

> The Ministry of Justice is applying a heavy-handed crackdown in order to solve the rising number of escaping industrial trainee-workers ... Outside the Shiwa Industrial Complex a foreign worker jumped from the second floor of a building to evade arrest from Immigration Officials ... The violence of the Immigration Officials is indiscriminate[;] they continue to harass churches, shelters for workers, and human rights supporters who help those workers who do not receive their salaries and are victims of factory accidents. Recently at the Protestant Foreign Workers Counseling Center in Ansan, 10 Immigration Officials threatened to arrest any one who came to the Center. (JCMK, 1996)

In the aftermath of a police raid of the Songnam Migrant Workers' House on 3 June 1996 and the ensuing arrest of Pastor Kim Haesong and two undocumented Nepalese workers, the JCMK's demands to the government expanded to include the rights of advocacy groups to counsel individuals and carry out public campaigns (JCMK 1996). In short, the movement was challenging the government to practice the democracy it was touting under the leadership of the first civilian president elected in over 30 years.

Transnational ideas, transnational action

The Asian financial crisis and the IMF bailout regimen have helped resuscitate the confrontational, 'us-against-them' rhetoric and style of struggle so familiar among labor activists in the earlier decades. Once again, the government is not to be trusted, and once again, big business is protected from fully paying for its sins. Despite the Korean labor unions' reluctance to shoulder the burden of the migrant workers' cause, the economic crisis has pushed labor activists (for Korean nationals and foreigners) to cast all workers in Korea as victims of government–business collusion, exploitative and abusive business practices, and Western neoimperialism. Both the moderate Federation of Korean Trade Unions and the more radical Korean Confederation of Trade Unions put forth position statements that condemned xenophobic reactions to and treatment of foreign workers in the midst of the economic crisis (Ahn 1997; Yoon 1997). An FKTU statement points out that 'some ... employers have made use of the forced departure policy of the government and they have delayed wage payment intentionally, dismissed unfairly, and unpaid [*sic*] the compensation of occupational diseases', and that 'this matter should be treated [the same as] domestic labour issues' (Ahn 1997). Such statements contrast with the explicit xenophobia expressed against foreign workers in Malaysia and Indonesia in the aftermath of the crisis.

In this context, the JCMK has emphasized the common interests of national and foreign workers rather than their conflicts. In its 1998 May Day message of worker solidarity at a rally of Korean and foreign workers at Myongdong Cathedral, the JCMK reiterated the sufferings of migrant workers and reminded Korean workers that 'like you and so many oppressed and exploited peoples throughout the world we are determined to forward the struggle against so-called Globalization' (JCMK 1998). They asserted that the forces of globalization – industrialized countries, the IMF, the World Bank and the World Trade Organization – not migrant workers, are to blame for 'taking jobs away from our people' (JCMK 1998). Specifically, the JCMK named Korean businesses' preference for flexibilization of labor as the main threat to workers' rights, job security and social benefits, a move also opposed by the KCTU and FKTU.

Whereas economic globalization has helped generate increased migration among low-skilled or unskilled workers from poorer countries into Korea and Japan, the normative facets of globalization – emphasis on human rights, democratization, and pluralism and cross-culturalism – have helped fuel the MWMs in both countries. The Korean movement, in particular, has used the more noble aspirations of globalization, touted repeatedly by government, business, media and academic elites under Kim Young Sam's presidency, as a tactical tool against elite-led globalization. For example, in a statement entitled, 'Message to Korean Government and People' (26 April 1996), the JCMK threw the 'globalization card' back at the government: *Segyehwa* (globalization) movement is a perfect lie, without the equal guarantee of the right to labor and human rights.' And in response to the government raid on the Reverend Kim Haesong's migrant workers' center in Songnam on 3 June 1996, the JCMK protested against 'the incredible situation where 500 armed police came to be involved in a situation of this kind, all this despite the Government's call for Globalization and Internationalization' (JCMK 1996). Moreover, the rhetoric employed by the JCMK challenges Koreans to transform their traditional parochialism into something akin to global citizenship, arguing that Koreans 'must find ways to live together harmoniously and overcome the existing system that unfairly persecutes and oppresses migrant workers'. The rationale is that 'such steps will ensure better ties with foreign nations and contribute to a smooth globalization process already in the making' (JCMK 1995).

Although the Japanese MWM has not employed the label of globalization to describe its struggle or to challenge government and business practices as explicitly as its Korean counterpart, the substance of the message is similar: human rights. The Japanese movement has instrumentally used existing international conventions and laws to point out where and how much the Japanese government falls short. As recently as the spring of 1999, the NNSMW appealed to international norms in an effort to oppose measures that would disadvantage migrant workers and foreign residents in the proposed revisions of the Immigration Control and Refugee Recognition Law and the Alien Registration Law pending in the Diet. In the first case, the NNSMW opposed the proposed measure to criminalize 'unlawful stay' and therefore make an undocumented person permanently subject to criminal prosecution, in contrast to the existing law that deems 'unlawful entry' a crime for a period of three years. The NNSMW also opposed the proposed increase in the length of the period (from one year to three to five years) before re-entry into Japan after compulsory repatriation. The umbrella organization for the MWM charged that the Japanese government would be violating rights established in the International Covenant on Civil and Political Rights and the Convention on the Rights of the Child, to which Japan is a signatory, by preventing families from living together for long periods of time through extending the period before permitted re-entry. The NNSMW also claimed that the government would be infringing on the 'right to residence' as established in the UN Convention on the Protection of All Migrant Workers and Members of Their Families (which Japan has not signed) by criminalizing the undocumented status of a foreigner for many years. In contrast to Japan's proposed measures, the NNSMW (1999b, 1–2) argues, 'In International Law and in the immigration and migration laws of many countries, it can be said that the right of residence is recognized.' Alternatively, the NNSMW proposes legalization, through amnesty, of 'illegals' residing in Japan.

Interviews in Tokyo, 14 April 1999, with Japanese and foreign staff members and several migrant workers at the Asian People's Friendship Society (APFS), one of the largest counseling and advocacy groups in Tokyo,[7] revealed that approximately 60 per cent of the undocumented foreign worker population in Japan has resided in the country for ten years or longer and that, on average, migrants stay between four and six years. Such long-term residents feel that they have earned the right of residency that the NNSMW and international norms refer to. But unless an undocumented foreign worker marries a Japanese national, which itself involves a long and arduous bureaucratic process, there is no way for him to apply for legal residency. The same holds true for women, with this exception: an 'illegal' foreign woman who is not married to a Japanese national can stay in Japan legally and qualify for the National Health Insurance only if she bears the child of a Japanese man who claims the child as his own (Interview with an attorney for migrant workers, 12 April 1999). As of 1999, the APFS has planned to test the waters by presenting to the government carefully selected cases among its members for 'special permission for residence'. An undocumented Bangladeshi man serving as a leader at the APFS believed that he had earned the right to reside in Japan after ten years of working, learning the language and culture, and befriending Japanese:

> I get human rights through residence. I have no human rights in Japan right now – I can't go get medical care because it is expensive, but later [with residence], I can get the National Health Insurance, and if I have no work, I can get unemployment insurance. I know Japan – this is the second country to me. (Interview, APFS, Tokyo, 14 April 1999)

In the second case of the proposed revision in laws, the NNSMW grants that the abolition of the required fingerprinting of foreign residents would be a substantive improvement. However, they argue that 'the requirement that under the penal law alien permanent residents must carry documentation at all times, while this does not apply to Japanese nationals, is not consistent with the Covenant [on Civil and Political Rights]', which Japan ratified in 1979. They emphasized that the UN Committee on Human Rights had 'urged twice in five years that Japan abolish the ARL's [Alien Registration Law] permanent pass possession requirement' and that the proposed revision 'is incompatible with Japan's responsibility under the International Covenants on Human Rights to bring domestic law into line with international law and should be vigorously criticized and opposed' (NNSMW 1999b, 2). During my field trip in Tokyo, the NNSMW and its supporting network of activists and NGOs were busy preparing for the Tokyo Parade for a Multiethnic, Multicultural Society (18 April 1999), which would emphasize opposition to the proposed changes in the immigration control laws and the ARL.

Like that of its Korean counterpart, the rhetoric and rationales of the Japanese MWM reveal the importance of 'accumulation' in the work of these movements. By accumulation, I refer to the legacy, experiences, personnel and even public clout that the movement has inherited or actively transferred from the social and political activism of the past. Japanese and migrant worker activists (in Japan) have seen the government's treatment of contemporary foreign workers as a continuation of its unequal treatment of long-term Korean residents and, more generally, its colonialist mentality. For example, the NNSMW argues that both proposed revisions of law amount to a 'surveillance system' akin to that of its colonial era:

> Under the pre-World War Two fascist system, foreigners residing in Japan (including people who had come from the Japanese colonies of Korea and Taiwan), were required to report to the police and get permission for work, residence, travel and other various aspects of life. It goes without saying that such a system caused many serious infringements of people's human rights. (NNSMW 1999a, 2)

It follows that the work of the Japanese MWM reflects not only the inequalities and injustices confronting contemporary foreigners from poorer countries living in Japan today but also those that continue for the foreign arrivals from past generations. It allows for collaborative activism with organizations and individuals that have been in the struggle against discrimination for several decades. For example, the NNSMW has been working with the Research/Action Institute for Koreans in Japan as well as other support groups for Korean residents to block the passing of the proposed legal revisions.

Individual activists themselves bring their political consciousness and experiences in past movements to their current work on behalf of the migrants. An attorney who is a representative of the Immigration Review Task Force (an NGO founded by citizens, lawyers and academics in 1994), which submitted its critique of the government to the UN Committee for Human Rights in 1998 (Immigration Review Task Force 1998), mentioned that his political awakening was greatly influenced by the student activism for Korean residents' rights when he was attending Waseda University in the 1970s. He focused on minority rights when he entered the legal profession in the early 1980s, which led him to his current work for migrant workers' rights (Interview, Tokyo, 12 April 1999).

In another case, one of the key staff members who addresses labor violations at CTIC has been active in the Japanese labor union movement for more than 20 years. Moreover, the MWM has as its outspoken leaders veterans from the Japanese women's movement: Yayoi Matsui, journalist, author, activist of international renown, and Shoji Rutsuko, the director of HELP, the first shelter/counseling center for female migrant workers and victims of trafficking in Japan. Both have continued to be relentless advocates of women's rights and other progressive causes in Japan and the Asian region and serve as two of the six codirectors of the NNSMW.

The particular role of transnational women's movements

It is important to point out that in both Japan and Korea, women's activism on matters concerning female migrant workers and victims of human trafficking served as the catalyst for greater attention to, and advocacy for, the general migrant worker population. Although viewed from the perspective of 'the internationalization of sexual exploitation' and not labor migration at the time, Asian women – particularly from the Philippines, Taiwan and Thailand – comprised the major inflow of migrants into Japan in the first half of the 1980s (Mori 1997, 71), the first decade of the contemporary migration boom in Northeast Asia. The head of Zentoitsu and other MWM activists mentioned that the women's organizations addressing the problems faced by female migrant workers – trafficking, sexual exploitation, harassment and violence, pregnancies, fraudulent marriages, unmet physical and mental health needs – served as the first groups to rally around human rights in order to assist and improve the lives of foreign women. The matter of general foreign workers' rights in the context of human rights grew out of that women's movement (Interview, Tokyo, 14 April 1999). It is also significant that the accumulation effect is at work in the women's movement on behalf of female migrant workers and victims of trafficking for the Japanese sex industry. One Yokohama shelter that assists such women started as an 'alternative movement after [the] Japanese "Women's Liberation Movement" in the late 1960s and the struggle in the 1980s for equal rights surrounding the Labor Standards Law and the protection of the rights of working women' (Azu 1997).

Although men and boys have composed the majority of the migrant inflow into Korea, as in Japan, activism on behalf of female migrant workers helped highlight the general problems of migrant workers. What began as a Catholic mass for seven to eight Filipinas, led by a

Korean and a Filipino nun in 1990, grew to a gathering of 100 female migrant workers within a year and led the Korean Catholic Church to respond institutionally to the plight of migrant female workers in 1992 (Interview, Seoul, 24 March 1999). Sister Lydia Paik, the director of the Foreign Workers' Labor Counseling Office of the Catholic Archdiocese of Seoul, established the first counseling center for migrant workers in Korea, which became a source of information about migrant workers' issues and needs for other NGOs and activists. The current head of the Association for Foreign Workers' Human Rights first learned of the exploitation and abuse of migrant workers through the Catholic sisters and their mission/counseling work, and soon after established the first secular migrant labor rights counseling center. He continues to be a key player in mobilizing and directing the MWM.

In addition to the accumulation of past efforts and experiences, the growing transnationalization of social movements – the expansion of regional and international networks/coalitions, use of the Internet to disseminate information and garner support, appeals to UN human rights mechanisms and international conventions – has helped empower the MWMs in Japan and Korea as human rights movements. Because migration is by definition a transnational and international issue, regional and international cooperation and coordination are both practical and necessary. The JCMK and the NNSMW try to create and maintain such cross-border ties in order to build support, share strategies and coordinate policies. The two have also been holding exchanges and seminars with each other, and some of the Korean activists who had visited Japan characterized the strengths and weaknesses of each movement this way: 'We must learn from the Japanese movement how to be more rational in organization and specialization of issue areas and expertise, and they must learn from us how to fight (the government and businesses) better.' Both organizations have also become determined to campaign in their respective country for the ratification of the UN Convention on the Protection of the Rights of All Migrant Workers and Members of Their Families. In this and other activities, both organizations network with the Asian Migrants Center of Hong Kong and other regional NGOs. In this way, these social movements are helping characterize migration and the increasing difficulty of governments in controlling immigration as 'a reflection of liberal developments in the international system, which are not purely economic but derive, in part, from political coalitions that seek to promote civil and human rights' (Cornelius, Martin and Hollifield 1994, 31).

Consequences

For these movements, which have small constituencies inside their national borders, international attention serves as a way to exert pressure on their home governments. An attorney who helps lead the Immigration Review Task Force in Japan summarized the role that the international human rights framework/movement plays in domestic society:

1. International norms and conventions, even when not binding, serve as legal/normative standards for activists to push for.
2. The UN Commission on Human Rights has the power to criticize a government's actions or inaction. In 1998, the commission issued a report heavily criticizing the Japanese government for its deportation practices and abusive treatment toward migrant workers and its inaction in preventing the trafficking of human beings for the sex industry, which was a huge blow to the Japanese Immigration Office.
3. Large international NGOs, such as Human Rights Watch and Amnesty International, help exert pressure on the government (Interview, Tokyo, 12 April 1999).

However, it is not solely pressure from below that leads to policy changes at the top. Governments and political leaders who demonstrate efforts to internationalize or globalize for whatever reason sometimes end up having to eat their own words; that is, organizations from below coopt government rhetoric and actions to suit their own agenda. For example, in the fall of 1997, the Korean government revised the citizenship law from patrilineage to bilineage, as long as the child was born in wedlock to a Korean citizen. It also established gender equality in the requirements for Korean citizenship for foreign-born spouses of Koreans, which had explicitly discriminated against women prior to the revision. One major daily called this an 'epoch-making' change in determining nationality (*Chungang Ilbo*, 21 September 1997). The newspaper *Hankyore Sinmun* (20 September 1997) described the revision as the 'government's attempt to modernize the Korean legal order in accordance with the era of globalization'. The *Chungang Ilbo* (20 September 1997) stated that the revision was a 'reflection of the government's attempt to observe the provisions against the discrimination of women ... as stipulated in the UN Convention for the Elimination of [All Forms of] Discrimination Against Women and the International Covenant on Human Rights, which the ROK [Republic of Korea] adopted respectively in 1984 and

1990'. The Korea Church Women United (KCWU), an umbrella organization for progressive Christian women's activism, had begun campaigning in 1996 for the revision of the citizenship law from patrilineage to bilineage. Although this had been a concern among Korean feminists, it had not become a salient issue until they were prompted by lawyers for migrant workers to address the plight of children born in Korea to a Korean woman and a male migrant worker. The KCWU organized demonstrations in front of Myongdong Cathedral, held petition drives, called for international solidarity through the Internet, and lobbied members of the National Assembly who might be sympathetic. The victory did not eliminate all forms of gender discrimination regarding citizenship entitlements, but it was a legal revolution for such an unapologetically patrilineal social system. And according to the KCWU official who initiated and led the campaign, it was not a hard victory: to her surprise, the government did not offer resistance, and the Ministry of Justice came up with its own initiative to change the laws soon after the first public demonstration. She attributed the government's responsiveness to the earlier adoption of CEDAW and noted that it was quite embarrassing for the government to have signed such a document yet continue to support old-fashioned laws (Interview, KCWU, Seoul, 7 April 1999).

It goes without saying that such international norms and conventions also have a spin-off effect on social movements that are not directly involved; a move toward women's equality has had some benefits for migrant workers as well. Japan's revision of the citizenship law had this effect, as did Korea's:

> Bowing to the United Nations Convention on the Elimination of All Forms of Discrimination against Women, Japan amended the nationality law in 1985 to allow Japanese nationality to be passed through either parent. The new nationality law represented a victory for feminists as well as Koreans and Japan's other immigrant groups. The majority (80 per cent) of ethnic Koreans marry Japanese nationals; their children now automatically become Japanese. It is premature to evaluate fully the amendment's impact, but it could portend wider acceptance of multiculturalism in a country that has long pretended to be monocultural. The recent emergence of the Japanese-Brazilian community will test further Japan's willingness to integrate immigrant groups, old and new. (Yamanaka 1994, 413–14)

Melucci (1996, 1) refers to contemporary social movements as 'disenchanted prophets', explaining that 'they are a sign, they are not merely an outcome of the crisis, the last throes of a passing society. They signal a deep transformation in the logic and processes that guide complex societies.' The success of the MWMs in Korea and Japan will hinge on their ability to help transform each society's nationalism and parochialism regarding not only citizenship but also economic contribution and cultural worth. All of the activists I interviewed in both countries viewed their compatriots' ignorance of different cultures and racism or ethnocentrism as the root cause of migrant workers' problems: labor exploitation, discrimination in social welfare provisions, physical violence, and social alienation. All stated that their long-term goal as individuals and movement leaders is a society accepting of foreigners and cultural differences and able to treat all persons as equals. All believed that the presence of migrant workers in their societies is a long-term phenomenon, despite each government's attempts to regard it as a short-term problem. For a start, despite the long economic repression in Japan and the IMF crisis in Korea, labor shortage in the low-value sectors in both countries is real; and unless global economic relations can simultaneously create wealth for all societies, which is not likely to happen in the foreseeable future, the relative poverty of their Asian and other neighbors will continue to send people in search of work across national borders. And unless Japan and Korea decide to swing back the pendulum of democracy and rights, the governments will be hard-pressed not to open the borders more to foreign workers. Cornelius's observation that 'it is the confluence of *markets* ... and *rights* that explains much of the contemporary difficulty of immigration control in Europe and the United States' applies also to Japan and Korea; 'recent efforts by democratic states to regain control of their borders all point to a gradual recognition that effective control of immigration requires a rollback of civil and human rights for noncitizens' (Cornelius, Martin and Hollifield 1994, 10). In their quest for a multicultural society and world of human rights, the movement activists have much ground to travel.

Notes

1. In this chapter, 'foreign worker' or 'migrant worker' refers only to foreign nationals who work in unskilled jobs. Unless specified otherwise, 'migrant workers' connotes undocumented or 'illegal' workers.
2. The NNSMW was formed in 1997 with about 70 groups, including Zentoitsu (All United Workers' Union), the Association in Kotobuki for Solidarity with Foreign Migrant Workers in Yokohama, Asian Women's Shelter HELP, the Kyoto YMCA, and RINK in Osaka. By June 1999, it had 86 member-affiliated groups.

3. The JCMK was established in 1995 by church groups, labor and human rights organizations, and the Korean Confederation of Trade Unions.
4. I use the term 'mission worker' to refer to those Christians attending to the needs and rights of migrant workers as a form of social outreach based on their faith, as distinct from a 'missionary', who might emphasize evangelism and conversion.
5. Cardinal Shirayanagi Seiichi, Archbishop of Tokyo, Pastoral Letter Concerning the Pastoral Care of Foreigners, 18 May 1997.
6. Interview, *Zentoitsu*, Tokyo, 14 April 1999. For example, the National Union of General Workers (*Ippan Roso*), which is composed of small- and medium-sized enterprises, and the National Machinery and Metal Workers' Union of Japan (*Zenkinzoku*), became two of the first *Rengo*-affiliated unions to support the conditional acceptance of unskilled foreign workers. See Komai (1995, 216).
7. In 1998, the APFS had 1862 members, 99 per cent of whom were undocumented. See *Nikkei Weekly*, 6 July 1998.

9
Conclusion: Pinpointing the Significance of Women's Empowerment, Recognizing Political Opportunities, Anticipating Transnational Coalitions

Craig N. Murphy

This study began with questions about the strategies and impact of different types of egalitarian social movements over the last 20 years. Since the late 1970s, the widespread adoption of neoliberal policies has meant the rapid marketization of more and more aspects of social life in all parts of world. Based on historical experience, we hypothesized that the prospects for any return back to 'society' from the market will depend on the success of those social movements. We noted global-level evidence that women's movements have been more successful than movements working to reduce class inequalities and regional inequalities, and hypothesized that this relative success reflected, in part, the strategies employed by women's and democracy movements.

A closer look at egalitarian politics in eight regions covering most of the world requires us to amend these simple hypotheses. The limited successes that some egalitarian movements have had so far may not presage a turn away from the market. Moreover, specific regional and national patterns of effective egalitarian politics reflect historical political opportunity structures that may or may not allow the formation of coalitions of the scale necessary to transform neoliberal globalization. Over the last two decades, egalitarian politics have made a difference; but they have not contained – and perhaps they cannot contain – the forces now working to make a less equal world.

The relative success of movements confronting different dimensions of inequality

The global evidence of increasing gender equality and formal political equality hides a more complex picture. In Chapters 1, 3 and 4, respectively, Mark Rupert, William Robinson and Filomina Steady remind us that although gaps between men and women's earned incomes may be shrinking in Africa and the Americas, household incomes of the poor have been stagnant or falling. In Eastern Europe, widening gaps between men and women accompany falling incomes for most families. Throughout the world, most women are working harder to help their families cope with growing class and regional inequality.

Nevertheless, in all regions except Eastern Europe, women have gained greater political and legal equality. Yet elite women's movements have been slow to recognize the economic and political forces that harm the vast majority of poorer women. Rupert demonstrates that mainstream women's organizations in the USA were slow to understand the threat of neoliberal policies. In China, as Marc Blecher points out in Chapter 6, the 'nonsocial' elite women's movement reflects a version of middle-class feminism of little relevance to China's rural poor. In Malaysia, as Christine Chin and Sylvia Tiwon show in Chapter 7, the state successfully marshaled the support of wealthier, active women against the peculiar coalition of transnational and popular forces calling for greater democratic accountability and openness.

Similarly, the democratic wave that hit Latin America, Eastern Europe and Africa in the 1980s and 1990s did nothing to level economic inequality. As Susan Strange argues (1996), transnational market forces and the neoliberal rollback of the state ensured that the new democratic governments had few tools that could be used to transform social inequities. The mid-twentieth-century apartheid state, for example, may have made it possible for Afrikaners to rise to the same level as South Africa's English-speaking ruling class; but the newly downsized South African democratic state of the 1990s cannot do the same for the country's black majority. Moreover, as Jane Dawson reminds us in Chapter 5, the communist era left Eastern European workers and women with limited organizational, ideological and political resources with which to seize the new political opportunities opened by formal democracy.

On the other hand, whereas the impact of women's democracy movements may have been less than we originally hypothesized, the role of some labor movements may have been greater. In China, Indonesia and Northeast Asia, more traditional labor movements (and illegal 'nonmovements') have played a socially transformative role, supporting democratization and helping to block both the excesses of transnationally sponsored neoliberal maketization and the conse-quences of xenophobic, precosmopolitan national policies. In Latin America, Robinson argues, 'globalization is generating the conditions for a new "social unionism" and alliances with other social movements are increasingly the fulcrum of the labor movement' (Chapter 3). It is far too early to assume that labor movements will play little role in any 'return to society' that follows the recent wave of marketization.

Robinson, Rupert and Steady, together with Joel Krieger (Chapter 2) and Katharine Moon (Chapter 8), all argue that the gendered impact of neoliberal globalization has created the beginnings of gender/class coalitions that have the greatest potential to reverse the recent global move toward the market. This may pinpoint the specific recent 'empowerment of women' that is relevant to the double-movement hypothesis. Rupert and Krieger point out ways in which the neoliberal attack on traditional labor organization and the end of the single-earner 'family wage' regime have created both new political incentives and new political space. Krieger notes further that

> the needs around which [Swedish] wage-earner feminists mobilized are widely supported by women throughout Western Europe … [T]he political agendas of women are driven by … an imperative to reconcile the demands of work and family responsibilities in a way that meets actual needs that are driven by the interactive effects of gender and class identities. (Chapter 2)

The same might be said for the agendas of women in the USA, in Latin America and in Africa (where Steady reports the similar concerns of activist women in the African National Congress who worked with pre-dominantly male labor leaders to create the outlines of the new state). Relatedly, successful actions by transnational women's movements in Japan and South Korea help provide both a strategy and a worldview, first for migrant workers' movements and then for a broader Japanese-Korean labor cooperation.

Specific histories and resulting political opportunities

Nevertheless, the same cases should make us cautious about all find-ings of great similarity across regions of the world. Krieger's emphasis on the flexible 'modularity' of contemporary identities and, hence, of contemporary politics was reinforced by the other studies of multiethnic and multireligious societies, such as those in Africa and Southeast Asia, where identity often trumps class or gender. Moreover, Krieger's argument has some validity almost everywhere that national identities have been promoted by national governments which, no matter how much they have been weakened by globalization, usually remain the site of the greatest consolidation of power that social movements can hope to channel toward their ends.

Different states create different kinds of political opportunities. In China, workers and peasants find no legal way to organize to press their interests, but the official Chinese women's association creates political space for an elite feminism, in much the same way that similar organizations created opportunities for feminist organization in authoritarian Nigeria. In supranational Europe, law and regime norms of the EU create opportunities for effective transnational coalitions to form. In modernizing South Korea (already signatory to the Convention on the Elimination of All Forms of Discrimination Against Women), claims about the need to bring local civil rights provisions up to 'international standards' gave women's and migrant workers' movements the opportunity to engineer radical changes in citizenship policy. To understand the structure of political opportunities open to a particular social movement, we must understand the history of the society in which that movement is embedded.

Such historical context is called for because not only do egalitarian social movements find different opportunities under different political systems but so do their opponents, and so do state leaders. As both Chin and Tiwon's chapter on Indonesia and Malaysia and Moon's on Korea and Japan point out, in many societies state leaders have effectively defined what 'equality' means. As Moon says, citizens in these societies 'traditionally have understood equality as stemming from one's membership in the ethnonational collective' (Chapter 8). For citizens in many parts of the world, there is no equality other than the equal citizenship they may enjoy in their own nation, which they often understand as unequally (in fact, especially) well blessed.

Opponents of egalitarian change may have the capacity to divide domestic egalitarian movements, find international support and close political space. As the cases of the East Asian migrants' movements demonstrate, however, these powers are never absolute. In Korea and Japan, a cosmopolitan movement leadership proposed and nurtured cosmopolitan identities as 'workers' and 'women' that have begun to bind together progressive political coalitions no longer in thrall to traditional national identity. In Malaysia, by contrast, antigovernment leaders have yet to offer an alternative vision of the people to be served by 'egalitarian' politics.

Transnational links and strategic choices

As Moon demonstrates, transnational links both emboldened and provided ideas for the cosmopolitan movements she investigated. The pattern in Northeast Asia also occurred in Indonesia, Africa, Europe and the Americas. In choosing to make and sustain transnational links, local social movements gained at least four strategic advantages: (1) they marshaled the power of like-minded foreign states; (2) they similarly marshaled the power of international organizations; (3) they learned from local struggles in other parts of the world; and (4) they gained the organizational support of a transnational leadership cadre. Their strategic gains should not be surprising; those egalitarian social movements that played significant roles in earlier 'returns to society' also understood the advantages of transnational coalitions.

Margaret Keck and Kathryn Sikkink's history of rights-oriented transnational social movements (1998) emphasizes the long tradition of movements marshaling like-minded states. This is what Keck and Sikkink call the 'boomerang effect': activists in one country want to change their government's policy. They seek the support of like-minded activists in other (often, more powerful) states, who lobby their own government to encourage the first government to change its policy.

Since the late 1970s, egalitarian movements have attempted to employ the boomerang effect, some successfully, many unsuccessfully, in the Americas, Europe, Africa and East Asia. Perhaps more common, in the current era, have been attempts to marshal the power of international institutions and to use the political space that they create. Steady and Moon both emphasize the significance of international standards and attempts to live up to international treaty commitments in the creation of national institutions supporting women and minorities. Krieger identifies some of the political space created by the supranational EU. More broadly, democracy movements have promoted linking political conditionality to intergovernmental development assistance and have convinced the central organs of the UN to aid almost every recent democratic transition (Sørensen 1993; Boutros-Ghali 1995; Joyner 1999).

Similarly, a willingness and ability to learn from parallel movements in other parts of the world has characterized the successful women's, democracy and human rights movements. Much of this transnational learning has taken place within regions. Steady emphasizes the importance of such learning to women's movements in Africa. Moon notes the cross-fertilization of ideas among migrant movements in East Asia. Chin and Tiwon suggest that a lack of willingness to learn from other regional cases – or a willingness to learn only the 'wrong' lessons – explains the different outcomes in Indonesia and Malaysia.

Transnational contacts also help build a transnational leadership cadre. Amy Higer's account of the international women's health movement (1997), historical accounts of the nineteenth-century antislavery movements (Goodman 1998), and the experience of nineteenth-century labor internationalism and twentieth-century anticolonialism make this point as well. To go back still further, to the very beginning of the social movement era, it may be that any successful movement needs its Thomas Paines (leaders who act in a number of states with the power to protect the egalitarian activists of one society by offering sanctuary or marshaling diplomatic pressure from another).

In fact, the antagonism of today's conservatives to the nongovernmental forums that regularly take place alongside intergovernmental meetings on human rights, women and development demonstrates the real significance of transnational contacts. Conservative legislators, including US Senator Jesse Helms, agree with social movement participants that the nongovernmental forums create space for international learning and serve as the primary locus for the development of transnational leadership cadres, which explains why conservatives have tried to end the global conference system (Fomerand 1996).

The experience of transnational social movements suggests one additional practical consideration for all egalitarian movements. John Braithwaite and Peter Drahos's extensive research of the origins of effective transnational business regulation (2000) emphasizes the significance of so-called model mongering, meaning the constant experimental promotion of an ever-growing array of possible solutions to the problems faced by governments and powerful social forces as a consequence of globalization. For example, small-scale gender-based lending, reproductive freedom, primary education for women, and other elements of a quarter-century-old Women in Development agenda have been well 'mongered' across a host of institutions. Although they are not primarily concerned with gender equality, these institutions have become convinced that such programs will reduce poverty, minimize costs of development assistance, placate an increasingly powerful Northern women's constituency, and help clean up the environment.

Nevertheless, although the studies in this volume identify strategic lessons for social movements attempting to counter accelerating social inequality, the authors are, at best, agnostic about the prospects for a Polanyian double movement. Rupert and Moon give examples of potentially transformative strategies employed in North America and Northeast Asia but make clear the limited scope of the social movements that currently employ those strategies. Krieger gives examples of potentially transformative politics in Europe, and Chin and Tiwon explain the rise of Indonesia's government whose local constituencies appear to be egalitarian movements; but both chapters explain why these seemingly progressive developments may prove illusory. Steady identifies significant African movements with coherent strategies but leaves the impression that they will have only a marginal impact given the continent's desperate political and economic dependency. Blecher and Dawson demonstrate the massive impediments to egalitarian change created by the power of China's Dengist state and the continuing political legacies of the Soviet system. Robinson sees little immediate prospect for transformation in Latin America and argues that critical scholars of globalization may most effectively exercise a 'preferential option' for the world's disadvantaged by uncovering 'the structural and historical context of the crisis of civilization we face, as well as the real inner workings and the contradictions of the emergent global social order' (Chapter 3).

Robinson and Jerry Harris (2000) have argued that the most salient development has been the rise of a truly transnational capitalist class whose political project has been the neoliberal globalization of the 1980s and 1990s. Braithwaite and Drahos (2000) demonstrate the range of contradictions that exist within that project and emphasize the range of ways in which different segments of the world's power structure understand and hope to cope with those contradictions (similarly, Murphy 1999). It is in the spaces created by those contradictions that Robinson sees opportunities for transnational social-labor coalitions and that Braithwaite and Drahos see ongoing opportunities for model mongering by egalitarian movements. It is in those spaces that the egalitarian politics in this age of globalization will continue to unfold.

References

ABANTU 1998. *African Women's Organisations in Civil Society: Transforming the State and the Economy*. London: ABANTU.

Abdalla, H. 1995. 'Women and Activism: The Nigerian Women's Movement', in A. Basu (ed.), *The Challenge of Local Feminisms: Women's Movement in Global Perspective*. Boulder, CO: Westview.

Adler, Nanci 1993. *Victims of Soviet Terror*. Westport, CT: Praeger.

AFL–CIO 1998. *The Union Difference*. Online at http://www.aflcio.org/union-difference/index.htm.

Ahn, Pong-Sul 1997. *Case Study on Employment and Social Safety Nets in Korea*. Seoul: International Relations Bureau of the Federation of Korean Trade Unions.

Albelda, Randy and Chris Tilly 1997. *Glass Ceilings and Bottomless Pits*. Boston, MA: South End.

Alt-WID 1993. *Breaking Boundaries: Women, Free Trade, and Economic Integration*. Washington, DC: Alt-WID.

——1997. *Reinventing Africa*. London: Zed Books.

Amin, Samir 1998. 'Globalization': A lecture series at the Massachusetts Institute of Technology, Cambridge.

Anderson, Benedict O. 1991. *Imagined Community: Reflections on the Origin and Spread of Nationalism*. London: Verso.

Anderson, Sarah and John Cavanagh 1996. *CEOs Win, Workers Lose: How Wall Street Rewards Job Destroyers*. Washington, DC: Institute for Policy Studies.

Aronowitz, Stanley 1992. *The Politics of Identity: Class, Culture, Social Movements*. New York: Routledge.

Ashwin, Sarah 1995. 'Russia's Official Trade Unions: Renewal or Redundancy?', *Industrial Relations Journal* 26(3): 192–203.

Aspinall, Edward 1996. 'The Broadening Base of Political Opposition in Indonesia', in G. Rodan (ed.), *Political Opposition in Industrialising Asia*. London: Routledge.

Aspinwall, Mark and Justin Greenwood 1998. 'Conceptualising Collective Action in the European Union: An Introduction', in J. Greenwood and M. Aspinwall (eds), *Collective Action in the European Union: Interests and the New Politics of Associability*. London: Routledge.

Azhgikhina, Nadezhda 1995. 'A Movement is Born', *Bulletin of Atomic Scientists* 51(4): 47–53.

Azu, Masumi 1997. *Migrant Women's Human Rights in G-7 Countries – Organizing Strategies*. Tokyo: Center for Women's Global Leadership.

Baglione, Lisa and Carol Clark 1998. 'The Challenge of Transforming Russian Unions', *Problems of Post-Communism* 45(1): 43–53.

Baker, Dean and Lawrence Mishel 1995. *Profits Up, Wages Down: Worker Losses Yield Big Gains for Business*. Washington, DC: Economic Policy Institute. Online at http://epn.org/epi/eppuwd.html.

Barkin, David, Irene Ortiz and Fred Rosen 1997. 'Globalization and Resistance: The Remaking of Mexico', *NACLA Report on the Americas* 30(4): 14–27.

Barrett, Michele 1988. *Women's Oppression Today: The Marxist/Feminist Encounter*, rev. edn. London: Verso.

Bauman, Zygmunt 1998. *Globalization: The Human Consequences*. New York: Columbia University Press.

Bell, Daniel 1975. 'Ethnicity and Social Change', in N. Glazer and D.P. Moynihan (eds), *Ethnicity: Theory and Experience*. Cambridge, MA: Harvard University Press.

Beneriá, Lourdes and Shelley Feldman, (eds) 1992. *Unequal Burden: Economic Crises, Persistent Poverty, and Women's Work*. Boulder, CO: Westview.

Blecher, Marc 1976. 'Income Distribution in Small Rural Chinese Communities', *China Quarterly* 68: 797–816.

—— 1997. *China Against the Tides*. London: Pinter.

Bonnell, Victoria (ed.) 1996. *Identities in Transition: Eastern Europe and Russia after the Collapse of Communism*. Berkeley, CA: University of California Press.

Borisov, Vadim, Simon Clarke and Peter Fairbrother 1994. 'Does Trade Unionism have a Future in Russia?', *Industrial Relations Journal* 25(1): 15–25.

Borisov, Vadim, Peter Fairbrother and Simon Clarke 1994. 'Is There Room for an Independent Trade Unionism in Russia?', *British Journal of Industrial Relations* 32(3): 359–79.

Boserup, Ester 1995. *Women's Role in Economic Development*. London: Earthscan.

Boutros-Ghali, Boutros 1995. 'Democracy: A Newly Recognized Imperative', *Global Governance* 1(1): 3–12.

Bowie, Alasdair and Danny Unger 1997. *The Politics of Open Economies: Indonesia, Malaysia, the Philippines, and Thailand*. Cambridge: Cambridge University Press.

Bowles, Samuel and Richard Edwards 1993. *Understanding Capitalism*. 2nd ed. New York: Harper Collins.

Braithwaite, John and Peter Drahos 2000. *Global Business Regulation*. Cambridge: Cambridge University Press.

Brennan, Martin 1982. 'Class, Politics, and Race in Modern Malaysia', *Journal of Contemporary Asia* 12(2): 188–215.

Brenner, Johanna 1993. 'The Best of Times, the Worst of Times: US Feminism Today', *New Left Review* 200: 101–59.

Bronfenbrenner, Kate 1997. 'We'll Close! Plant Closings, Plant-Closing Threats, Union Organizing and NAFTA', *Multinational Monitor*, March: 8–13.

Brown, David 1994. *The State and Ethnic Politics in Southeast Asia*. London: Routledge.

Bunce, Valerie 1992. 'Comparing East and South', *Journal of Democracy* 6(3): 87–100.

Buroway, Michael 1979. *Manufacturing Consent: Changes in the Labor Process under Capitalism*. Chicago, IL: University of Chicago Press.

Buzan, Barry 1991 'The Idea of the State and National Security', in N. Glazer and D. P. Moynihan (eds), *Perspectives on World Politics*, 2nd edn. London: Routledge.

Calderon, Fernando 1995. *Movimientos Sociales y Politica: La Decada Ochenta en Latinoamerica*. Mexico: Siglo Veintiuno.

Carre, Francoise and Chris Tilly 1998. 'Part-Time and Temporary Work: Flexibility for Whom?', *Dollars and Sense*, January–February: 22–5.

Castells, Manuel 1983. *The City and the Grassroots: A Cross-Cultural Theory of Urban Movements*. London: Arnold.

Chase-Dunn, Christopher 1998. 'Globalization from Below in Guatemala': Paper presented at the 'Conference on Guatemalan Development and Democracy: Proactive Responses to Globalization', Guatemala City, 26–28 March.

Chin, Christine B. N. 1998. *In Service and Servitude: Foreign Female Domestic Workers and the Malaysian Modernity Project*. New York: Columbia University Press.

Chin, Christine B. N. and James H. Mittelman 1997. 'Conceptualising Resistance to Globalization', *New Political Economy* 2(1): 25–37.

China Statistical Abstract (Zhongguo tongji zhaiyao) 1996. Beijing: China Statistical Press (Zhongguo tongji chubanshe).

China Statistical Yearbook 1995–98. Beijing: China Statistical Press.

Chirot, Daniel 1995. 'Modernism without Liberalism', *Contention* 13 (Fall): 1–12.

Christensen, Paul 1997. 'Why Russia Lacks a Labor Movement', *Transitions* 14(7): 44–51.

Cohen, Jean 1985. 'Strategy or Identity', *Social Research* 52(4): 663–716.

Comision Economica para América Latina 1993. *Panorama Social de América Latina*. Santiago, Chile: CEPAL/UN.

Committee Against Repression in the Pacific and Asia (CARPA) 1988. *Tangled Web: Dissent, Deterrence and the 27 October 1987 Crackdown in Malaysia*. Kuala Lumpur: CARPA.

Cook, Linda 1995. 'Workers in the Russian Federation', *Communist and Post-Communist Studies* 28(1): 13–42.

Cornia, Giovanni 1987. 'Adjustment at the Household Level: Potentials and Limitations of Survival Strategies', in Giovanni Cornia, R. Jolly and F. Stewart (eds), *Adjustment with a Human Face*. New York: Oxford University Press.

Cornelius, Wayne A. 1994. 'Japan: The Illusion of Immigration Control', in W. A. Cornelius, P. L. Martin and J. F. Hollifield (eds), *Controlling Immigration: A Global Perspective*. Stanford, CA: Stanford University Press.

Cornelius, Wayne, Philip L. Martin and James F. Hollifield 1994. 'Introduction: The Ambivalent Quest for Immigration Control', in W. A. Cornelius, P. L. Martin and J. F. Hollifield (eds), *Controlling Immigration: A Global Perspective*. Stanford, CA: Stanford University Press.

Crone, Donald K. 1991. 'Military Regimes and Social Justice in Indonesia and Thailand', *Journal of Asian and African Studies* 26(1–2): 96–113.

Crowley, Stephen 1994. 'Barriers to Collective Action: Steelworkers and Mutual Dependence in the Former Soviet Union', *World Politics* 46(4): 589–615.

——1995. 'Between Class and Nation', *Communist and Post-Communist Studies* 28(1): 43–69.

Cunningham, Shea and Betsy Reed 1995. 'Balancing Budgets on Women's Backs', *Dollars and Sense*, November–December: 22–25.

Dalton, Russell 1994. *The Green Rainbow*. New Haven, CT: Yale University Press.

Dalton, Russell J. and Manfred Kuechler (eds) 1990. *Challenging the Political Order: New Social and Political Movements in Western Democracies*. New York: Oxford University Press.

Dawson, Jane 1996. *Eco-Nationalism: Anti-Nuclear Activism and National Identity in Russia, Lithuania, and Ukraine*. Durham, NC: Duke University Press.

Dembele, D. 1998. 'The Political Economy of Debt, Adjustment, and Globalization', *Echo: Bilingual Quarterly Newsletter of the Association of African Women Organized for Research and Development* (AAWORD) 3 (Fall): 1.

Deng, Lual, M. Kostner and M. Crawford Young (eds) 1991. *Democratization and Structural Adjustment in Africa in the 1990s*. Madison, WI: University of Wisconsin African Studies Program.

Dudley, Steven 1998. 'Walking Through the Nightscape of Bogota', *NACLA Report on the Americas* 32(2): 10–14.

Eckholm, Erik 1998. 'Divorce Curb is Dividing Feminists in China', *New York Times*, 18 November.

ECLAC 1985–93. *Annual Reports*. Santiago, Chile: UN.

—— 1994–95. *Economic Survey of Latin America and the Caribbean 1994–1995*. Santiago, Chile: UN.

Economic Policy Institute (EPI) 1997. *Profits Fax: Corporate Profit Rates Hit New Peak*. Washington, DC: EPI. Online at http: //epinet.org/pr970328.html.

Eldridge, Philip J. 1995. *Non-Government Organisations and Democratic Participation in Indonesia*. Kuala Lumpur: Oxford University Press.

Enloe, Cynthia 1995. 'The Globetrotting Sneaker', *Ms.*, March–April: 10–15.

Ericson, Richard 1995. 'The Russian Economy since Independence', in G. Lapidus (ed.), *The New Russia*. Boulder, CO: Westview.

Esping-Andersen, Gosta 1990. *The Three Worlds of Welfare Capitalism*. Princeton, NJ: Princeton University Press.

Fairbrother, Peter and Vladimir Ilyn 1996. 'Where are Miners' Unions Going? Trade Unions in Vorkuta, Russia' *Industrial Relations Journal* 27(4): 304–16.

Fall, Yassine 1998. *Association of African Women Organized for Research and Development (AAWORD)*. Dakar: AAWORD.

Farrell, Amy 1995. 'Like a Tarantula on a Banana Boat: *Ms.* Magazine, 1972–1989', in M. M. Femee and P. Y. Martin (eds), *Feminist Organizations*. Philadelphia, PA: Temple University Press.

Feminist Majority 1997. 'Women's Groups Demand Nike End Sweatshop Labor', *Feminist Majority Report* (Fall). Online at http://www.feminist.org/research/report/93_twelve.html.

Fernández-Kelly, Maria Patricia 1994. 'Political Economy and Gender in Latin America: The Emerging Dilemmas': Working Paper of the Latin America Program No. 207. Washington, DC: Woodrow Wilson Center.

Fish, M. Steven 1991. 'The Emergence of Independent Associations and the Transformation of Russian Political Society', *Journal of Communist Studies* 7(2): 14–37.

Fodor, Eva 1997. 'Gender in Transition', *East European Politics and Societies* 11(3): 470–500.

Folbre, Nancy 1995. *The New Field Guide to the US Economy*. New York: New Press.

Fomerand, Jacques 1996. 'UN Conferences: Media Events or Genuine Diplomacy?', *Global Governance* 2(3): 361–77.

Forney, Matt 1997. 'We Want to Eat', *Far Eastern Economic Review*, 26 June.

Freeman, Gary P. and Jongryn Mo 1996. 'Japan and the Asian NICs as New Countries of Destination', in P. J. Lloyd and Lynne S. Williams (eds), *International Trade and Migration in the APEC Region*. New York: Oxford University Press.

Freeman, Richard and James Medoff 1984. *What do Unions Do?* New York: Basic.

Frege, Carola 1997. 'Does Economic Transformation Undermine Union Collectivism?', *Industrial Relations Journal* 28(3): 163–73.

Gabriel, Christina and Laura Macdonald 1994. 'NAFTA, Women, and Organizing in Canada and Mexico', *Millennium* 23: 535–62.

Gellner, Ernest 1994. *Conditions of Liberty: Civil Society and its Rivals*. New York: Allen Lane.

Gereffi, Gary and Donald Wyman (eds) 1990. *Manufacturing Miracles: Paths of Industrialization in Latin America and East Asia*. Princeton, NJ: Princeton University Press.

Gibbon, P., Y. Bangura and O. Ofstad (eds) 1992. *Authoritarianism, Democracy, and Adjustment: The Politics of Economic Reform in Africa*. Seminar Proceedings No. 26. Uppsala, Sweden: Scandinavian Institute of African Studies.

Gibney, Mark 1997. 'Prosecuting Human Rights Violations from a Previous Regime', *East European Quarterly* 31(1): 93–111.

Gill, Stephen 1998. 'European Governance and New Constitutionalism: Economic and Monetary Union and Alternatives to Disciplinary Neoliberalism in Europe', *New Political Economy* 3(1): 3–14.

Gilroy, Paul 1993. *Small Acts: Thoughts on the Politics of Black Cultures*. London: Serpent's Tail.

Goldfarb, Jeffrey 1997. 'Why is there No Feminism after Communism?', *Social Research* 64(2): 235–38.

Goldfield, Michael 1997. *The Color of Politics*. New York: New Press.

Gomez, Edmund Terence and K. S. Jomo 1997. *Malaysia's Political Economy*. Cambridge: Cambridge University Press.

Goodman, Paul 1998. *Of One Blood: Abolitionism and the Origin of Racial Equality*. Berkeley, CA: University of California Press.

Gordon, David, Richard Edwards and Michael Reich 1982. *Segmented Work, Divided Workers*. Cambridge: Cambridge University Press.

Gordon, Leonid and Eduard Klopov 1992. 'The Workers' Movement in Postsocialist Perspective', in Bertram Silverman, Robert Vogt and Murray Yanowitch (eds), *Labor and Democracy in the Transition to a Market System*. Armonk, NY: M.E. Sharpe.

Gramsci, Antonio 1971. *Selections from the Prison Notebooks*, Edited and translated by Quentin Hoare and Geoffrey Nowell Smith. New York: International Publishers.

Greenhouse, Steven 1997a. 'In Shift to Labor, Public Supports UPS Strikers', *New York Times*, 17 August.

—— 1997b. 'Nike Supports Women in its Ads, but Not its Factories, Groups Say', *New York Times*, 26 October.

Greider, William 1987. *Secrets of the Temple*. New York: Simon & Schuster.

—— 1997. *One World, Ready or Not: The Manic Logic of Global Capitalism*. New York: Touchstone.

Habermas, Jürgen 1981. 'New Social Movements', *Telos* 48: 33–7.

Hall, Stuart 1992. 'The Question of Cultural Identity', in Stuart Hall, David Held and Tony McGrew (eds), *Modernity and its Futures*. Cambridge: Polity.

Hallas, Karin 1994. 'Difficulties with Feminism in Estonia', *Women's Studies International Forum* 17(2–3): 229–300.

Hart, Gillian, Andrew Turton and Benjamin White, with Brian Fegan and Lim Teck Ghee 1989. *Agrarian Transformations: Local Processes and the State in Southeast Asia*. Berkeley, CA: University of California Press.

Heitlinger, Alena 1993. 'The Impact of the Transition from Communism on the Status of Women in the Czech and Slovak Republics', in Nanètte Funk and Magda Mueller (eds), *Gender Politics in Communism*. New York: Routledge.

—— 1996. 'Framing Feminism in Post-Communist Czech Republic', *Communist and Post-Communist Studies* 29(1): 77–93.

Henderson, Callum 1998. *Asia Falling? Making Sense of the Currency Crisis and its Aftermath*. Singapore: McGraw-Hill.

—— 1997a. 'Dow 7000', *Left Business Observer* 76, 18 February.

Henwood, Doug 1997b. 'Earnings', Online at *Left Business Observer* website: http://www.panix.com/~dhenwood/Stats_earns.html.

—— 1997c. 'Measuring Privilege', *Left Business Observer* 78, 17 July.

Heryanto, Ariel 1996. 'Indonesian Middle-Class Opposition in the 1990s', in G. Rodan (ed.), *Political Opposition in Industrializing Asia*. London: Routledge.

Hewett, Edward A. 1991. 'The New Half-Measures', in Edward A. Hewett and Victor H. Winston (eds), *Milestones in Glasnost and Perestroyka*. Washington, DC: Brookings Institution.

Heyzer, Noeleen 1995. 'Towards New Government-NGO Relations for Sustainable and People-Centred Development', in Noeleen Heyzer, James A. Riker and Antonio B. Quizon, *Government–NGO Relations in Asia: Prospects and Challenges for People-Centered Development*. New York: St Martin's.

Higer, Amy J. 1997. 'Transnational Movements and World Politics: The International Women's Health Movement and Population Policy', PhD dissertation, Department of Politics, Brandeis University, Waltham, MA.

Hinton, Carma 1986. *All Under Heaven*. Pittsburgh, PA: New Day Films.

Hobsbawm, Eric 1996. 'Identity Politics and the Left', *New Left Review* 217: 40–51.

Hoffer, C. 1973. 'Madam Yoko: Ruler of the Kpa Mende Confederacy', in M. Z. Rosaldo and L. Lamphere (eds), *Woman, Culture and Society*. Stanford, CA: Stanford University Press.

Holmgren, Beth 1995. 'Bug Inspectors and Beauty Queens: The Problems of Translating Feminism into Russian', *Genders* 22: 15–31.

Howell, Chris 1996. 'Women as the Paradigmatic Trade Unionists? New Work, New Workers and New Trade Union Strategies in Conservative Britain', *Economic and Industrial Democracy* 17: 511–43.

——2000. 'Unforgiven: The Crisis of British Trade Unionism', in George Ross and Andrew Martin (eds), *The End of Labor's Century?* Providence, RI: Berghahn.

Howell, Jude 1993. *China Opens its Doors*. Hemel Hempstead: Harvester Wheatsheaf.

Huber, Evelyn and John D. Stephens 1998. 'Internationalization and the Social Democratic Model: Crisis and Future Prospects', *Comparative Political Studies* 31(3): 353–97.

Hunt, Swanee 1997. 'Women's Vital Voices', *Foreign Affairs* 76(4): 2–7.

Immigration Review Task Force. 1998. *The Actual Status of the Deportation Procedures and Immigration Detention Facilities in Japan*. Tokyo: Immigration Review Task Force.

Indonesia Labour Information Institute (LIPS) 1999. *LIPS: Quarterly Report*. Jakarta: LIPS, January–March.

Jaquette, Jane S. (ed.) 1994. *The Women's Movement in Latin America*. Boulder, CO: Westview.

JCMK 1995. 'The Situation of Foreign Workers in Korea and Measures to Ensure their Protection', Online at http://kpd.sing.kr.org/jcmk/situation/situation_engl.html.

—— 1996. 'Forced Intrusion of Songnam Migrant Workers' House', undated but probably June. Online at http://kpd.sing-kr.org/sniwh/overseas1.html.

—— 1998. 'A Solidarity Message for Korean Workers and for all Koreans, 1 May', Online at http://labournet.org.uk/1998/May/jcmk.html.

Jelin, Elizabeth (ed.) 1990. *Women and Social Change in Latin America*. London: Zed Books.

Jenkins, J. Craig 1983. 'Resource Mobilization Theory and the Study of Social Movements', *Annual Review of Sociology* 9: 527–53.

Johnson, Chalmers 1987. 'Political Institutions and Economic Performance: The Government–Business Relationship in Japan, South Korea, and Taiwan', in F. C. Deyo (ed.), *The Political Economy of the New Asian Industrialism*. Ithaca, NY: Cornell University Press.

Jomo, K. S. and Patricia Todd 1994. *Trade Unions and the State in Peninsular Malaysia*. Kuala Lumpur: Oxford University Press.

Jones, Derek 1992. 'The Transformation of Labor Unions in Eastern Europe: The Case of Bulgaria', *Industrial and Labor Relations Review* 45(3): 452–70.

—— 1995. 'Successor Unions in Transitional Economies: Evidence from St. Petersburg', *Industrial and Labor Relations Review* 49(1): 39–55.

Jowitt, Kenneth 1992. *New World Disorder: The Leninist Extinction*. Berkeley, CA: University of California Press.

—— 1998. 'Challenging the "Correct Line"', *East European Politics and Societies* 12(1): 87–106.

Joyner, Christopher 1999. 'The United Nations and Democracy', *Global Governance* 5(3): 33–58.

Judd, Karen and Sandy Morales Pope 1994. 'The New Job Squeeze', *Ms.*, May–June: 86–90.

Kabira, Wanjiku Mukabi, J. Odoul and M. Nzomo (eds) 1993. *Democratic Change in Africa: Women's Perspective*. Nairobi: AAWORD and ACTS Gender Institute.

Kadetsky, Elizabeth 1994. 'The Human Cost of Free Trade', *Ms.*, January–February: 12–15.

Kamenitsa, Lynn 1997. 'East German Feminists in the New German Democracy', *Women and Politics* 17(3): 41–66.

Kameri-Mbote, A. P. and Kiwutha Kibwana 1993. 'Women, Law, and the Democratization Process in Kenya', in Wanjiku Kabira *et al.* (eds), *Democratic Change in Africa: Women Perspective*. Nairobi: AAWORD and ACTS Gender Institute.

KCTU (Korean Confederation of Trade Unions) 1998a. 'Hyundai Motor Workers Lead the Struggle', *KCTU Action Alert*, 22 July.

—— 1998b. 'Kim Dae Jung Set To Emulate Past Dictators?', *KCTU Action Alert*, 22 July.

—— 1998c. 'Statement by the KCTU Ulsan Regional Council and the Ulsan Alliance of the National Alliance for Democracy and Reunification in Korea (NADRK): Stop the Repression of Labour and People's Movements. Immediately Release Those Arrested!', *KCTU Action Alert* 22 July.

Keck, Margaret E. and Kathryn Sikkink 1998. *Activists Beyond Borders: Advocacy Networks in International Politics*. Ithaca, NY: Cornell University Press.

Kemp, A., Z. Madlala, A. Moodley and E. Salo 1995. 'The Dawn of a New Day: Redefining South African Feminism', in Amrita Basu (ed.), *The Challenge of Local Feminisms: Women's Movement in Global Perspective.* Boulder, CO: Westview.

Khan, Azizur Rahman and Carl Riskin 1988. 'Income and Inequality in China', *China Quarterly* 154 (June): 242–67.

Khasiani, S. A. and A. Njiro (eds) 1993. *The Women's Movement in Kenya.* Nairobi: AAWORD.

Kim, Sunhyuk 1997. 'State and Civil Society in South Korea's Democratic Consolidation: Is the Battle Really Over?', *Asian Survey* 37(12): 11–41.

Kitschelt, Herbert 1986. 'Political Opportunity Structures and Political Protest: Anti-Nuclear Movements in Four Democracies', *British Journal of Political Science* 16: 58–95.

Klandermans, Bert 1986. 'New Social Movements and Resource Mobilization: The European and American Approaches', *International Journal of Mass Emergencies and Disasters* 4: 13–39.

Komai, Hiroshi 1995. *Migrant Workers in Japan.* London: Kegan Paul International.

Korea Labor and Society Institute. 1998. 'Labor on the Second Tripartite Commission: Why Korean Labor was so Reluctant to Participate. 8 June', Online at http:kctu.org/links.html.

Kotz, David M., Terrence McDonough and Michael Reich 1994. *Social Structures of Accumulation: The Political Economy of Growth and Crisis.* Cambridge: Cambridge University Press.

Krieger, Joel 1999. *British Politics in the Global Age: Can Social Democracy Survive?* Cambridge: Polity.

Kriesi, Hanspeter *et al.* 1995 *New Social Movements in Western Europe: A Comparative Analysis.* Minneapolis, MN: University of Minnesota Press.

Lapidus, Gail 1989a. 'Gorbachev's Nationalities Problem', *Foreign Affairs*, Fall: 92–108.

—— 1989b. 'State and Society: Toward the Emergence of Civil Society in the Soviet Union', in Seweryn Bialer (ed.), *Politics, Society, and Nationality: Inside Gorbachev's Russia.* Boulder, CO: Westview.

Latinamerica Press. 1995. 'Special Issue: The Face of Human Rights in the '90s', *Latinamerica Press* 27(10).

—— 1997. 'Special Issue: Women and Power: The Road to Equality', *Latinamerica Press* 29(32).

—— 1998. 'Prisons Bursting at the Seams', *Latinamerica Press* 30(10): 4.

Lee, Hye-kyung 1997. 'The Employment of Foreign Workers in Korea: Issues and Policy Suggestions', *International Sociology* 12(3): 40–65.

Lim Mah Hui 1985. 'Affirmative Action, Ethnicity, and Integration: The Case of Malaysia', *Ethnic and Racial Studies* 8(2): 250–74.

Linz, Juan 1964. 'An Authoritarian Regime: Spain', in E. Allardt and Y. Littunen (eds), *Cleavages, Ideologies and Party Systems.* Helsinki: Academic Bookstore.

Lovenduski, Joni 1997. 'Gender Politics: A Breakthrough for Women?', *Parliamentary Affairs* 50(4): 708–19.

Mahon, Rianne 1991. 'From Solidaristic Wages to Solidaristic Work: A Post-Fordist Historic Compromise for Sweden?', *Economic and Industrial Democracy* 12(3): 295–326.

—— 1996. 'Women Wage Earners and the Future of Swedish Unions', *Economic and Industrial Democracy* 17(4): 540–52.

Marchand, Marianne 1996. 'Selling NAFTA: Gendered Metaphors and Silenced Gender Implications', in E. Kofman and Gillian Youngs (eds), *Globalization: Theory and Practice*. London: Pinter.

Marciniak, Piotr 1992. 'Polish Labor Unions: Can They Find a Way Out?', *Telos* 92: 149–57.

May, Martha 1990. 'The Historical Problem of the Family Wage', in E. C. du Bois and V. L. Ruiz (eds), *Unequal Sisters*. London: Routledge.

Mba, N. 1989. *Nigerian Women Mobilized*. Berkeley, CA: University of California Institute of International Studies.

McAuley, Alastair 1995. 'Inequality and Poverty', in David Lane (ed.), *Russia in Transition*. New York: Longman.

McDowell, Linda 1991. 'Life without Father and Ford', *Transactions of the Institute of British Geographers* 16: 400–19.

McGinn, Mary 1995. 'How GATT Puts Hard-Won Victories at Risk', *Ms.*, March–April: 15.

Means, Gordon P. 1991. *Malaysian Politics: The Second Generation*. Singapore: Oxford University Press.

Melucci, Albert 1985. 'The Symbolic Challenge of Contemporary Movements', *Social Research* 52(4): 789–816.

—— 1996. *Challenging Codes: Collective Action in the Information Age*. New York: Cambridge University Press.

Milanovic, Branko 1994. *Rossiia: Bednost*. Washington, DC: World Bank.

—— 1995. *Income, Inequality, and Poverty during the Transition*. Washington, DC: World Bank.

—— 1999. *True World Income Distribution, 1988 and 1993: First Calculation Based on Household Surveys Alone*. Washington, DC: World Bank.

Milbraith, Lester 1965. *Political Participation*. Chicago, IL: University of Chicago Press.

Miller, Francesca 1995. 'Latin American Women and the Search for Social, Political, and Economic Transformation', in Sandor Halebsky and Richard L. Harris (eds), *Capital, Power, and Inequality in Latin America*. Boulder, CO: Westview.

Milne, R. S. and Diane K. Mauzy 1978. *Politics and Government in Malaysia*. Singapore: Federal Publishers.

Mishel, Lawrence 1997. 'Behind the Numbers: Capital's Gain', *The American Prospect* 33 (July–August): 71–3. Online at http://epn.org/prospect/33/33mishf.html.

Mishel, Lawrence, Jared Bernstein and John Schmitt 1997. *The State of Working America, 1996–97*. Armonk, NY: M.E. Sharpe.

Molyneux, Maxine 1995. 'Review Essay: Gendered Transitions in Eastern Europe', *Feminist Studies* 21(3): 637.

Moody, Kim 1988. *An Injury to All: The Decline of American Unionism*. London: Verso.

—— 1997. *Workers in a Lean World*. London: Verso.

Mori, Hiromi 1997. *Immigration Policy and Foreign Workers in Japan*. London: Macmillan.

Morris, Aldon and Carol Mueller (eds) 1992. *Frontiers in Social Movement Theory*. New Haven, CT: Yale University Press.

Mugyeni, M. 1988. 'Development First – Democracy Second: A Comment on Minimalist Democracy', in W. Ogunyi *et al.* (eds), *Democratic Theory and Practice in Africa* Portsmouth, NH: Heinemann.

Murphy, Craig N. 1994. *International Organization and Industrial Change: Global Governance since 1850*. Cambridge: Polity.

—— 1999. 'Inequality, Turmoil, and Democracy: Global Political-Economic Visions at the End of the Century', *New Political Economy* 4(2): 289–304.

Nasution, Adnan Buyung 1992. *The Aspiration for Constitutional Government in Indonesia: A Socio-legal Study of the Indonesia Konstituante 1956–1959*. The Hague: CIP-Gegevens Koninklijke Bibliotheek.

Nevitt, Christopher Earle 1996. 'Private Business Associations in China: Evidence of Civil Society of Local State Power', *The China Journal* 36(July): 25–46.

Ng, Cecilia and Chee Heng Leng 1996. 'Women in Malaysia: Present Struggles and Future Directions', *Asian Journal of Women's Studies* 2: 192–210.

Nkomo, Maria 1993. 'Engendering Democratization in Kenya', in Wanjiku Kabira *et al.* (eds), *Democratic Change in Africa: Women's Perspectives*. Nairobi: AAWORD and ACTS Gender Institute.

NNSMW 1999a. *Migrant Network News* 11 (February).

—— 1999b. *Migrant Network News* 12 (March).

Norris, Christopher 1990. *What's Wrong with Postmodernism: Critical Theory and the Ends of Philosophy*. Baltimore, MD: Johns Hopkins University Press.

O'Barr, Jean 1976. 'Pare Women: A Case for Political Involvement', *Rural Africana* 29: 121–34.

O'Brien, Kevin 1994. 'Implementing Political Reform in China's Villages', *The Australian Journal of Chinese Studies* 32 (July): 33–59.

—— and Li Lianjiang 1995. 'The Politics of Lodging Complaints in Chinese Villages', *China Quarterly* 143 (September): 756–83.

Offe, Claus 1985. 'New Social Movements: Challenging the Boundaries of Institutional Politics', *Social Research* 52: 817–68.

Ohmae, Kenichi 1990. *The Borderless World: Power and Strategy in the Interlinked Global Economy*. New York: Harper Business.

Oka, Takashi 1994. *Prying Open the Door: Foreign Workers in Japan*. Washington, DC: Carnegie Endowment for Peace.

Okonjo, K 1981. 'Women's Political Participation in Nigeria', in Filomina C. Steady (ed.), *The Black Woman Cross-Culturally*. Cambridge, MA: Schenkman Books.

Ostrovska, Ilze 1994. 'Women and Politics in Latvia', *Women's Studies International Forum* 17(2–3): 301–3.

Papanek, Gustav F. (ed.) 1980. *The Indonesian Economy*. New York: Praeger.

Park, Heh-Rahn 1996. 'Narratives of Migration: From the Formation of Korean Chinese Nationality in the PRC to the Emergence of Korean Chinese Migrants in South Korea', PhD dissertation, Department of Political Science, University of Washington, Seattle.

Park, Young-bum 1996. 'Labour Market Developments and Foreign Worker Policy in the Republic of Korea', in *Migration and the Labour Market in Asia: Prospects to the Year 2000*. Paris: OECD.

Petras, James 1997. 'Imperialism and NGOs', *Monthly Review* 49(7): 10–27.

—— 1997–98. 'A Marxist Critique of Post-Marxists', *Links* 9: 27–48.

Pinheiro, Paul Sergio 1996. 'Democracies without Citizenship', *NACLA Report on the Americas* 30(2): 17–23.

Polanyi, Karl 1957. *The Great Transformation. The Political and Economic Origins of Our Time*. Boston, MA: Beacon Press.

Pollert, Anna and Irera Hradecka 1994. 'Privatization in Transition: The Czech Experience', *Industrial Relations Journal* 25(1): 52–63.

Pontusson, Jonas 1992. *The Limits of Social Democratic Power: Investment Politics in Sweden*. Ithaca, NY: Cornell University Press.

Poulgrain, Greg 1997. *The Genesis of Malaysian Konfrontasi: Brunei and Indonesia 1945–1965*. Hindmarsh, Australia: Crawford House.

Pritchett, Lant 1995. 'Divergence, Big Time', World Bank Policy Research Working Paper No. 1522. Washington, DC: World Bank.

Przeworski, Adam 1995. *Sustainable Democracy*. New York: Cambridge University Press.

Ramasamy, P 1994. *Plantation Labour, Unions, Capital and the State in Peninsular Malaysia*. Kuala Lumpur: Oxford University Press.

Remington, Thomas 1999. *Politics in Russia*. New York: Longman.

Robinson, William I 1996a. 'Globalisation: Nine Theses of our Epoch', *Race and Class* 38(2): 13–31.

—— 1996b. *Promoting Polyarchy: Globalization, US Intervention, and Hegemony*. Cambridge: Cambridge University Press.

—— 1998a. 'Beyond Nation-State Paradigms: Globalization, Sociology, and the Challenge of Transnational Studies', *Sociological Forum* 13(4): 561–94.

—— 1998b. '(Mal)development in Central America: Globalization and Social Change', *Development and Change* 29(3): 467–9.

—— Robinson, William I. and Jerry Harris 2000. 'Towards a Global Ruling Class? Globalization and the Transnational Capitalist Class', *Science and Society* 64(1): 11–54.

Robison, Richard 1996. 'The Middle Class and the Bourgeoisie in Indonesia', in R. Robinson and D. S. G. Goodman (eds), *The New Rich in Asia: Mobile Phones, McDonalds, and Middle Class Revolution*. London: Routledge.

Rochon, Thomas R. 1990. 'The West European Peace Movement and the Theory of New Social Movements', in Russell J. Dalton and Manfred Kuechler (eds), *Challenging the Political Order: New Social and Political Movements in Western Democracies*. New York: Oxford University Press.

Rodney, Walter 1981. *How Europe Underdeveloped Africa*. Washington, DC: Howard University Press.

Roeder, Philip 1991. 'Soviet Federalism and Ethnic Mobilization', *World Politics* 43(2): 196–232.

Rogers, Barbara 1980. *The Domestication of Women: Discrimination in Developing Countries*. London: Tavistock.

Rosenburg, Tina 1995. *The Haunted Land*. New York: Random House.

Ross, Andrew (ed.) 1997. *No Sweat: Fashion, Free Trade, and the Rights of Garment Workers*. London: Verso.

Ross, George 1998. 'European Integration and Globalization', in R. Axtmann (ed.), *Globalization and Europe: Theoretical and Empirical Investigations*. London: Pinter.

Rozelle, Scott 1988. 'Stagnation Without Equity: Patterns of Growth and Inequality in China's Rural Economy', *The China Journal* 35: 63–92.

Rucht, Dieter 1995. 'The Impact of National Contexts on Social Movement Structures: A Cross-Movement and Cross-National Comparison', in John McCarthy *et al.* (eds), *Opportunities, Mobilizing Structures, and Framing: Comparative Applications of Contemporary Movement Theory*. New York: Cambridge University Press.

Rueschemeyer, Marilyn (ed.) 1994. *Women in the Politics of Postcommunist Eastern Europe*. Armonk, NY: M.E. Sharpe.

Runyan, A. S. 1996. 'The Places of Women in Trading Places', in E. Kofman and Gillian Youngs (eds), *Globalization: Theory and Practice*. London: Pinter.

Rupert, Mark 1995. *Producing Hegemony: The Politics of Mass Production and American Global Power*. Cambridge: Cambridge University Press.

—— 1997. 'Contesting Hegemony: Americanism and Far-Right Ideologies of Globalization', in Kurt Burch and Robert Denemark (eds), *International Political Economy Yearbook* 10, Boulder, CO: Lynne Rienner Publishers. pp. 113–38.

—— 1998. 'Re-Engaging Gramsci: A Response to Germain and Kenny', *Review of International Studies* 24: 427–34.

Rutland, Peter 1990. 'Labor Unrest and Movements in 1989 and 1990', *Soviet Economy* 6(3): 345–84.

Safa, Helen 1994. *The Myth of the Male Breadwinner: Women and Industrialization in the Caribbean*. Boulder, CO: Westview.

—— 1995. 'Women's Social Movements in Latin America', in C. E. Bose and E. Acosta-Belen (eds), *Women in the Latin American Development Process*. Philadelphia, PA: Temple University Press.

Sarris, A. and H. Shams 1991. *Ghana under Structural Adjustment: The Impact on Agriculture and the Rural Poor*. Albany, NY: New York University Press.

Sawa-Czajka, Elzbieta 1996. 'Are There Female Political Elites in Poland?', *Journal of Women's History* 8(2): 103–9.

Sayer, Andrew and Richard Walker 1992. *The New Social Economy*. Oxford: Basil Blackwell.

Scheper-Hughes, Nancy 1997. 'People who get Rubbished', *New Internationalist* 295: 20–2.

—— and Daniel Hoffman 1994. 'Kids out of Place', *NACLA Report on the Americas* 27(6): 298–335.

Schmitter, Philippe and Terry Carl 1991. 'Modes of Transition in Latin America, Southern and Eastern Europe', *International Social Science Journal* 138: 35–47.

Sen, Gita and C. Grown 1987. *Development Crises and Alternative Visions: Third World Women's Perspectives*. New York: Monthly Review Press.

Siklova, Jirina 1998. 'Why We Resist Western-Style Feminism', *Transitions* 5(1).

Smith, Kathleen 1996. *Remembering Stalin's Victims*. Ithaca, NY: Cornell University Press.

Solomon, M. Scott and Mark Rupert 1999. 'Eight Theses in Search of a Nail: Historical Materialism, Ideology, and the Politics of Globalization'. Paper presented at the workshop on Historical Materialism and Globalization, Centre for the Study of Globalization and Regionalization, University of Warwick, 15–17 April.

Sørensen, Georg (ed.) 1993. *Political Conditionally*. London: Frank Cass.

Sparr, Pamela 1992. 'How We Got Into This Mess and Ways to Get Out', *Ms.*, March–April: 29–36.

Sperling, Valerie 1999. *Organizing Women in Contemporary Russia: Engendering Transition*. Cambridge: Cambridge University Press.

Stahl, Karin 1996. 'Anti-Poverty Programs: Making Structural Adjustment More Palatable', *NACLA Report on the Americas* 29(6): 32–36.

Steady, Filomina C 1975. *Female Power in African Politics: The National Congress of Sierra Leone*. Pasadena, CA: Munger Africana Library.

Stephen, Lynn 1998. *Women and Social Movements in Latin America*. Austin, TX: University of Texas Press.

Strange, Susan 1996. *Retreat of the State*. Cambridge: Cambridge University Press.

Streeck, Wolfgang 1997. 'German Capitalism: Does It Exist? Can It Survive?', *New Political Economy* 2(2): 237–56.

Suny, Ronald 1995. 'State, Civil Society and Ethnic Cultural Consolidation in the USSR', in Alexander Dallin and G. Lapidus (eds), *The Soviet System: From Crisis to Collapse*. Boulder, CO: Westview.

Suryakusuma, Julia I 1996. 'Murder, Gender, and the Media: Sexualizing Politics and Violence', in Laurie J. Sears (ed.), *Fantasizing the Feminine in Indonesia*. Durham, NC: Duke University Press.

Susskind, Yifat 1998. 'What's So Liberal About Neo-Liberalism?', *MADRE Speaks*, Fall: 3–8.

Tang Tsou 1986. *The Cultural Revolution and the Post-Mao Reforms*. Chicago, IL: University of Chicago Press.

Tarrow, Sidney 1994. *Power in Movement: Social Movements, Collective Action, and Mass Politics*. New York: Cambridge University Press.

—— 1995. 'States and Opportunities: The Political Structuring of Social Movements', in John McCarthy *et al.* (eds), *Opportunities, Mobilizing Structures, and Framing: Comparative Applications of Contemporary Movement Theory*. New York: Cambridge University Press.

—— 1998. 'Building a Composite Polity: Popular Contention in the European Union', Paper presented at the Center of International Security and Arms Control, Stanford University, California.

Tismaneanu, Vladimir 1998. *Fantasies of Salvation*. Princeton, NJ: Princeton University Press.

Tiwon, Sylvia 1996. 'Articulating the Female in Indonesia', in Laurie J. Sears (ed.), *Fantasizing the Feminine in Indonesia*. Durham, NC: Duke University Press.

Touraine, Alain 1981. *The Voice and the Eye*. New York: Cambridge University Press.

Tzannatos, Zafiris 1998. 'Women and Labor Market Change in the Global Economy: Growth Helps, Inequalities Hurt and Public Policy Matters', World Bank Social Protection Discussion Paper No. 9808. Washington, DC: World Bank.

Uchitelle, Louis 1997. 'Gap Between Full-Time and Part-Time Workers has Widened', *New York Times*, 8 August.

UN 1989–99. *The World's Women: Trends and Statistics*. New York: UN.

UN Department for Economic and Social Information and Policy Analysis. 1995. *World Economic and Social Survey 1995*. New York: UN.

UNDP 1995–99. *World Development Reports*. New York: Oxford University Press.

UN ECA 1998. *African Economic Report*. Online at http://www.un.org/Depts/eca/divis/espd/aer98.htm.

UN Environmental Program 1991. *Report of the Global Assembly of Women and the Environment*. Nairobi: UN Environmental Programme.

UN Industrial Development Organization 1993. *Global Report 1993/94*. Vienna: UN.

Upchurch, Martin 1995. 'After Unification: Trade Unions and Industrial Relations in Eastern Germany', *Industrial Relations Journal* 26(4): 280–91.

US Bureau of Labor Statistics 1997. 'Union Members in 1996'. Online at http://stats.bls.gov/news.release/union2.nws.htm.

US Census Bureau 1992. 'Workers with Low Earnings, 1964 to 1990', *Current Population Reports*, 60–178.

—— 1996. 'A Brief Look at Postwar US Income Inequality', *Current Population Reports*, 60–191.

van der Pijl, Kees 1997. 'The History of Class Struggle: From Original Accumulation to Neoliberalism', *Monthly Review* 49(1): 28–44.

Veltmeyer, Henry 1997. 'Latin America in the New World Order', *The Canadian Journal of Sociology* 22(2): 197–242.

Volkov, Iurii 1992. 'The Transition to a Mixed Economy and the Prospects for the Labor and Trade Union Movement', in Bertram Silverman, Robert Vogt and Murray Yanowitch (eds), *Labor and Democracy in the Transition to a Market System*. Armonk, NY: M. E. Sharpe.

Wachtel, Howard 1990. *The Money Mandarins*. Armonk, NY: Sharpe.

Wang Zheng 1997. 'Maoism, Feminism, and the UN Conference on Women', *Journal of Women's History* 8(4): 126–52.

Wapner, Paul 1996. *Environmental Activism and the World Civic Politics*. Albany, NY: State University of New York Press.

Ward, Kathryn B. (ed.) 1990. *Women Workers and Global Restructuring*. Ithaca, NY: ILR Press.

—— and Jean Larson Pyle 1995. 'Gender, Industrialization, Transnational Corporations, and Development', in Christine E. Bose and Edna Acosta-Belen (eds), *Women in the Latin American Development Process*. Philadelphia, PA: Temple University Press.

Ward, Michael D., John O'Loughlin, Jordin S. Cohen, Kristian S. Gleditsch, David S. Brown, David A. Reilly, Corey L. Lofdahl and Michael E. Shin 1999. 'The Diffusion of Democracy, 1946–1994', *Annals of the Association of American Geographers* 88: 545–74.

Wiener Institut für Internationale Wirtschaftsvergleiche 1995. *Transition Countries: Economic Situation in 1994 and Outlook*. Vienna: Wiener Institut für Internationale Wirtschaftsvergleiche.

Wilkie, James W. (ed.) 1995–97. *Statistical Abstract of Latin America*. Los Angeles: UCLA Latin American Center Publications.

Williamson, John (ed.) 1990. *Latin American Adjustment*. Washington, DC: Institute for International Economics.

—— 1993. 'Democracy and the "Washington Consensus"', *World Development* 21(8): 1329–36.

Winters, Jeffrey A 1996. *Power in Motion: Capital Mobility and the Indonesian State*. Ithaca, NY: Cornell University Press.

Wolff, Edward N. 1995. *Top Heavy*. New York: Twentieth Century Fund.

Wolin, Sheldon S. 1988. 'On the Theory and Practice of Power', in Jonathan Arac (ed.), *After Foucault: Humanistic Knowledge, Postmodern Challenges*. New Brunswick, NJ: Rutgers University Press.

'Women: Changing Roles' 1995. Special issue of *Transition* 1(16).

World Bank 1988–96. *World Development Report*. New York: Oxford University Press.

World Bank 1993–94. *The East Asian Miracle: Economic Growth and Public Policy*. Washington, DC: World Bank.

——1997. *Poverty and Income Distribution in Latin America: The Story of the 1980s*. Washington, DC: World Bank.

Yamanaka, Keiko 1994. 'Commentary: Theory versus Reality in Japanese Immigration Policy', in Wayne A. Cornelius, Philip L. Martin and James F. Hollifield (eds), *Controlling Immigration: A Global Perspective*. Stanford, CA: Stanford University Press.

Yoon, Jin-Ho 1997. *IMF Bailout and Employment Crisis: The Labour Response*. Seoul: KCTU.

Young, Katherine 1996. 'Loyal Wives, Virtuous Mothers', *Russian Life* 39(3): 4–14.

Zdravomyslova, Olga 1995. 'The Position of Women', in David Stuart Lane (ed.), *Russia in Transition*. New York: Longman.

Zulu, Lindiwe 1998. 'The Role of Women in the Reconstruction and Development of the New Democratic South Africa', *Feminist Studies* 24(1): 46–75.

Index

Abacha, Sani, 86
ABANTU for Development (London), 92, 93
abbreviations, viii–ix
Abdalla, H., 89, 95(n2), 212
Abdurrahman Wahid, 154
ABIM (an Islamic Youth Movement, Malaysia), 167
abortion, 106, 112, 113
accidents, 175, 187–8, 190, 191
accountability, 170, 206
accumulation, 60, 69, 75(n4)
Aceh (Sumatra), 151, 157, 172, 173(n3)
affirmative action, 63, 84, 104, 159, 166
Africa, 1, 3, 5, 58, 174
  conclusion, 206–10
  engendering change through egalitarian movements, 77–95
  marginalization, 56, 61, 79, 80
  underdevelopment, 80
African Economic Report, 80
African National Congress (ANC), 89, 90, 94, 207
African-Americans, 11–12
Agence France-Presse (AFP), 125
Agricultural Bank of China, 143
agriculture, 58, 60, 64, 80, 85, 86, 87, 90, 96, 99, 127–8, 142, 156, 176, 186
AKINA MAMA AFRICA (London), 92
Albania, 121
Albelda, Randy, 23, 212
Ali Moertopo, General, 172(n1)
Alien Registration Law (ARL, Japan), 197–8
  proposed revisions (1999), 196
All-Union Central Council of Trade Unions (USSR), 107
Alliance Party (Malaya/Malaysia), 158, 159
Alternative Women-in-Development (Alt-WID) working group, 28–9

'American Dream', 19, 20
American Federation of Labor and Congress of Industrial Organizations (AFL–CIO), 12, 20, 109
Amnesty International, 116, 201
ANC Women's League (1913–), 89
Anderson, Benedict O., 148, 212
Ansan, 192, 193, 194
anti-Semitism, 123(n6)
anticolonialism, 210
antinuclear movement, 38
antireform forces (Russia/Eastern Europe), 117
antislavery movements, 210
Anwar Ibrahim, 158, 163–8, 170
apartheid, 78, 89–90, 92, 206
Arco Oil, 151
Argentina, 62, 63, 71, 126, 184
Asahi News Service, 184, 185
Asia, 3, 6, 146, 164, 166, 172, 174
Asian financial crisis (1997–), 58, 101, 119, 123(n1), 144, 146, 155, 163–5, 166–7, 169, 170, 177, 183, 194–5
  Russia (1998–), 99–100, 119, 123(n1)
Asian Migrants' Centre (Hong Kong SAR), 193, 200
Asian People's Friendship Society, 196–7, 204(n7)
Asiaweek, 168
Aspinwall, Mark, 50(n1), 212
Association of African Women Organized for Research and Development (AAWORD), 93, 94
Association for Foreign Workers' Human Rights (South Korea), 180, 193, 200
Association in Kotobuki for Solidarity with Foreign Migrant Workers (Yokohama), 203(n2)
Austria, 41